T0326780

ILEX FOUNDATION SERIES 10

ON THE WONDERS OF LAND AND SEA

Also in the Ilex Foundation Series

Dreaming across Boundaries:
The Interpretation of Dreams in Islamic Lands
edited by Louise Marlow

Strī:
Women in Epic Mahābhārata
by Kevin McGRATH

Persian Literature and Judeo-Persian Culture:
Collected Writings of Sorour S. Soroudi
edited by Houchang Chehabi

The Rhetoric of Biography:
Narrating Lives in Persianate Societies
edited by L. Marlow

Jaya:
Performance in Epic Mahābhārata
by Kevin McGRATH

The History *of Beyhaqi (The History of Sultan Masʿud*
of Ghazna, 1030–1041) by Abu'l-Fażl Beyhaqi
translated and with commentaries by Clifford Edmund Bosworth
fully revised and with further commentary by Mohsen Ashtiany

The Last of the Rephaim:
Conquest and Cataclysm in the Heroic Ages of Ancient Israel
by Brian R. Doak

Ruse and Wit:
Humorous Writing in Arabic, Turkish, and Persian Narrative
edited by Dominic Parviz Brookshaw

ON THE WONDERS OF LAND AND SEA

PERSIANATE TRAVEL WRITING

Edited by
Roberta Micallef and Sunil Sharma

Ilex Foundation
Boston, Massachusetts
and
Center for Hellenic Studies
Trustees for Harvard University
Washington, D. C.

Distributed by Harvard University Press
Cambridge, Massachusetts, and London, England

On the Wonders of Land and Sea: Persianate Travel Writing
Edited by Roberta Micallef and Sunil Sharma

Published by Ilex Foundation, Boston, Massachusetts and the Center for Hellenic Studies, Trustees for Harvard University, Washington, D.C.

Distributed by Harvard University Press, Cambridge, Massachusetts and London, England

Production editor: Christopher Dadian
Cover design: Joni Godlove
Printed in the United States of America

The image on the front cover is an artist's rendition, based on the 1864 map of Asia of S. A. Mitchell Jr. and Mullā Fīrūz's *Dīn-khirad*, Meherjirana Library MS F-82, f. 1.

Library of Congress Cataloging-in-Publication Data

On the wonders of land and sea : Persianate travel writing / edited by Roberta Micallef and Sunil Sharma.
p. cm. -- (Ilex Foundation series ; 10)
Includes bibliographical references and index.
ISBN 978-0-674-07334-0 (alk. paper)
1. Travel in literature. 2. Travelers' writings, Persian--History and criticism. 3. Travelers' writings--History and criticism. 4. Middle East--Description and travel. 5. India--Description and travel. 6. Europe--Description and travel. 7. Muslim travelers--Middle East. 8. Muslim travelers--India. 9. Muslim travelers--Europe. I. Micallef, Roberta editor of compilation. II. Sharma, Sunil, 1964- editor of compilation..
PN56.T7O53 2013
809'.9332--dc23

2013005872

CONTENTS

List of Illustrations

1. A portrait of Mullā Fīrūz b. Kā'ūs (1758-1830). Photograph by Daniel Sheffield. (*Courtesy* Dadyseth Atash Behram, Mumbai.)
2. Mullā Fīrūz's *Dīn-khirad.* Photograph by Daniel Sheffield. (*Courtesy* Meherjirana Library, Navsari.)
3. A studio photograph of Māṇekji Limji Hāṭaria (1813-90). Photograph by Daniel Sheffield. (*Courtesy* K. R. Cama Oriental Institute, Mumbai.)
4. The title page of Māṇekji Limji Hāṭaria's *Risāle Ezhār-e Siāt-e Irān.* Photograph by Daniel Sheffield. (*Courtesy* Meherjirana Library, Navsari.)
5. A stele from Persepolis. Photograph by Daniel Sheffield. (*Courtesy* Meherjirana Library, Navsari.)
6. Caravanserai on the road from Isfahan to Shiraz (litho), Flandin, Eugene (1809-76). (*Courtesy* Bibliothèque des Arts Decoratifs, Paris, France / Archives Charmet / The Bridgeman Art Library.)
7. Portrait of Mahdi Hasan Fath Nawaz Jang. (*Courtesy* Omar Khalidi.)
8. Portraits of Mahmud and Ghulam Muhammad Tarzi, as depicted in *Siyāḥatnāma-yi sih qiṭ'a-yi rū-yi zamīn dar bīst o no rūz* (1915). (*Courtesy* Thomas Wide.)
9. The Fyzee sisters and others on their 1908 European tour, as depicted in *Sair-yi Yurop* (1909?). (*Courtesy* Sunil Sharma.)
10. Qazi Abdul Ghaffar and family. (*Courtesy* Omar Khalidi.)
11. A portrait of Halide Edib. (*Courtesy* Public domain image available on Wikimedia Commons at: http://commons.wikimedia.org/wiki/File:Halide-edip-adivar-b3.jpg)

Foreword

It is a pleasure to welcome *On the Wonders of Land and Sea: Persianate Travel Writing* into the Ilex Foundation Series. This fine collection of seven articles devoted to Persianate travel writing from the late eighteenth to the early twentieth century constitutes a major contribution to a neglected area within the study of modern travel literature. The expansion of research related to travel writing in recent decades has greatly advanced scholarship at the intersection of historical and literary studies, and the publication of numerous travel-related memoirs, many of them composed during the period under study in the present volume, has provided a growing readership with access to a far more numerous and diverse set of individual voices than was previously available. The overwhelming majority of these studies, however, have concerned the travels of Europeans, especially in lands to the south and east of Europe, and in regions with significant Muslim populations. As Roberta Micallef and Sunil Sharma indicate, "internal" travel within the Muslim-majority world of the period has, until recently, received very little scholarly attention. This neglect is all the more regrettable and surprising given the volume, range and interest of the literature generated by such travel, and its very considerable historical importance.

In seven independent but interrelated essays, the present collection rectifies this deficit with reference to travels to, from and within the Persianate world. The contributions highlight the experiences, observations and insights of a diverse group of men and women, whose writings document and illuminate a world in the midst of rapid change. Each contributor situates his or her traveler(s) in historical and literary context, and readers will note the countless ways in which various imperial projects underway in the region impinge on the travelers' journeys and their lives. The focus of the collection, however, lies in the importance of the travelers' literary representations as media for exploring differing constructions of self and identity, home and community, gender and generation, in the course of the planned and unplanned encounters thrown up by their travels. Unexpected intersections and coincidences across the collection offer particular moments of interest and delight, such as when two of the travelers turn out to have attended performances of *Lohengrin*, or when one traveler's observations and reactions prefigure another's.

Collectively, the essays demonstrate the degree to which Persianate societies of the period formed a linked cultural region, within which travelers confronted at once difference and familiarity. The Persian language, moreover, made available to travelers who chose to adopt it the rich tradition of the *safarnāma*, on which many authors drew even as they adapted a lively variety of forms from other literatures and genres. In this connection, the volume offers further an exploration of the status of Persian during this period, and the meanings it carried for authors, often already multilingual, at a time when vernacular languages on the one hand and European languages on the other added new alternatives.

In short, this excellent collection introduces readers to an engaging set of individual travelers, and combines close readings of their writings with their careful location in the rapidly changing world that both stimulated their production and elicited their comment. A broad readership will find itself indebted to the editors and contributors for not only extending an important body of interdisciplinary scholarship but also opening new paths of research.

LM

Introduction

Roberta Micallef and Sunil Sharma

On the Wonders of Land and Sea: Persianate Travel Writing is the outcome of two workshops held at Boston University over the course of two years, 2007-9. Five papers were presented at the workshops and two were solicited for this volume. Our aim in this initiative was to make an intervention in the flourishing field of travel writing studies by focusing attention on modern travelogues in an attempt to examine nineteenth- and early twentieth-century travel writing from a lens other than that of Orientalism or post-colonial studies. If the West was also invested in exploring, colonizing, and writing about the exotic East during this period, there was a surge in South Asians and Middle Easterners traveling and writing about their experiences in Europe, Asia and Africa. What is missing in the recent body of scholarship on travelogues is a comparative and nuanced analysis of works by authors, whether they be North Africans, Turks, Iranians or Indians, travelling and writing in the eastern Islamic or Persianate world. Nor has there been a sufficient understanding of the ways in which certain features of traditional travelogues survived into the modern period, while absorbing new narrative techniques from a variety of sources. Instead of merely excluding the West as a reference point of travel writers to ruminate on a number of issues, other linked cultural regions with a history going back several centuries have been integrated into the field of study.

The writing of travel literature is a broad field that encompasses several genres and disciplines, mainly in historical, literary and cultural studies. Too often travelogues are mined for the information they can provide and it is well to be reminded that, "Travel writing is not a literal and objective record of journeys undertaken. It carries preconceptions that, even if challenged, provide a reference point. It is influenced, if not determined, by its authors' gender, class, age, nationality, cultural background and education. It is ideological."[1] The study of texts in a cultural and historical context brings several pertinent subjects to the forefront of scrutiny: the large-scale global movement of peoples and the existence of expatriate communities in far-flung places at the advent of modernity, the impact of print culture in the writing and circulation of travel books, and the choice of language in

1. Youngs 2006, 2.

an age when multilingualism was more prevalent than it is today. Our travel writers were often transnational individuals, heirs to more than one cultural and literary tradition, who attempted to negotiate the differences and distances between cultures, but also between expatriate communities and the homeland. It is also noteworthy that many of these travelers were also literary authors who variously wrote poetry, novels, and essays, and their travelogues evince features of their creative side.

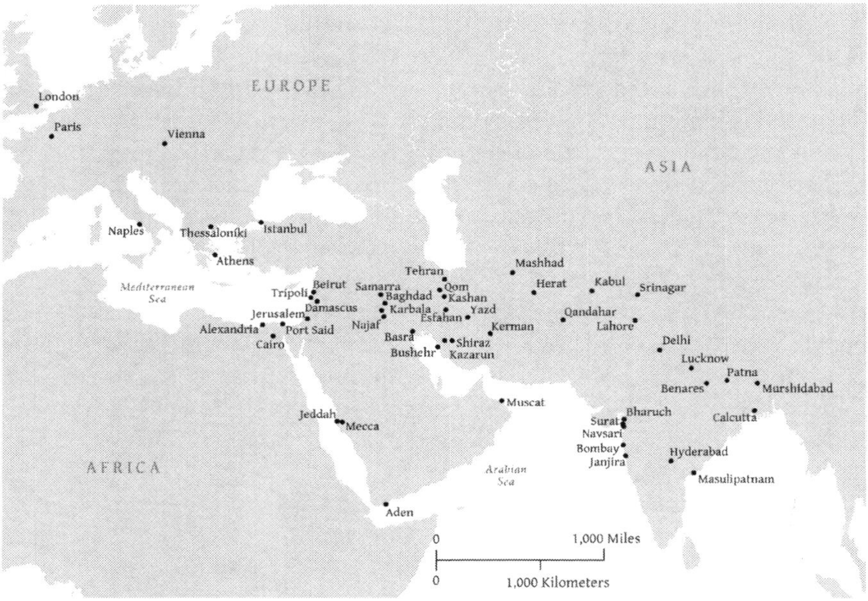

The World of the Persianate Traveler, 1786–1935

Scholars who work on travel literature acknowledge that "[c]ritical reflection on travel literature, however, is a relatively new phenomenon" for "[m]ost texts which we today include in the category of "travel writing", because of their largely non-fictional and/or hybrid generic status, were located beyond the scope of most scholars' academic research."[2] Although "non-English travel writing has often been influential in English and published in Britain, with translations appearing soon after original publication, and travel writing has played an important role in recent years in the creation of an international literary field,"[3] scholarly and translation efforts

2. Moroz and Sztachelska 2010, ix; also Hulme and Youngs 2002, 1.
3. Hulme and Youngs 2002, 1. Translations of travelogues from other languages also played an important role in nineteenth-century Persian literary culture (Afshar 2002, 155).

continue to privilege premodern narratives or those that are in dialogue with the West. This is, of course, not a negative comment on this trend for, according to a recent work, "Feminist and post-colonial studies have become two fields that have concentrated on the texts of travel literature in the most sustained and fruitful ways; the former exposing its patriarchy and redressing the balance between the attention paid of female versus male travelers and travel writers, the latter being keen to prove travel writing's and travel writers' (often unconscious) complex involvement and implication in the projects of Orientalism, colonialism, imperialism and post-colonialism."[4] The recent rise in interest in autobiographies and the history of the self has been another avenue by which the study of travel literature has gained acceptance in a variety of diciplines.[5]

In a more specific way, the travel narratives discussed in these essays follow those introduced by Alam and Subrahmanyam in their study of classical Indo-Persian travel literature. In this volume we are concerned with what the two historians have identified as "the moment of colonization—some moment between 1800 and 1850—that defines the end of the Indo-Persian travel-text; there are certainly travel-accounts written in Persian after this date, but they belong largely to an Iran that has increasingly turned its back on South Asia and the larger Persophone world."[6] The terminus point of this volume is the early twentieth century, the highpoint of nationalism across vast areas of the world and the twilight of colonialism and imperialism. From another point of view, it takes us to the time just before commercial flights changed the patterns and routes of travelers, ushering in a new era of travel writing. As part of the long nineteenth-century world-wide phenomenon in the increase in the mobility of travelers, Iranians, Turks, Afghans and Indians not only visited and wrote about Europe but also ventured out of their own corner of the Islamic or Persianate world, as the case may be, and expressed their awareness of a connected history with others. Such modern accounts have not received their due notice for we are hard put to name Turkish accounts of India after the sixteenth-century seafarer Sidi Ali Reis or Arab accounts of India and Iran after the fourteenth-century globetrotter Ibn Battuta, although such works do exist. Similarly, the full picture of Iranian accounts of travel to India in the post-Safavid period, not to mention the vast body of untranslated Safavid accounts of India in prose and verse, is quite unclear and only beginning to be explored. When it comes to women's

4. Moroz and Sztachelska 2010, ix.

5. See Blanton 2002 and Majeed 2007 on the representation of the self in the autobiography and travel genres.

6. Alam and Subrahmanyam 2007, 360.

writing, with rare exceptions, travel writing by female Muslims makes an appearance at the moment of modernity in several cultures and offers startling points of comparison and contrast to their male counterparts.[7]

A preliminary foray into the texts of the late early modern and modern period shows that some of the same reasons continued to motivate later travelers as earlier ones, but on a geographically larger scale and in more complex historical circumstances. There has been significant empirical and theoretical scholarship on travel for the sake of learning and education and pilgrimage, whether on hajj or to Shiʿite locales, and this scholarship allows one to view the long-term patterns in and routes of journeys, as well as to undertake comparative studies.[8] Recent anthologies that include excerpts of travel writings by Muslims or Asians and Africans also enable comparisons between premodern and modern accounts.[9] The decision by Indian travelers to write in vernacular languages, as opposed to the almost exclusive use of Persian in earlier times, and the preference for English, the new cosmopolitan language of the modern world, or to choose the form of a diary, or to decide to publish and translate works in this genre for a wide audience, are all features of modern travel writing literary culture. In his discussion on the problems of studying the nineteenth-century Persian travelogue, William L. Hanaway writes, "Until the twentieth century, when Persian sensibility changed under the influence of European Romanticism, Persian travel accounts remained quite strictly dynamic and utilitarian."[10] Paying particular attention to the literary aspects of the travelogues reveals links to traditional forms of narrative, such as the reaction of travelers to wonders (*ʿajāʾib*) or the beauty of cities and people (*shahrāshūb*), or the introduction of new forms of discourse, such as the benefits of modernization and technology.

A traveler's choice of form or genre, from poetry with conventional metaphors to a polished introspective narrative, results from choices that are both literary and personal. A text with a more documentary record of people met and places seen requires a different kind of reading, but offers some of the same possibilities of understanding the author's attempt at self-fashioning as a more autobiographical work does.[11] Not all travelogues are

7. Lambert-Hurley 2008. There is no anthology of Asian and/or Middle Eastern women travelers although several collections of writings by European and American women have been published.

8. Euben 2006; Eickelman and Piscatori 1990. Euben emphasizes the need for comparative studies: "I seek to shift the theoretical perspective by bringing into view the ways in which travelers of all kinds, past and present and from many directions, produce knowledge about others and themselves comparatively," Euben 2006, 8.

9. For instance, see Khair 2006.

10. Hanaway 2002, 249-50.

11. Rahimieh's pertinent question and comment can be applied to travel writing from

great literary works, of course, but that does not provide the justification for taking a positivist attitude towards them. For instance, they also have a place in the study of the formation of a register of language particularly suited to dealing with a world quickly becoming modern; as Iraj Afshar suggests, "travelogues were one of the practical means for the arrival and dissemination of foreign words in Persian and the development of Persian literary style."[12] In the academic study of travel writing, the definition of a travelogue has been broadened to include works of fiction or imaginary voyages, topics that are not touched upon in this volume, not deliberately but due to the serendipitous collocation of topics and inter-related texts in Persian, Urdu, Gujarati and English.

Coming from various disciplines, we collectively address the issues discussed above and other pertinent subjects such as the difference in the nature of travel writing when the traveler is traveling within his/her own culturally familiar space as opposed to going to a foreign land, the politics implicit in these works whether in a colonial or post-colonial world, and the role of gender and national identity on the perspectives of the authors. The essays in this collection span the late eighteenth, nineteenth and early twentieth century and include travel by male and female, Muslim and Parsi/Zoroastrian, travelers in the Hijaz, Iraq, Egypt, Turkey, Iran, Afghanistan, India and Europe. Additionally, India (South Asia) figures as the point of departure or destination of each traveler. Thus, the designation of "Persianate" for the travelogues, on the one hand, indicates their geographic ambit, and on the other hand, signifies certain generic and cultural connections with the medieval and early modern Arabic, Persian and Ottoman Turkish *rihla* and *safarnāma*. The idea of the Persianate ecumene, comprising cultural regions where Persian served as the main, if not the only, cultural lingua franca for elites until modern times, overlaps to some degree with the Islamicate world, in the influences on the cultural lives and practices of non-Muslims. Thus, the early twentieth-century traveler Halide Edib's reaction to India as a familiar place is due to the Islamicate elements in Turkish and Indian societies of the time. In this regard, the city of Istanbul (Constantinople) is of significance because it is both Persianate by virtue of the Ottoman-Persian cultural and literary connections, but also because it figures largely in the Indo-Muslim and Afghan imagination of the modern period. "Persianate" can have a religiously diverse and slightly different cultural connotation;

---

neighboring cultures: "[W]hat might we find by assuming that Persian life writing occurs at the intersections of social history, political memoir, travelogues, and diaries? ... [W]riting about the self is always irrecovably bound to the communal and the political. But this notion of the self has not remained static throughout Persian history" (2001, 17).

12. Afshar 2002, 149.

the place of Iran in the Parsi worldview contrasts with the way it was regarded by Indian Muslims or Hindus. Each essay then is about the theme of travel and investigates a Muslim or Persianate traveler, whether to Europe or to another part of the Persianate world, and explores how the narrator represents what s/he sees while drawing on and reshaping the genre of travel writing itself. Our general map, which includes most of the cities our travelers visited, demonstrates that Persianate and Islamicate travels linked various parts of the world in a way that was transformed in the twentieth century when national borders changed modes of travel. We hope that this collection will be a step toward a more sustained critical and comparative discussion of travelogues by Muslim and Persianate travelers in dialogue with other Persianate, Muslim and European travelers. In terms of gaps, a piece on travel in Central Asia or on a work by a traveler from there would have added another dimension to the study of the Persianate travelogue.

Daniel Sheffield's contribution compares two travelogues of Indian Zoroastrians who visited Iran during the eighteeenth and nineteenth centuries: the Persian *Dīn-khirad* (Wisdom of the Religion) of Mullā Fīrūz b. Kā'ūs (1786), and Māṇekji Limji Hāṭariā's Gujarati *Risāle Ezhār-e Siāt-e Īrān* (Exposition of Travels in Iran) (1865). Read along with the texts discussed in Mana Kia's paper, the works studied here challenge the standard definition of the Persianate travelogue, often predetermined by European or better known Islamic models. These texts are situated within the contemporary debates concerning religious authority in the Zoroastrian community. Following sociologist Eviatar Zerubavel's definition of Zoroastrianism as a group of communities connected in their social construction of shared memory through common narratives, commemoration of sacred places, and through shared, periodically repeated activities, Sheffield demonstrates how the mnemonic landscape of Iran itself became a locus of the controversies of the eighteenth and nineteenth century that ultimately split the Parsi community into two groups, only one of which continued to recognize the authority of the Iranians. By reading these texts alongside an examination of the contemporary debates and the anxieties which constitute them, Sheffield explores the complexity of these texts, and demonstrates some ways in which they reflect the tensions within the Indian Parsi community in their very depictions of landscape and peoples of Iran.

Mana Kia's paper investigates two early nineteenth-century works by Persian Shi'a Muslims, 'Alī Mīrzā Maftūn's *Zubdat al-akhbār fi savāniḥ al-afsār* (1826-7) and Aqā Ahmad Behbahānī's narrative, *Merāt al-aḥvāl-i jahān-numā* (1805-10). Kia examines the perceptions of their places of origin and destination of two travelers who travel between Iran and India in opposite directions. She argues for a particular meaning of geography common to a shared Persianate culture that gives meaning to the experiences of travel and representation of places, while pinpointing the specificities of each text. In contrast to Behbahānī's heavily autobiographical travel narrative, Maftūn's text is a *hajjnāma*, with additional trips to Shi'ite places of pilgrimage in Iran, thus being a variation on the more frequently encountered hajj travelogues and experiences of a pilgrim in the Hijaz, such as the one by a Sunni Afghan discussed in Thomas Wide's paper. Each narrative has different concerns and views, but they nevertheless evince a shared understanding of the significance of Iran and India as places. *'Ajam* was not merely a geographic designation for these travelers, but rather a set of cultural practices that softens the discomfort of travel.

Omar Khalidi's piece is a close reading of the Mahdi Hasan Khan Fath Nawaz Jang's travel diary about his travels to England in 1888. It is noteworthy that many travelers from Hyderabad wrote travelogues in this period, as compared to some other parts of South Asia. Khalidi presents the reader with an Indian aristocrat's representation of Victorian Britain from an 'official' and political point of view. Written in English and subsequently translated into Urdu, this work seems dry in comparison to earlier travelogues, and is also devoid of the anti-colonial passion that is seen later, as discussed in Daniel Majchrowicz's paper. Khalidi's essay is particularly important for the history of Muslim travelogues because it frames Fath Nawaz Jang's travel diary in the context of other Persian, Urdu and English narratives of the period, as well as his own life. A close analysis of this work reveals the shifting attitudes among the Muslim elites of Hyderabad and Lucknow in the critical post-1857 period.

Thomas Wide's essay is about a Persian travel-account written by the Afghan intellectual, statesman and exile Mahmud Tarzi of a trip he made through the Ottoman Empire as a young man accompanying his father on the hajj in 1891, and published in 1915. Wide's focus on "mobility" and "transnationalism" allows him to examine Afghanistan in its regional and trans-regional context, with its strong cultural and historical links to Iran on one side and India on the other. Through a study of the text and its context Wide demonstrates that Mahmud Tarzi's travelogue is at once a case study and an example of "the steam-powered intellectual" whose travels transformed their perspective, and "a testament to wider patterns of interaction and integration between parts of the world that were formerly distinct." Studying Tarzi and his travelogue through the lens of hybridity rather than alteritism, and tracing the encounters between Tarzi and larger movements and communities of Afghan travelers scattered across the Ottoman Empire,

Wide examines larger issues in Tarzi's text such as identity and homeland. This approach allows him to argue that Tarzi's text is not only an interesting travelogue by a new type of "transcultural traveler" but also an attempt to write peripheral regions such as Afghanistan back into global history.

Sunil Sharma examines the narratives from 1906-8 of Atiya Fyzee and Nazli Begum, two Muslim sisters from Bombay. Their travelogues drew on traditional forms of discourse, especially in reacting to new places and people, while employing subversive strategies used to express their emotions within the boundaries of what was allowed to be expressed in women's writings. The travel diaries of the two sisters include a substantial autobiographical content, and the detailed descriptions they provide about public and domestic life in Europe and the Middle East, their meetings with Indian expatriates as well as Europeans, including former colonial administrators, gentry and even rulers, are replete with important information for social historians. This essay is relevant to scholars of women's and gender studies in that it explores a different perspective than that evident in the travelogues written by male authors. The Fyzee sisters often reacted to the same places, people and situations in markedly different ways than male travel writers of this time. It would seem that they had not lost the capacity to feel wonder and express joy. In another instance, it is instructive to contrast Mahdi Hasan's report on Richard Wagner's opera *Lohengrin*, as discussed in the previous piece, with Nazli Begum's dramatic encounter with an effeminate dandy, which is linked to a particularly sensitive emotional juncture in her life. Her worries about the erosion of Indian masculine values look forward to the same anxiety expressed by a male traveler a few years later, as discussed in the next piece.

Daniel Majchrowicz explores how another Indian traveler Qāẕī 'Abdul Ġaffār, who traveled to Europe as part of the Indian *Khilāfat* committee in 1924, rejects colonial discourse and affirms his own version of Indian nationalism in his Urdu chronicle, *Naqsh-i firang*. Just as 1857 marked a turning point in the shift in tone in Indo-Muslim travelogues, this period of the end of the Islamic caliphate and rising nationalism can be seen as another period of transition. This work is marked by a strong degree of political consciousness and is not merely a straightforward acount of an Anglophile colonial subject going in to the heart of the empire, as was quite frequent in late nineteenth-century Indian travel books. The narrative that initially allows the traveler to reverse myths about the Oriental in Europe also provides him with the means to narrate and resolve his contentious existence through the act of writing. The literary value of the text, written by a man of letters, and its semiotic connection to the author's autobiography links it to the last essay in this volume.

Roberta Micallef's essay examines three linked autobiographical narratives by the Turkish intellectual, Halide Edib Adivar. In her essay Micallef explores Edib's journey from the semiotic to the symbolic by tracing her life stories, which begin with her childhood home and take her to India; thus she travels in the opposite direction from the Fyzee sisters. Edib's gaze, with respect to what she sees and how she sees India in 1935, is demonstrably tempered by her point of origin. Like the other travel narratives discussed in this volume, Edib's narrative reveals as much about her own place in Turkey as it does about her views on India. She acquires an adult public speaking voice from her journeys, both literal and figurative, as her travels involve historical encounters with modernity, changing borders and boundaries of both the nation and the individual, all against the backdrop of a collapsing Ottoman empire, the emerging Turkish Republic, and the eve of partition in India. Edib's sympathetic reaction to India and Indians is part of the familiarity of Persianate cultural values and connected history.

We have provided a General Bibliography, by no means comprehensive, at the end of this volume. Its purpose is two-fold: one, to compile a list of translations of travelogues from the period under study in this volume, intended particularly for teachers and students; two, to bring together critical studies on the subject for the use of other scholars. In the first regard, the reader will be struck by how little is available in translation from this period. This neglect can perhaps be explained by the discomfort of some translators with texts that are situated between the disciplines of literature and history. In any event, given the paucity of translations, we have allowed authors to quote generously in translation from the original sources instead of summarizing the contents of individual works. Travelogues written in English are excluded from the bibliography of primary texts because there were just too many of them in this period, although a database of such works would be an extremely valuable tool. The transliteration of Persian and Urdu is consistent within the essays but not necessarily across them.

We would like to thank Boston University's Center for the Humanities and the Institute for the Study of Muslim Societies and Civilizations for their support of our workshops. We are also indebted to Naghmeh Sohrabi for her animated and engaged participation in our workshops and for suggesting the title for this volume; we regret her inability to offer a written contribution. Mana Kia and Daniel Majchrowicz provided valuable help in finalizing the introduction and bibliography respectively, while Scott Walker at Harvard's Map Collection kindly prepared the map. We would also like to thank our colleagues Shankar Raman (Massachusetts Institute of Technology) and Keith Vincent (Boston University) for serving as discussants at our secondworkshop. Louise Marlow, our Ilex editor, and Christopher Dadian, production editor, deserve our special thanks for their exemplary support and encouragement. This volume is dedicated to the memory of Dr. Omar Khalidi, who was enthusiastic about this project from its inception and provided assistance in the form of references and books, but left us while the collection was still in preparation.

Bibliography

Afshar, Iraj (2002), "Persian Travelogues: A Description and Bibliography," in: Elton L. Daniel (ed.), *Society and Culture in Qajar Iran: Studies in Honor of Hafez Farmayan*, Costa Mesa, Cal.: Mazda, 145-62.

Alam, Muzaffar and Sanjay Subrahmanyam (2007), *Indo-Persian Travels in the Age of Discoveries, 1400-1800*, Cambridge: Cambridge University Press.

Anderson, Jaynie (ed.) (2009), *Crossing Cultures: Conflict, Migration and Convergence*. Melbourne: Miegunyah Press.

Bentley, Jerry H., Renate Bridenthal, and Káearen Wigen (ed.) (2007), *Seascapes: Maritime Histories, Littoral Cultures, and Transoceanic Exchanges*, Honolulu: University of Hawaii Press.

Bhattacharji, Shobhana (2008), *Travel Writing in India*, New Delhi: Sahitya Akademi.

Blanton, Casey (2002), *Travel Writing: The Self and the World*, New York: Routledge.

Bose, Sugata (2006), *A Hundred Horizons: The Indian Ocean in the Age of Global Empire*, Cambridge: Harvard University Press.

Burton, Antoinette (1998), *At the Heart of the Empire: Indians and the Colonial Encounter in Late-Victorian Britain*, Berkeley: University of California Press.

Chandra, Nandini (2007), "The Pedagogic Imperative of Travel Writing in the Hindi World: Children's Periodicals (1920-1950)," *South Asia: Journal of South Asian Studies* 30/2: 293-325.

Chatterjee, Kumkum (1999), "Discovering India: Travel, History and Identity in Late 19th and Early 20th Century Colonial India," in: Daud Ali (ed.), *Invoking the Past: The Uses of History in South Asia* , Delhi, Oxford University Press, 192-230.

Despoix, Philippe and Justus Fetscher (2004), *Cross-cultural Encounters and Constructions of Knowledge in the 18th and 19th century: Non-European and European Travel of Exploration in Comparative Perspective*, Kassel: Kassel University Press.

Eickelman, Dale F. and James Piscatori (1990), *Muslim Travellers: Pilgrimage, Migration, and the Religious Imagination*, London: Routledge.

Euben, Roxanne L. (2006), *Journeys to the Other Shore: Muslim and Western Travelers in Search of Knowledge*, Princeton: Princeton University Press.

Fisher, Michael H. (2004), *Counterflows to Colonialism: Indian Travellers and Settlers in Britain 1600-1857*, Delhi: Permanent Black.

Ghanoonparvar, M.R. (1993), *In a Persian Mirror: Images of the West and Westerners in Iranian Fiction*, Austin: University of Texas Press.

Göçek Fatma Müge (1987), *East Encounters West: France and the Ottoman Empire in the Eighteenth Century*, New York: Oxford University Press.

Grewal, Inderpal (1996), *Home and Harem: Nation, Gender, Empire, and the Cultures of Travel,* London: Leicester University Press.

Hanaway, William L. (2002), "Persian Travel Narratives: Notes towards the Definition of a Nineteenth-Century Genre," in: Elton L. Daniel (ed.), *Society and Culture in Qajar Iran: Studies in Honor of Hafez Farmayan,* Costa Mesa: Mazda, 249-68.

Herzog, Christoph and Raoul Motika (2000), "Orientalism "*alla turca*": Late 19th/Early 20th Century Ottoman Voyages into the Muslim Outback," *Die Welt des Islams* 40/2 (July): 139-95.

Hooper, Glenn and Tim Youngs (ed.) (2004), *Perspectives on Travel Writing,* Aldershot: Ashgate.

Hulme, Peter and Tim Youngs (ed.) (2002), *Cambridge Companion to Travel Writing*, Cambridge: Cambridge University Press.

Khair, Tabish, Martin Leer, Justin D. Edwards and Hanna Ziadeh (ed.) (2006), *Other Routes: 1500 Years of African and Asian Travel Writing,* Bloomington: Indiana University Press.

Lambert-Hurley, Siobhan (2008), "Afterword: Muslim Women Write Their Journeys Abroad," in: *A Princess's Pilgrimage: Nawab Sikandar Begum's A Pilgrimage to Mecca*, Bloomington: Indiana University Press, 155-71.

——— and Sunil Sharma (2010), *Atiya's Journeys: A Muslim Woman from Colonial Bombay to Edwardian Britain*, New Delhi: Oxford University Press.

Leask, Nigel (2002), *Curiosity and the Aesthetics of Travel Writing, 1770-1840: 'From an Antique Land'*, Oxford: Oxford University Press.

Majeed, Javed (2007), *Autobiography, Travel and Postnational Identity: Gandhi, Nehru and Iqbal*, Hampshire: Palgrave Macmillan.

Matar, Nabil (2009), *Europe through Arab Eyes, 1578-1727,* New York: Columbia University Press.

Mohanty, Sachidananda (ed.) (2003), *Travel Writing and the Empire,* New Delhi: Katha.

Moroz, Grzegorz and Jolanta Sztachelska (2010), *Metamorphoses of Travel Writing: Across Theories, Genres, Centuries and Literary Traditions*, Newcastle upon Tyne: Cambridge: Scholars Publishing.

Pearson, Michael N. (1996), *Pilgrimage to Mecca: The Indian Experience, 1500-1800*, Princeton: Markus Wiener.

Pratt, Mary Louise (1992), *Imperial Eyes: Travel Writing and Transculturation,* London: Routledge.

Rahimieh, Nasrin (2001), *Missing Persians: Discovering Iranian Cultural History,* Syracuse: Syracuse University Press.

Rastegar, Kamran (2007), *Literary Modernity between the Middle East and Europe: Textual Transactions in Nineteenth Century Arabic, English, and Persian Literatures*, London: Routledge.
Ringer, Monica M. (2002), "The Quest for the Secret of Strength in Iranian Nineteenth-Century Travel Literature: Rethinking Tradition in the *Safarnameh*," in: Nikki Keddie and Rudi Matthee, (ed.), *Iran and the Surrounding World, 1501-2001: Interactions in Culture and Cultural Politics*, Seattle: University of Washington Press, 146-61.
Sohrabi, Naghmeh (2012), *Signs Taken for Wonder: Nineteenth Century Travel Accounts from Iran to Europe*, Oxford: Oxford University Press.
Tavakoli-Targhi, Mohamad (2001), *Refashioning Iran: Orientalism, Occidentalism, and Historiography*, New York: Palgrave.
Ursinus, Michael (ed.) (2000), "Ottoman Travels and Travel Accounts from an Earlier Age of Globalization," *Die Welt des Islams* 40/2 (July): 133-334.
Youngs, Tim (ed.) (2006), *Travel Writing in the Nineteenth Century: Filling the Blank Spaces*, London: Anthem.
Zilcosky, John (2011), *Writing Travel, the Poetics and Politics of the Modern Journey*, Toronto: The University of Toronto Press.

A portrait of Mullā Fīrūz b. Kā'ūs (1758–1830). Photograph in the collection of Daniel Sheffield. (Courtesy Dadyseth Atash Behram, Mumbai.)

Iran, the Mark of Paradise or the Land of Ruin?

Historical Approaches to Reading Two Parsi Zoroastrian Travelogues

Daniel Sheffield

I. Introduction

SINCE THEIR EMIGRATION TO INDIA, the idea of Iran has played a prominent, yet complicated role in the Parsi Zoroastrians'[1] imaginary topography. Ancient Iran, as the ancestral homeland of the community and the setting of pre-Islamic Zoroastrian mytho-history, has always been a *locus memoriae* and an important part of Parsi communal identity,[2] yet attitudes towards contemporary Iran, as ruled by a succession of Islamic dynasties, changed significantly over time. In this paper, I investigate aspects of two Parsi narratives of travel to Iran, the *Dīn-khirad* (*The Wisdom of the Religion*) of Pishūtan, the son of Kā'ūs (better known as Mullā Fīrūz), a versified Persian account written in 1786, and Māṇekji Limji Hāṭariā's *Risāle Ezhār-e Siāt-e Īrān*[3] (*An Account of a Journey to Iran*), published in Gujarati in 1865. Using these two works, written a little less than a century apart from each other, I will trace the ways in which the Parsi community's views of Iran and its co-religionists living there shifted dramatically during the years leading up to the onset of colonial modernity. I argue that these shifts in perspective, though related to the great hardships Iranian Zoroastrians faced in the wake of the fall of the Zands and the rise of the Qājār dynasty, are ultimately

1. For the purposes of this paper, the term Parsi refers to the descendants of the Zoroastrian communities that settled in Western India during the latter quarter of the first millennium CE. For the sake of convenience, the term Irani Zoroastrian refers to later Zoroastrian migrants from Iran to the Indian subcontinent, while Iranian Zoroastrian refers to the Zoroastrian communities that remained in Iran, concentrated for most of the early modern period near the cities of Yazd and Kerman. Obviously, these categories are somewhat permeable.

2. My interest in the role of place in the Parsi collective memory originates in my reading of Pierre Nora's *Realms of Memory*. Nora 1996, vii, defines a *locus memoriae* as "a symbolic element of the memorial heritage of any community."

3. The title is the Gujarati transcription of the Persian *Risāla-yi Iẓhār-i Siyāḥat-i Īrān*.

projections originating in changing social currents within the Parsi community itself.

Social theorist Ashis Nandy famously characterized the colonialist enterprise in South Asia as accompanied by the loss and the recovery of selfhood.[4] As I have argued elsewhere, the Parsi encounter with colonial modernity too is characterized by, on the one hand, the loss of an Indo-Persianate identity that had developed over the course of centuries of inter-communal interaction in Gujarat, and on the other, the recovery of a constructed ancient Iranian identity, a recovery made possible through the newly introduced colonial sciences of philology, archaeology, and ethnology.[5] In this paper, examining the writings of Mullā Fīrūz, one of the last representatives of the long Parsi engagement with the Indo-Persian literary tradition, and Māṇekji Limji Hāṭariā, an influential figure in the shaping of Iranian identity both among the Parsis and in Iran itself, I contend that this shift in the Parsi notion of selfhood is intimately linked with how the Parsi community constructs discourse around Iran.

II. Relations between Indian and Iranian Zoroastrians

Both Mullā Fīrūz and Māṇekji Limji Hāṭariā were sent to Iran through the patronage of Parsi community members on missions to the Iranian Zoroastrian communities. In order to understand what impelled their journeys, it is therefore necessary to say a few words about the historical relations of the Iranian and Parsi Zoroastrian communities. According to most normative twentieth-century Parsi historiography, the predecessors of the Parsi community emigrated from Iran sometime in the eighth or ninth century to escape "persecution" at the hands of Muslim rulers;[6] such narratives usually continue that for those Zoroastrian communities which stayed in Iran, oppression and persecution continued to such an extent that the community was reduced to crippling material and intellectual poverty by the nineteenth century.[7] While affirming that Iranian Zoroastrians have faced considerable persecution over time, such universally condemnatory narratives might seem, at best, essentialist, often denying agency to the very

4. See Nandy 1983.

5. See Chapter 5 of my dissertation, *In the Path of the Prophet: Medieval and Early Modern Narratives of the Life of Zarathustra in Islamic Iran and Western India* (Harvard University, 2012).

6. For the debate on the traditional dates of the Parsi migration, see Modi 1905 and Hodivala 1920, as well as the discussion in Williams 2009, 205–17. For general surveys of the history of the Parsi community in India, see *inter alia*, Karaka 1884, Paymaster 1954, Kulke 1974, and Palsetia 2001.

7. Surveys of Iranian Zoroastrian history after the coming of Islam can be found in Amighi 1990 as well as Namīrānīyān 1387/2009.

group for which they purport to elicit sympathy. Even Mary Boyce, often cited as the twentieth century's leading expert on Zoroastrianism, refers to Iranian Zoroastrians after the Islamic conquest of Iran as an "intellectually starved minority which remained in ignorance of any scientific developments after the ninth century CE, [...] spared the need to struggle with new knowledge, or to re-examine the dogmas of their ancient faith."[8]

For many Parsis, like other mercantile communities on the western coast of India and throughout the Persian Gulf, Iran historically has played a very significant role as a partner in maritime trade. Contrary to the normative view of Parsi history described above, recent research has shown that the initial Zoroastrian settlements in Western India may have had as much to do with this trade as they did with religious persecution.[9] Though during the centuries following the fall of the Sasanian Empire in 651 CE, the Zoroastrians of India seem to have only been in contact with the Zoroastrians who remained in Iran very sporadically, communication between the communities was re-established in the fifteenth century, and Iran became the center of Zoroastrian priestly authority. Questions were asked via couriers sent from Indian priests and communal leaders to their Iranian counterparts, and Indian priests were encouraged to travel to the Iranian Zoroastrian centers in the area of Yazd and Kerman in order to undergo religious training. This exchange of religious knowledge lasted until the eighteenth century, and over the course of the three centuries of correspondence, more than twenty texts exchanged between the Indian and Iranian communities (collectively referred to as the *Persian Rivāyats*) are extant.[10]

Already in the earliest of the *Persian Rivāyats*, Indian priests are advised to visit Iran in order to study religious texts and learn correct ritual practice. Thus, from the *Rivāyat of Narīmān Hūshang* (1478 AD) (Unvala 1922 v. 2, 380), we learn that:

> The worst thing is when *herbeds* [Zoroastrian priests] do not know how to use the (ritual) implements properly, nor do they know about the decisions, or the religious authorities, or purity or pollution. It is incumbent, therefore, that two knowledgeable *herbeds* should come to learn Pahlavi script and find out what is and what is not proper (*shāyist va nā-shāyist*), and then attend to the religion of Ohrmazd in that region [India] and be diligent in performing meritorious actions (*kirfa kardan*),

8. Boyce 1972, 19.

9. See, in particular, Wink 1990, 104–8, who argues that the Zoroastrian migrations to India were the result of an intensification of intercourse with older trading contacts made possible by the burgeoning commercial links between Islamic Iran and India.

10. See Unvala 1922 for the Persian edition and Dhabhar 1932 for a translation of most of these documents.

> so that they might reach Garōthmān, the best of existences and the place of the Righteous ones (*ashōvān*). It is (quite) near by the land route. From Qandahār to Sīstān is the shortest (way), and there is no worry (going) from Sīstān to Yazd.

And likewise, from the *Rivāyat of Bahman Pūnjiya* (1626 AD) (Unvala 1922 v. 1, 586):

> Whenever a suitable *herbed* comes here [Iran] and stays here for a year, (if) he comes here, learns all the rituals, and masters (*ustād shavad*) them, when he goes back to that region [India], it is fitting, otherwise if he does not see (what he is supposed to do) and does not learn it, it is not fitting. There are sayings and writings about this matter.

When Mullā Fīrūz was born in the city of Bharuch in 1758, the social and commercial networks of Indian and Iranian Zoroastrians had changed considerably in the three centuries since the beginning of the *Rivāyat* period, witnessing political instability in Iran, the influx of European merchants in the Persian Gulf and Indian Ocean, and the decline of the port of Surat in Gujarat.[11] New Parsi elites, who successfully exploited connections with European traders, were no longer content to be subjugated to the religious authority of the Iranian Zoroastrians. Matters came to a crucial turning point when it was suggested that the Iranian and Parsi religious calendars, which differed by one month, be synchronized. The politics of memory about Iran came to center on the calendar, upon which all acts of religious com-memoration (that is, "remembering together") rely, but which can also overtly mark sectarian differences in the case of differing praxes. Trivial as it might seem, the question of whether a leap year ever existed in the Zoroastrian religious calendar was the most debated topic in the Parsi priestly community for more than a century.

As early as the *Rivāyat of 1635*, it was noticed that the Iranian calendar was one month ahead of the Indian calendar.[12] In 1722, an Iranian named Jāmāsp Ḥakīm b. Ardashīr Vilāyatī came to Gujarat from Iran bearing a response to religious enquiries, and again observed the one month discrepancy between the Indian and the Iranian religious calendars. Dastur Jāmāsp apparently attracted a significant following among local priests in the city of Surat, among whom he was held in high regard—so much so that a con-

11. See Nadri 2009, 9–21 for a brief account of the history of the economic world in Gujarat.

12. See Vitalone 1992. The probable explanation for this is identified in de Blois 1996 and supported in 2003, namely that a leap month was added in 375 AY but was rejected by the Magians of Khurasan. However, this argument was unknown during the eighteenth and nineteenth centuries.

temporary Parsi author named Jiji Jamshedji Modi[13] composed a poem in Persian verse praising him and his activities in India (University of Mumbai Library Persian MS 48, f. 1v)

> Expert in astrology, skilled in the reading of *Pāzand*, with good intention, good character, and good speech,
> With mercy in his heart and power in the hand of his charity, his pure heart full of joy,
> He came to India from Iran; he came with love in his heart along with his companions. (...)
> He dignified India with his presence and opened the door of knowledge to those in India.

The manuscript goes on to describe Dastur Jāmāsp correcting a number of practices current among the Indian priests, even redacting the Avestan text and Pahlavi commentary of the Vīdēvdād, the scripture which formed the core of many of the most important Zoroastrian rituals.[14] Unlike his predecessors, he encouraged the Parsis to rectify their calendar and religious praxis with that of Iran. Jāmāsp was apparently the first to ascribe the calendrical difference between the Iranians and the Indians to a phenomenon referred to in Arabic and Persian as *kabīsa* or intercalation, namely the addition of a month to the calendar every one hundred and twenty years.[15] According to Jāmāsp, the custom of adding a leap month to the calendar, which was current neither among Iranian Zoroastrians nor among Parsis, had existed during the Sasanian period. Jāmāsp and his followers held that the Parsis of India had at some point erroneously added one leap month when their Iranian Zoroastrian coreligionists did not do so.[16]

Unlike the author of the *Rivāyat of 1635*, Jāmāsp suggested that the Parsis adopt not only the Iranian calendar but also other Iranian practices, such as pronouncing Avestan prayers with the pronunciations used in Iran rather than those current in India. However, the various parties who were

13. On Modi, see Karaka 1884 v. 2, 55.

14. See Cantera & Andrés Toledo 2008. This reworked manuscript is presumably alluded to in the same manuscript, f. 4v, "He wrote a book with his own hand (...), a *Vandīdād* (i.e., a *Vidēvdād*) with complete meaning." See also Vafadari 2003.

15. It should be noted that the length of the *actual* solar year was presumably well known to anyone in the eighteenth century, having been calculated millennia before this controversy. Intercalary months were already added by the Babylonians, and according to Ptolemy, the length of the tropical year had already been calculated by Hipparchus of Nicæa in the second century BCE to be 365 days, 3 hours, 48 minutes, and 49 seconds. See Meeus and Savoie 1992. The only other scholar who has drawn attention to the importance of the *kabīsa* controversy for the study of the history of early modern Zoroastrianism is Maneck 1997, 128–159. See also Coorlawala 1918 and Patel 1900.

16. This account of Jāmāsp's teachings is largely based on Mullā Fīrūz 1830, 12–20.

struggling for elite status within the Parsi community perceived Jāmāsp's suggestions as further subordination to the priests of Iran, resulting in a schism in the community, with the majority of the community questioning the right of the Iranians to continue to assert religious authority over the Parsis. The rift concerning the calendar split the community into two groups: the first, who became known as the *Shahanshāhīs*,[17] who maintained the Indian calendar, and the second, the *Qadīmīs*,[18] who synchronized their calendar with that of the Iranians. Shahanshāhī Parsis argued that the intercalation was part of the Zoroastrian religious calendar although it had been abandoned sometime after the fall of the Sasanian Empire, whereas Qadīmī and Iranian Zoroastrians argued that intercalation was never part of the religious calendar, at most only part of the civic calendar. More importantly, the Shahanshāhī group, which formed the majority of the Parsi community, ceased to recognize the authority of the Iranian priests, stopped participating in the *Rivāyat* correspondence, and instead asserted local priestly hierarchies in India, with the Bhagariā lineage of Navsari eventually becoming the most prominent.[19]

III. The End of the Rivāyat Era: The Dīn-Khirad of Mullā Fīrūz

By the 1760s, when Mullā Fīrūz (1758–1830) set out with his father, a Qadīmī priest, for Iran to receive the last of the *Persian Rivāyats*, Qadīmī Parsis were primarily active in the cities of Surat and Bharuch in Gujarat. At the time, the Shahanshāhīs and the Qadīmīs were led by two prominent businessmen,

17. Meaning "Imperialists" — so called because they held that intercalation was part of the Imperial Sasanian religious calendar. This group was also insultingly referred to as *Rasmī* or "Traditionalist," presumably along the lines of "those who care more about tradition than what is correct."

18. Meaning "Ancients," apparently because the Zoroastrian month names were called *qadīm* or "ancient" as opposed to their Islamic counterparts. This group also had an insulting nickname, *Chūrīgarī* or "Bangle-maker," referring, apparently, to the lower-class origins of some members of the group.

19. See Hinnells 2008. It should be noted that at the same time as the early *kabīsa* controversy, a number of rifts had formed among the Shahanshāhīs in Navsari — the Bhagariā *anjuman* was split on the question of whether laity could choose which priest could perform rites for them, or whether such rites should only be performed by designated individuals (a group known as the Minocher Homjis held the former view and founded their own fire temple); by 1733, another group of priests belonging to the Sanjānā *panthak* (one of five priestly genealogies in India), who were responsible for the care of the sacred *Ātash Behrām* fire transported the fire out of the city, until it was lodged in the village of Udvada in 1742. Despite this, strong connections with the communities in the trading centers of Surat and Bombay allowed the Bhagariā *panthak* to maintain its authority.

named Mancherji Kharshedji and Dhanjishāh Manjishāh respectively. The two were bitter opponents and collaborated with opposing commercial interests, Mancherji with the Dutch and Dhanjishāh with the English. Amidst debate between the two groups of Parsis, Dhanjishāh brought the matter of the Zoroastrian calendar to the court of the Muslim *navāb* of Bharuch in 1767 for adjudication. The *navāb*, who consulted the *panchāyats* of Navsari and Surat, declared that the Shahanshāhīs were correct and that all other *panchāyats* should emulate their practice.[20] This ruling did not please Dhanjīshāh, and violent incidents between the two groups began to arise. A Dutch record tells us that

> On April 1st 1768, a Parsi servant of Mancherji Khurshedji, a merchant and broker of the Dutch Company, came to Surat to whom another Parsi servant of Dhanjishah, a merchant under the English protection, asked wherefrom he came and without any further argument he inflicted a blow with his fist to the first mentioned who then fell down and meanwhile he gave him a slap, then the defender inflicted two pricks with his knife to the offender; many people witnessed this fight, and the Parsi who still had the knife in his hand, was attacked with bamboos with such force that the knife fell from his hand, he was further beaten up till he fell down.[21]

After failing to obtain affirmation by the *navāb* of Bharuch, Dhanjishāh Manjishāh sought affirmation from the Iranian Zoroastrians. He commissioned a leading Qadīmī priest of Bharuch, Kā'ūs b. Rustam, to go to Iran to obtain another *Rivāyat* about the calendar. But though this was to be the last *Rivāyat* to be obtained from Iran, the circumstances of this *Rivāyat*'s acquisition are remarkably preserved in the earliest extant Parsi travelogue:[22] entitled the *Dīn-khirad (Wisdom of the Religion)*, this text was written in Persian

20. This story is preserved not only in Parsi tradition, but also in an early Urdu versified history of the fall of the Nawab of Bharuch, called the *Qiṣṣa-i Ghamgīn*, written by Munshī 'Abbās 'Alī. See the edition by Misra 1975, 7–11. According to the text, Dhanjīshāh held a grudge after the Nawab decided in favor of Mancherji and wrote to the English to remind them that the Nawab owed them money from forty years ago, an event that the author of the *Qiṣṣa* sees as instrumental in the Nawab's downfall. That this may have been the case seems to be borne out by British records, which state "[Dhanjishāh] was of service as to the two expeditions [that against Surat and that leading to the conquest of Broach in the early 1770s]" (see Torri 1998, 286–7, esp. n. 111, *pace* Misra 1975, 15: "there is no hint of this in the Surat or Bombay documents"). The implications of the *Qiṣṣa* were already discussed in Modi 1908. See also the documents contained in Gense and Banaji 1937, 137–8.

21. Cited from Nadri 2007, 315.

22. An earlier travelogue, entitled the *Qiṣṣa-yi Kā'ūs va Afsād*, was composed by an Iranian Zoroastrian merchant named Kā'ūs b. Farīburz who was shipwrecked in Gujarat in the early sixteenth century. Consult Meherjirana Library MS F45 and Mulla Firuz Library MS R VII 119.

verse by Kā'ūs's son Pishūtan (later known as Mullā Fīrūz),[23] who accompanied his father on his twelve-year journey to Iran.

The text describes a debate between the *Shahanshāhīs* and the *Qadīmīs* held in Surat in 1768, which led to the journey of Pishūtan with his father (First Dastoor Meherjirana Library MS F-82, 16–19):[24]

> The debate went on to such an extent that many people gave their lives to that matter.
> Finally, it was put forth by both sides, "There are many knowledgeable *dastūrs* in Iran.
> We shall ask them and keep fear away from our minds. We will keep their responses close to our hearts."
> It was such that before this there was nothing left but the name of the religion of Zarathustra in India.
> No one was aware of the religion or the path—they were all deluded by the Hindu religion (*dīn-i hindū*).
> No one knew any of the Zend-Avesta, and each was firm on the road of deviation (*rāh-i bī-rāhī*).
> Finally, when they realized that, they sought the way to the *dastūrs* of Iran.
> When they realized that they were in disagreement and were not living according to the religion but were on the wrong path,
> They asked about the religion from top to bottom. Upon the reply, the religion would become strong again.
> A thousand disputes arose before them, but the correct path appeared out of all the deceptions.
> "Now this dispute is very large—it is like a wolf in the flock of the religion.
> We must send two people, no matter from where, who will put matters of religion aright for us."
> They investigated the priests (*radān*) of the religion, with a hundred announcements, a hundred examinations and scrutiny,
> They made up their minds on this matter, but the group of ignorami were upset out of their places.
> They sat and argued. They said much and heard much that was said.
> They said, "This is not what we want—What will we get from this besides shame?

23. For a general survey of the lives of this father and son based on the text of this travelogue, see Paymaster 1931 and Shahmardān Īrānī 1967 and 1984.

24. The text of Mullā Fīrūz's travelogue was published in 1999 by Shāyista Akhtar Jāved. Unfortunately, the edition is full of errors. The page numbers quoted in this paper are from MS F-82, preserved in the First Dastoor Meherjirana Library, Navsari, rather than the printed edition.

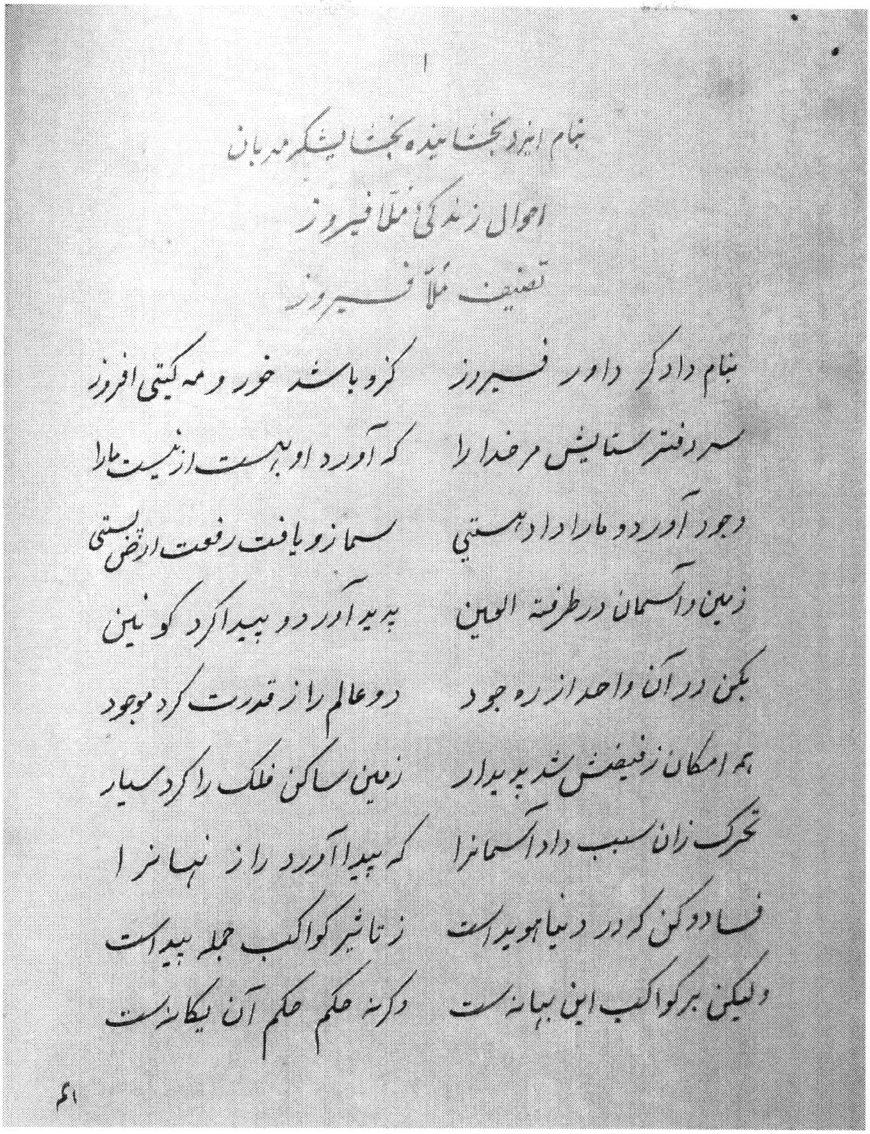

۱

بنام ایزد بخشاینده بخشایشگر مهربان

احوال زندگی ملا فیروز

تصنیف ملا فیروز

بنام دادگر داور فیروز — کزو باشد خور و مه گیتی افروز

سر دفتر ستایش مر خدا را — که آورد او بهست از نیست ما را

وجود آورد و ما را داد هستی — سما زو یافت رفعت ارض پستی

زمین و آسمان در طرفة العین — پدید آورد و پیدا کرد کونین

بکن در آن واحد از ره جود — دو عالم را ز قدرت کرد موجود

همه امکان ز فیضش شد پدیدار — زمین ساکن فلک را کرد سیار

تحرک زان سبب داد آسمانرا — که پیدا آورد راز نهانرا

فساد و کون که در دنیا هویداست — ز تاثیر کواکب جمله پیداست

ولیکن بر کواکب این بهانه ست — دگرنه حکم حکم آن یگانه ست

Mullā Fīrūz's *Dīn-khirad.* Photograph by Daniel Sheffield. (Courtesy Meherjirana Library, Navsari.)

We live according to the path and custom of our mothers and fathers
—we aren't looking for a bookish way or custom.
Our book is the way of our forebears—how is abandoning this just?"

The text narrates the journey of Kā'ūs and Pishūtan from Surat to Yazd via Muscat and Bandar Abbas. In Yazd, the two were welcomed by the Zoroastrian community, which the text describes as "illuminated, worthy, and magnificent" (*pur-nūr u pur-arj u khurrahmand*).[25] Further, the text continues (First Dastoor Meherjirana Library MS F-82, 29):

In Yazd, there was a great man (*kadkhudā*) of abundant good qualities
and a man of God.
He was the ruler and a man of rank. His gold and silver abounded in
Yazd.
He was called Bahrām because he was peaceful (*ba-ārām*) and good
(*bih*). His goblet was never empty of wine.

Upon arriving in Yazd, Mullā Kā'ūs presented two letters from the Qadīmī Parsis of Surat to the high priests there. The priests convened an assembly, and (First Dastoor Meherjirana Library MS F-82, 30–31):

After their conversation, they responded. They gave a very pleasant
and joyous reply, saying:
"A letter for the questions is required—we will make a suitable
response for every matter.
But as for the month controversy, let it be sufficient not to write about
it.
We have written about the month many times. Because of the
remaining doubt, we are leaving it aside.
One answer to the question is enough. The writing has been repeated
with proofs.
But in India, the priests and laity engage in partisanship (*ta'aṣṣub
mīkunand*) regarding the religion.
They consider taking care of the fire something lowly. They have
nothing to do with the religion or the customs.
Those who nourish speech are foreign to the religion. (Instead) they
keep lies and falsehood with them at home.
They know nothing but useless prayers. They are vacant of learning
or intellect.
They are careless towards God and incompetent towards Zarathustra.
They know nothing but ignorance.
If what they do were not ignorance, it would be easy and simple to
account for it.

25. Meherjirana Library MS F-82, 28.

> They consider going astray a gift. They don't believe in counting the cycles of the sun.
> In the open is self-indulgence. Hidden is the religion of God.
> Truthfully, they hold arrogance and self-worship as their profession in their minds where they think.
> They talk about knowledge and matters for discussion, but they don't understand the meaning of these words."

In Yazd, the young Pishūtan underwent priestly training while his father traveled to Kerman to study astrology. The text describes this vividly (First Dastoor Meherjirana Library MS F-82, 31–34):

> I was happily entrusted to a teacher (*ustād*) to learn to read Zend.
> When I finished the Yasna (*yazishn*) and the Visperad, I completed the Khurda Avesta.
> They performed for me the Barashnūm in the correct way—eleven times, I remember.
> In the month of Ardībihisht, on the day Dīn, thus there was the true path and custom.
> 1141 years had passed since the last king was seated in Iran.
> By the command of God, I became *nawzūd*. I came into the ritual area (*urvīs*) and sat there.
> The priest of the age came before me, perfected in the knowledge of the religion, Marzubān by name.
> He gave me much advice and admonition as to the religion, saying, "Never choose anything but goodness." (...)
> That teacher came as the *Rāspī*, and in the *urvīs*, he set up all the utensils of the religion.
> I quickly invoked the name of the *Zūd*, tied (my *kushtī*), and began to utter prayers (*zamzam*).
> Then, I took the *bāzh* and *barsum* quickly, in the way in which my *Zūd* had shown me.
> (It was as though) a world had assembled from the city and from the lanes to watch that ceremony and feast.
> According to the custom of the religion and the command of the pure creator, all that business was performed beautifully.
> The leader of the priests brought me to his house out of kindness with no pretense.
> Then he said to my father, "Fīrūz mustn't consume just a small grain of the *Avesta*.
> After bringing him into my house, I shall teach him. I shall open all the locks of the religion for him."
> He had a young son named Suhrāb who was well-spoken, well-mannered, and with good character.

He entrusted me to him and said to him, "Son, be the authority (*dastūr*) to this one for matters of religion."
Teach him everything that he needs to know—never rest from this either by night or by day.
Teach him from the Vendīdād, along with the (way to consecrate) the ritual milk and the materials for the *haoma*!" And he strove a great deal.
In picking the *barsum*, in bringing the *haoma*, and in cutting the pomegranate twigs (*urvarām*) from their place,
Of the strips of leaf (*'ayvangīn*), whether of cherry or of pomegranate, which are used to tie the *barsum*,
He taught me also about the hair of the bull (*vars*) and the consecrated bull's urine (*nīrang*), and he illuminated my soul with knowledge of the religion.

Pishūtan became one of the last Parsi priests to receive religious training in Iran. Years later, when he returned with the sobriquet Mullā Fīrūz to India, he advocated that religious ceremonies be performed in the Iranian way, and in Qadīmī fire temples, rituals are to this day performed as Mullā Fīrūz established them in the early 1800s.

After finally receiving a response to the religious questions posed by the Qadīmī group in Surat, Kā'ūs and Pishūtan set out for Esfahan, where a *maḥżar* about the Zoroastrian calendar was obtained from the Muslim ulema, and where Kā'ūs predicted Karīm Khān's victory over the Ottoman Turks in Basra in 1775. When Karīm Khān Zand heard of Kā'ūs's skill as an astrologer, he and his son were summoned to the Zand court in Shīraz, where they stayed for several years.

While in Shiraz, Kā'ūs and Pishūtan met two Zoroastrians from Kerman. They had been waiting for a year and a half to present a petition at court about the *jizya*. According to this pair (First Dastoor Meherjirana Library MS F-82, 67–8):

There was oppression in Kerman on the Zoroastrians. No one could repel it.
Too much poll-tax (*jizya*) was taken from them. Things were difficult for those poor souls.
The reason was that in an earlier time, there was an abundance of Zoroastrians in Kerman.
Their number was written in a book, and that amount (of tax) was taken from them.
All at once, there was a massacre in Kerman, and many Zoroastrians died therein.

Thousands of Zoroastrians died—their lives perished.
Not one in ten people remained alive. Bodies, hands, heads, and feet were strewn about all over.
But the poll-tax was as before. Nothing was changed in it.

With the help of their Muslim supporter, Ḥājjī Muḥammad Khān, the governor of Esfahan, a petition was prepared for court, and upon hearing it, Karīm Khān immediately ordered the *jizya* to be recalculated (First Dastoor Meherjirana Library MS F-82, 71):[26]

When the *vakīl* [Karīm Khān] became aware of their plight, the hardship of the oppressed was lessened.
The auspicious one quickly issued a command, saying "Tyranny is rare in our age."
A scribe came and wrote the command to the tax collectors (*'ummāl*) and governor (*vālī*) of Kerman
As follows: "We have knocked down the foundation of tyranny. We have thrown it out of every place and every spot.
We want the subjects to be happy, for the kingdom flourishes through its subjects.
I have observed this tyranny in Kerman on the Zoroastrians (*majūs*). I have heard of a peculiar tyranny upon them.
From now on one should take what is fixed—shun away from repeating it -
You must not take more than this—since when did one equal ten?"

Kā'ūs and Fīrūz remained at the court of the king for three and a half years. One day, the father and son were calculating the "mystery of the turning celestial sphere" (*rāz-i charkh-i girdūn*) when they realized that the king did not have long to live. Kā'ūs decided that it was finally time to leave Iran. Wanting first to visit Istanbul, the two were stranded for a time in Baghdad before finally reaching Surat via Basra in 1780.

In the course of the fourteen years that the two had been away, Fīrūz had become thoroughly Persianate, having adopted the dress, ritual practice, and the language of his Iranian brethren who had trained him in the religion. For Mullā Fīrūz, Iran remained the land of religious authority, a place where the religious traditions had lived more or less unbroken for more than eleven hundred years since the last Sasanian monarch.

26. Curiously, given the importance of the *jizya* for the "continuous decline" model, this achievement by Mullā Kā'ūs is almost universally forgotten.

IV. The Iranian Zoroastrian Amelioration Fund, Māṇekji Limji Hāṭariā, and the Risāle Ezhār-e Siāt-e Īrān

Already during Mullā Fīrūz's lifetime, *Shahanshāhī* priests had started to claim that the priests in Iran no longer had authority over the Indian community. Iran was thrown into chaos with the rise of Āqā Muḥammad Khān, who decimated the areas around Yazd and especially Kerman.[27] Streams of Irani Zoroastrians along with Iranian Muslims began immigrating to Bombay in order to escape the ensuing chaos. A Danish Orientalist named Nils Ludvig Westergaard visited Yazd and Kerman in 1843, and found a very different place than that which Fīrūz had witnessed some fifty years before. A letter from Westergaard, published in the *Journal of the Royal Asiatic Society*, described the condition of the Zoroastrians of Yazd:

> Now, for the Gabrs [Zoroastrians] in Yazd. There are in all one thousand Gabr houses in Yazd, in the mahalla or quarter named Pusht-i Khána Ali, where alone they live, and in the surrounding villages. A few only are merchants; the most part live poorly and wretchedly by tilling the ground, and other manual occupations. As one can scarcely reckon more than four, or four and a half, to each house, the whole population does not amount to more at any rate than five thousand, including men, women, and children. A few merchants travel now and then to Shiraz, Teherán, and Káshán; but their families remain at Yazd . . . They stand far below, I will not say the Pársís, but below the lowest Hindús. Of their religion they know nothing whatever; in the temple they light the fire only for a few hours during the beginning of the night. They consider smoking as improper for the Dasturs only; and the Dastur himself offered me a kalian in his own house, when I did him the honour to call on him the first time. There are few dasturs — Námdár, Rashíd, Rustam, Dinyar; the first two are sons of Kai-Khúsrú and Sharivar, who both are said to have been good Zand and Pahlavi scholars (*inter cœcos regnat luscus* [In the country of the blind, the one-eyed man is king]).[28]

Though the Parsis in Bombay were aware of the political situation in Iran, still Westergaard's account of the state of Iranian Zoroastrians must have caused a shock. According to the *Oriental Christian Spectator*, the journal of the Free Church of Scotland missionaries in Bombay which reprinted Westergaard's letter, some *Qadīmīs* apparently denounced this report and called Westergaard an enemy of the religion (*dīnno duśmen*). The Rev. John Wilson,

27. See *CHI* 7, 125–6.
28. Westergaard 1846, 349.

A portrait of Māṇekji Limji Hāṭaria (1813-90) and his wife. Photograph by Daniel Sheffield. (Courtesy K. R. Cama Oriental Institute, Mumbai.)

the most prominent of the Bombay missionaries to the Parsi community at the time, writes in *The Oriental Christian Spectator* (June 1848, 228–229):

> The publication in our last number of Professor Westergaard's letter on the state of the Gabars [Zoroastrians] of Persia, has caused a considerable excitement among the Zoroastrians of Bombay. The reason is this. The Kadimí sect, of whom the late learned Mulláh Fīrūz was the head and ornament, have been accustomed to fortify themselves in the position which they occupy in the Kabisah or Intercalary controversy, by an appeal to the practices and observances of their Irání brethren, which they allege to be similar to their own. The testimony of the learned Dane as to the depression of the Persian Gabars, and their violation of Pársí customs in the comparative neglect of their fire-temples and their practice of smoking, is construed as hostile to that deference which the Kadímís show to them in reference to the time of observing the festivals. The Jám-i-Jamshíd [a *Shahanshāhī* paper], who properly gives the professor due credit for truthfulness, boldly says, "Now, we ask, whether those Behdín, or Mobeds, or Dastúrs, who may be keeping fire in their temple only for a few hours of the day, and may be thinking it right and proper to smoke the huká, can be called Zoroastrians?—And whether such persons ought to be appointed as the expounders of religion?—And whether the opinions given by them in religious matters, ought to be considered as true?" We leave the Pársís to reply.

Months later, the issue was brought up again (*Oriental Christian Spectator*, December 1848, 468–9):

> Our attention has been invited to an article which was published three days ago in the Guzerattee Paper, called Chábuk. It relates to the state of the Pársís in Persia, which it represents to be of the most painful description. Subsequent to the death of the late Sháh, they have been subjected to a persecution of the harshest and most blood-thirsty kind. Robbery, murder, and torments await them, so that of 500 residing at Kermán many have fled to the mountains in order to preserve their lives. The unfortunate sufferers have sent a petition to the influential Pársís of Bombay praying for assistance, which it is said many are anxious to send –but they do not know how to afford it permanently to their unfortunate co-religionists. The Chábuk quotes the name of the man who has supplied him with the information on this subject. While those complaints have come from Kermán other accounts of a similar nature have arrived from Yazd, for which place the Pársís entertain the highest veneration. The plundering of the Merchants and Caravans from Cabul, Candahar and Turkestan are also quoted,—and a lamentable picture is drawn of the state of "Irán," which as a Pársí Gentleman stated yesterday

> in the sincerity of his heart—he wished the British Government would conquer and undertake to govern, for he pitied the fate of the descendants of the ancient Parthians, who are still subject to cruel persecutions— after having groaned during 13 centuries under the yoke of the Moguls [i.e., Muslims of Turkic origin]. It is undoubtedly a high compliment to the British Authorities to find Parsís thus express a wish that the men who have preserved the faith of Zoroaster in Persia, should be protected by the laws of England and governed by the English system, but we doubt whether the English would gain any advantage from the conquest.

Enough of a controversy had been stirred up that calls for a "charitable fund" were raised to benefit the impoverished Zoroastrians in Yazd and Kerman. By 1854, the Iranian Zoroastrian Amelioration Fund been formed,[29] and their representative, Māṇekji Limji Hāṭariā, was sent to Yazd and Kerman. Māṇekji (1813–90), a layman and successful merchant, is still remembered for his role in the abolition of the *jizya* under Nāsir al-Dīn Shāh Qājār in 1882[30] and is regarded as a pivotal figure in the history of Iranian Zoroastrianism, so much so that Malcolm Deboo, a prominent interfaith activist working with the Zoroastrian Centre in London, has referred to him as the "Martin Luther King of Zoroastrianism."[31]

Unlike the idealized Iran of Mullā Fīrūz's memories, for Māṇekji, Iran was a ruined land, a shadow of its ancient grandeur, a land in which his coreligionists lived in squalor and intellectual poverty. Māṇekji came to Iran at a time in which a new generation of English-educated Parsi intelligentsia, fascinated by the colonial sciences of philology, archaeology, and ethnology, were intent on restoring what they believed to be the ancient Zoroastrian religion by removing supposed later corruptions from the religion. In Bombay in 1851, one early reformer, Sorābji Śāpurji Baṅgāli, had started an illustrated Gujarati magazine entitled the *Jagatpremi*, "Friend of the World," in part dedicated to the dissemination of new discoveries of ancient Iranian archaeology. For the first time, average Parsis of Bombay could see reconstructions of Achaemenid and Sasanian archaeological sites, and Parsis began to identify symbols derived from ancient Iranian iconography as part of their own communal identity.[32]

When Māṇekji set out for Iran, then, he went with certain ideas in mind.

29. See the early reports of the fund, published in 1865–67, as well as the documents collected in Amini 2001.

30. As we have seen above, the *jizya* was also ameliorated by Karīm Khān at the request of Mullā Kā'ūs, but this event has been forgotten in the Parsi collective memory.

31. Deboo 2006.

32. On the life of Baṅgāli, see Bengalee 1904.

Māṇekji was a very well-connected man — as a practicing Freemason, he came into close contact with European diplomats and Iranian elites[33] — and he dedicated much of his life to bettering the lives of Zoroastrians in Iran. He corresponded with such figures as the Qājār prince Jalāl al-Dīn Mīrzā, for whose *Nāma-yi Khusrawān* he composed a *History of the Parsis* (*Tārīkh-i Pārsīyān*), which appears as an appendix to the first volume.[34] He commissioned a mytho-historical narrative of ancient Iranian history to be written by Mīrzā Ismā'īl Tūsirkānī, governor of Yazd, called the *Farāzistān* (published in 1894 AD). He sponsored the early archaeological activities of Muhammad Nāsir Fursat Shīrāzī, resulting in the publication of *Āthār-i 'Ajam* (1894). In addition to his interest in ancient history, Māṇekji was an early advocate for the use of pure Persian (*pārsī-yi sara*), that is Persian purged of most of the Arabic element, and he commissioned a grammar of pure Persian called the *Mīzān-i Pārsī* (1231 AH).[35] He also corresponded extensively with Bahā'ullāh, urging him to write in pure Persian, to which Bahā'ullāh complied in his response (now canonized by the Bahā'ī community as the *Lawḥ-i Mānikjī Ṣāḥib*).[36] Besides, he interacted with the British Envoy at Tehran, noted archaeologist Sir Henry Rawlinson, the French diplomat and orientalist Arthur de Gobineau, the Japanese envoy Masaharu Yoshida,[37] and met the English missionary Napier Malcolm, as well as orientalists Sir Edward G. Browne and Valentin Zhukovskiĭ.

Māṇekji's role in instigating social reform for the Zoroastrians of Iran is well known,[38] and his participation along with other prominent figures in reshaping Iranian national identity through increased awareness of its ancient past has now been investigated by Mohammad Tavakoli-Targhi and more recently Afshin Marashi.[39] But he also played a significant role in shaping how Parsis think about Iran, and it is this topic that I would like to investigate briefly here.

In 1865, Māṇekji published his Gujarati-language *Risāle Ezhār-e Siāt-e Irān* ("Treatise Expounding upon a Trip to Iran"),[40] which paints a radically different picture of the state of Iranian Zoroastrians from that of Mullā Fīrūz.

33. On the history of Freemasonry in Iran, see Shāhābādī 2000–10.

34. Mīrzā 1868. On the thought of Jalāl al-Dīn Mīrzā, see Amānat 1999.

35. Hurmuzdān Hurmuzd Pārsī 1866. On this work, see Jeremiás 2006.

36. See Bahā'ullāh 2006 for a translation.

37. Masaharu 1894. Masaharu's visit to the archaeological site of Persepolis (*takht-i Jamshīd*) leads him to an investigation of ancient Iranian history, in the course of which, he discusses the Zoroastrian religion with Māṇekji. See Masaharu 1994, 115–26.

38. See Ringer 2009 and Boyce 1969.

39. Tavakoli-Targhi 2001, Marashi 2008

40. See Stausberg 2003 as well as Giara, Karanjia & Stausberg 2004.

The book was intended for urban Parsis, and makes several appeals for donations to the cause of the Amelioration Fund. It was quickly abridged and translated into Persian for the growing Irani population of Bombay as well as for distribution in Iran. The work is notable for a number of reasons. As documentation of the social customs and practices of Iranian Zoroastrians in the mid-nineteenth century, the work is unique. But Māṇekji's travelogue is also the first published instance of a different way of thinking about Iran and its Zoroastrians, one which is necessitated, I think, by the mnemonic break with the Iranian Zoroastrians caused by the calendar controversy and the rediscovery of ancient Iran by the Bombay reformers. Rather than ascribing the hardships faced by the Zoroastrians of Iran to the difficulties brought on by the beginning of the rise of the Qājārs, Māṇekji was the first to posit the "continuous decline" model of post-Sasanian Zoroastrian history that became very important in the development of Iranian nationalism in the nineteenth and twentieth centuries, and almost paradigmatic among Parsi and even many Western historians of Zoroastrianism.

Māṇekji begins his travel report with a review of Iran's past (Hāṭariā 1865, 2):

> The first rulers of the country of Iran, which is the land of the kingdom of the ancestors of the Parsi people and their homeland (*janmabhumi*), called it "Iran, the mark of Paradise" (*irān mino-niśān*) on account of the good qualities of its climate and land, that is, Iran, the land which bears the mark of Paradise (*sarzamin beheśtni niśānvāli*), and whether or not there is some exaggeration, still whoever sees this land's climate, the yield of its plants, and its agricultural cycle wherein all things become possible, this land was like the garden of paradise (*beheśtnā bāg*), and it still is—in this, there is no doubt.

But, as Māṇekji goes on to narrate, before the coming of Islam, Iran was full of peace, the center of culture and the arts, and so on; whereas afterwards, in his words (Hāṭariā 1865, 3–4):

> It cannot be unknown to any scholar that by the oppression of time, rule slipped out of the hands of the Parsi people, and it is now 1200 years that Muslims, Arabs, Afghans, Mongols, Tartars, and different groups have, by ruling with greed and covetousness, constantly been encouraging plunder and tumult. [...] Thereby, what at first was "Iran the mark of Paradise" (*irān mino-niśān*) should now be called "Iran the ruined" (*irān verāṇ*), since the angels (*ferestā*) which once inhabited this pure land which was like the garden of paradise have disappeared, and now the land of the demons (*devo*) has increased, for as every scholar says, Iran itself is paradise, but it has fallen into the hands of the denizens of hell (*dozakhio*).

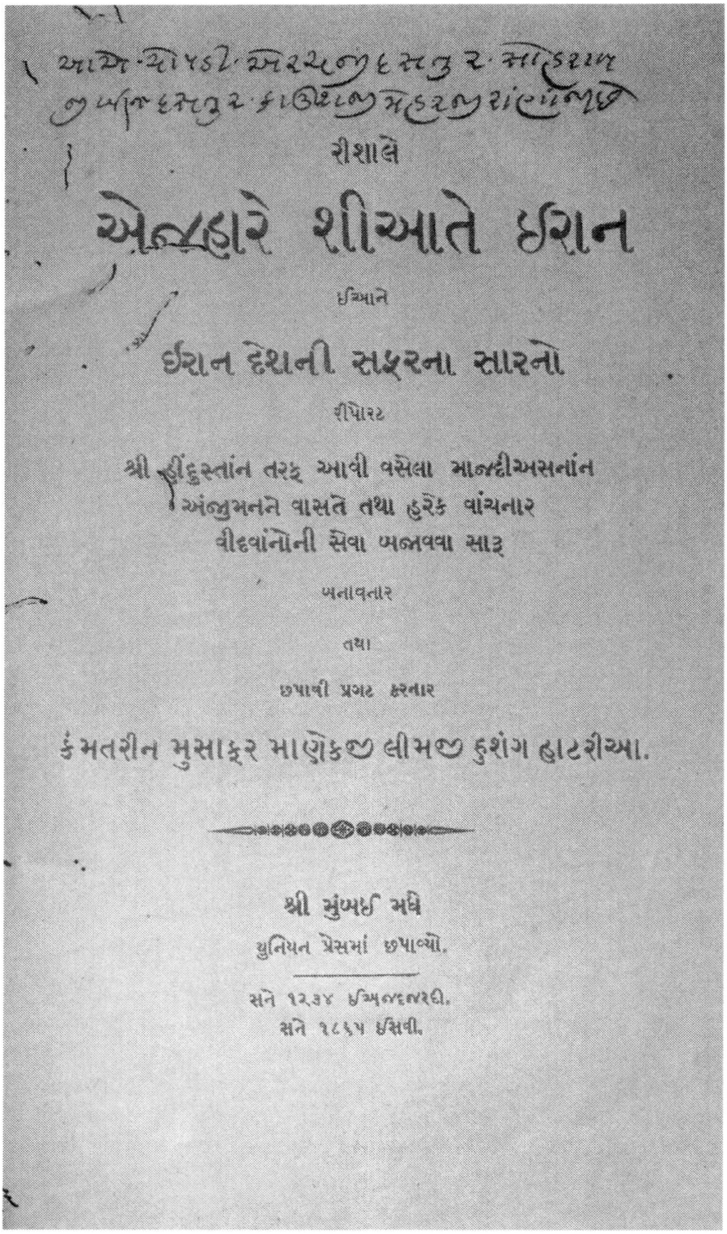

The title page of Māṇekji Limji Hāṭaria's *Risāle Ezhār-e Siāt-e Irān*. Photograph by Daniel Sheffield. (Courtesy Meherjirana Library, Navsari.)

A stele from Persepolis as depicted in Furṣat-i Shīrāzī's 1894 *Āthār-i 'Ajam*, (plate facing p. 178). Photograph by Daniel Sheffield. (Courtesy Meherjirana Library, Navsari.)

Given Māṇekji's delineation between pre-Islamic Iran and Iran after the coming of Islam, it is probably unsurprising that apart from Yazd and Kerman, most of the places he describes in his travelogue are actually or supposedly pre-Islamic sites. In cataloging and describing the extant sites of pre-Islamic Iran, Māṇekji is effectively forging a new topography of memory in which the rediscovered ancient Iranian past still dwells. Throughout the entire text of his description of ancient Iran and its places, Māṇekji constantly uses variations of the Gujarati expression *hatũ ne che,* "was and is," affirming the connection between ancient and modern Iran. For instance, in his description of the sites near Shiraz, Māṇekji writes (Hāṭariā 1865, 82):

> In some places near Takht-e Jamshīd, Takht-e Tāqdīs, the Dakhma of Jamshid, the Dakhma of Faridun, the Dakhma of Zartusht, the Ka'ba of Zartusht, and Naqsh-e Rustam, every one of the Persian kings had inscribed many images and mysterious meanings (*bhedbharelā māenāo*)[41] during the rites of appointing their heirs to the crown and throne, festival assemblies, and while holding courts of justice, and they are (still there).

However, Māṇekji reinforces the point that the present-day Iranian Zoroastrian community is ignorant of their connection to these sites (Hāṭariā 1865, 78):

> It is clear to every scholar that it has now been twelve hundred years since the ancestors of the Mazdayasnian Parsis who have come to settle in India emigrated after leaving their homeland. From then till now, no one has known whether there was any sign or trace left over from the hands or time of their good ancestors who ruled over the land of Iran for thousands of years. Even now, the Parsis left over in Iran likewise were and are completely ignorant, since they have not been able to and still cannot travel very far from the vicinity of their homes.

By contrasting the ignorance of contemporary Iranian Zoroastrians with the embedded secrets of the supposedly "ancient" Iranian topography, Māṇekji suggests that the ways of ancient Iran are to be discovered and renewed, in the process lifting up the Zoroastrians of Iran. At the same time, the publication of his travelogue in Bombay kindled further interest in visiting the archaeological monuments of ancient Iran which had become linked with Parsi identity. Māṇekji's imagination of ancient Iran had lasting effect on

41. Interestingly, Māṇekji throughout his life maintained a firm belief in a form of Zoroastrian mysticism, profoundly influenced by the works of the seventeenth century mystic Āẓar Kayvān and his followers. These books, which were published in India in the first half of the nineteenth century, were very popular in Iran and important in shaping early Iranian conceptions of the pre-Islamic past.

Iranian nationalists of the late nineteenth and early twentieth centuries, many of whom drew inspiration from works like the *Āthār-i 'Ajam*, the extensive archaeological guide the earliest stages of which had been sponsored by Māṇekji.

In some sense, both Mullā Fīrūz and Māṇekji Limji Hāṭariā are attempting to achieve a similar goal through their texts: namely, to strengthen some sort of an identity through an appeal to shared mnemonic links with Iran. For Mullā Fīrūz, and for the early Qadīmī priests, these mnemonic links were to be found in the religious calendar, which, as sociologist Eviatar Zerubavel writes, is an "extremely useful social site of memory [...] As a cycle of "holy days" specifically designed to commemorate particular historical events, the calendar year usually embodies major narratives collectively woven by mnemonic communities from their past."[42] By visibly marking their difference from other Indian Zoroastrian communities through the calendar, Mullā Fīrūz and the other Qadīmī priests deliberately associated themselves with the authority of the Iranian priests, an authority which they presented as having been transmitted directly since the time of the Sasanian Empire. On the other hand, Shahanshāhī Zoroastrians in the eighteenth and early nineteenth century, as well as later groups, who were no longer concerned with the priestly legitimacy of the Iranian priests, instead sought to associate themselves with the past glories of Iran, glories which by seeking to reform the conditions of their contemporary coreligionists they sought to renew. As such, parts of Māṇekji Limji Hāṭariā's travelogue can be read as a discovery of a mnemonic topography, based on Māṇekji's idiosyncratic understanding of Iranian and Zoroastrian history. The importance of Māṇekji's travelogue within the Parsi community was tremendous, and it was soon followed by several antiquarian guides to the sites of Iran, notably Kavasji Dinshaw Kiash's trilingual *Ancient Persian Sculptures* (1889), Cooverbai Manockji Dhalla's *Irān ane Irākmā Musāfari* (1922), Jivanji Jamshedji Modi's *Māri Muṃbai Bahārni Sehel* (1926), and Rustom Kharegat's *Tourist Guide to Iran* (1935). It is interesting to note that even today, religious tours to Iran for Parsis and diaspora Zoroastrians follow a virtually identical route to that of Māṇekji in his travelogue.

In any case, what I hope to have demonstrated is that the way in which Parsis have remembered Iranian history was very much determined by contemporary notions of Parsi identity. For Mullā Fīrūz, who relied upon the Iranians for priestly authority, the link of his contemporary peers in Iran to ancient Iranian mytho-history was paramount. On the other hand, Māṇekji, who was confronted with a community injured after the turmoil in Iran

42. Zerubavel 2003, 30.

surrounding the rise of the Qajar dynasty, hearkened to an ancient Iranian heritage which he believed should be restored after more than a millennium of degradation. One cannot simply take either of these narratives at face value. Due to circumstances in the development of the Parsi community as well as the historiographical tradition, Māṇekji's narrative model of Iranian history has become dominant in the shaping of the modern Zoroastrian identity, while Mullā Fīrūz's travelogue is almost entirely unknown by either Parsis or by scholars. Mullā Fīrūz and his father Kā'ūs, are today almost forgotten as the last standard-bearers of the Parsi Indo-Persian tradition. On the other hand, Māṇekji is regarded as a hero of the Parsi community, embodying the recovery of an ancient Iranian selfhood characteristic of colonial modernity.

Appendix: Parsi Travelogues in Gujarati Published before 1950 (excluding serials)

Karākā, Dosābhāi Frāmji. 1861. *Greṭ Briṭan khāteni Musāfari.* [*Journey to Great Britain*]

Ek Pārsi Gharhastho. 1864. *Amerikānī Musāfari.* [*Journey to America*]

Hāṭariā, Māṇekji Limji. 1865. *Risāle Ezhār-e Siāt-e Irān, yāne Irān Deśni Safarnā Sārno Riporṭ.* [*Treatise Expounding upon a Trip to Iran, i.e., a Report About a Trip to the Land of Iran*]

Tāleyārkhān, Dinśāh Ardesar. 1870. *Hindusthān (Dakṣin)mā Musāfari.* [*A Journey in (South) India*]

Mus, Ardesar Frāmji 1871. *Hindusthānmā Musāfari.* [*Journey in India*]

Jijibhāi, Pirozśāh Mervānji. 1879. *Hindusthānmā Musāfarini Keṭlik Nondh.* [*Some Notes on a Journey in India*]

Keāś, Kāvasji Dinśā, 1882. *Irānmā Musāfari.* [*Journey in Iran*]

Piṭiṭ, Frāmji Dinśāji. 1883. *Muṃbaithi Yurop Tarafnā Pravāsnī Noṃdh.* [*Remarks on a Journey from Mumbai to Europe*]

Marzbān, Jahāngir Behrāmji. 1887. *Muṃbaithī Kāśmir.* [*From Bombay to Kashmir*]

Piṭiṭ, Frāmji Dinśāji. 1889. *Yurop, Amerikā, Jāpān ane Chin tarafni Musāfarini Nodh.* [*Remarks on a Journey to Europe, America, Japan, and China*]

Master, Pestonji Jivanji. 1892. *Pārsi Krikeṭ Klabni Musāfarino Ramuzi Hevāl.* [*An Amusing Account of the Parsi Cricket Club's Journey*]

Piṭiṭ, Bamanji D. 1895. *Dakhaṇ Hindustān tarafni Musāfarini Ṭuṃk Nodh.* [*Short Remarks on a Journey to South India*]

Peṭivāḷā, Ādarji Dādābhai. 1899. *Inglāṇḍ ane Āfrikāno Jaḷ Pravās.* [*A Water Journey to England and Africa*]

Marzbān, Jahāngir Behrāmji. 1906. *Modikhātethi Mārsels.* [*From Modi Bandar to Marseilles*]

Marzbān, Jahāngir Behrāmji. 1915. *Gorā Yuropnũ Gaḷyũ Dāstān.* [*A Sweet Story of White Europe*]

Shroff, Śāvakśā D. 1917. *Belārḍpiyarthi Briṭan.* [*From Ballard Pier to Britain*]

Confectioner, Nādir A. 1920. *Kolābāthi Kāśmir.* [*From Colaba to Kashmir*]

Dhāllā, Kuverbāi Māṇekji. 1922. *Irān ane Irākmā Musāfari.* [*Journey in Iran and Iraq*]

Modi, Jivanji Jamśedji, 1926. *Māri Muṃbai Bahārni Sehel: Yurop ane Irānni Musafārina 101 Patro.* [*My Excursion Out of Bombay: 101 Letters of a Journey in Europe and Iran*]

Mullā, Māṇek Fardunji. 1928. *Iran Bhumino Bhomiyo: Irān ane Irākmā Māri Kidheli Musāfarini Nodho.* [*A Guide to the Land of Iran: Notes on My Travels in Iran and Iraq*]

Fitter, Kaykhusro A. 1929. *Māri Irānni Dāyarimā Ḍokyũ.* [*A Peep in My Iran Diary*]

Anklesariā, Meherbānu Behrāmgor. 1932. *Pahlavi Irānmā Musāfari.* [*A Journey in Pahlavi Iran*]

Bharuchā, Mancerśā. 1933. *Amāri Duniyāni Musāfari.* [*A Journey in Our World*]

Dāvar, Nānābhāi. 1936. *Vicitra Ladākh Traṇ Māsni Manzal.* [*Three Months' Stay in Strange Ladakh*]

Desāi, Sunāmāi Bamanji. 1942. *Māri Kāśmirni Ṭur ane Darjiliṃgni Musāfarinũ Varṇan.* [*My Tour of Kashmir and a Description of Travels in Darjeeling*].

Balsara, Frām N. 1950. *Mādar Vatan Irān: Irānni Musāfarinũ Rasilũ Dāstān.* [*The Motherland Iran: An Enjoyable Story*]

Bibliography

Amānat, ʻA. (1999), "Pūr-i Khāqān va Andīsha-yi Bāz-yābī-yi Tārīkh-i Millī-yi Irān: Jalāl al-Dīn Mīrzā va *Nāma-yi Khusrawān*," *Irānnāma* 17: 5–54.

Amighi, J. (1990), *The Zoroastrians of Iran: Conversion, Assimilation, or Persistence*, New York: AMS Press.
Amīnī, T. (1380/2001), *Asnādī az Zartushtiyān-i Mu'āṣir-i Īrān (1258–1338 Shamsī)*, Tehran: Sāzmān-i Asnād-i Millī-yi Īrān.
Bahā'ullāh (2006), *The Tabernacle of Unity: Bahá'u'lláh's Responses to Mánikchí Sáhib and Other Writings*, Haifa: Baha'i World Centre.
Bengalee, N. S. (1904), *The Life of Sorabjee Shapoorjee Bengalee, C. I. E.* Bombay: Times of India Press.
Boyce, M. (1969), "Manekji Limji Hataria in Iran," in: N. D. Minocher-Homji & M. F. Kanga (ed.), *K. R. Cama Oriental Institute Golden Jubilee Volume*, Bombay: K.R. Cama Oriental Institute, 19–31.
—— (1977), *A Persian Stronghold of Zoroastrianism*, Oxford: Clarendon Press.
Cama, K. R. (1870), *Yazdejardī Tārīkh*, Muṃbaī: Daftar Āśkārā Chāpkhānū.
Cantera, A. & M.-Á. Andrés Toledo (2008), "The transmission of the Pahlavi Vīdēvdād in India after 1700 (I) – Jāmāsp's visit from Iran and the rise of a new exegetical movement in Surat," *Journal of the K. R. Cama Oriental Institute* 68: 81–142.
Coorlawala, D. N. (1918), "The Last Kabiseh," in: *The Dastur Hoshang Memorial Volume*, Bombay: Fort Printing Press, 143–60.
de Blois, F. (1996), "The Persian Calendar," *Iran* 34: 39–54.
—— (2003), "The Reform of the Zoroastrian Calendar in the Year 375 of Yazdgird," in: C. Cereti & F. Vajifdar (ed.), *Ātaš-e Dorūn: The Fire Within: Jamshid Soroush Soroushian Commemorative Volume*, Bloomington: 1st Books, 139–45.
Deboo, M. (2006), "Seth Maneckji Limji Hataria: The Martin Luther King of Zoroastrianism & the Struggle for Zoroastrian Civil Rights in Iran," available online at http://www.zoroastrian.org.uk/vohuman/Article/Seth Maneckji Limji Hataria.htm. Accessed on June 5, 2011.
Dhabhar, B. N. (1932), *The Persian Rivayats of Hormazyar Framarz and Others*, Bombay: K.R. Cama Oriental Institute.
Furṣat-i Shīrāzī, M. N. (1312/1894), *Āthār-i 'Ajam*. Bombay: Maṭba'-i Nādirī.
Gense, J. H. and D. R. Banaji (1937), *The Gaikwads of Baroda II: Fatesingrao (1771-1776)*, Bombay: D.B. Taraporewala.
Giara, M., R. Karanjia, and M. Stausberg (2004), "Manekji on the Religious Ritual Practices of the Iranian Zoroastrians," in: L M. Stausberg (ed.) *Zoroastrian Rituals in Context*, Leiden: Brill, 481–515.
Hāṭariā, M. L. (1865a), *Risāle Ezhār-e Siāt-e Īrān*. Bombay: Union Press.
—— (1865b), *Tarjuma-yi Iẓhār-i Siyāḥat-i Īrān*. Persian tr. by Bāqir Kirmānshāhānī. Bombay: Bombay Education Society.
Hinnells, J. (2007), "Changing Perceptions of Authority among Parsis in

British India," in: J. Hinnells and A. Williams (ed.), *Parsis in India and the Diaspora*, London: Routledge, 100–18.
Hodivala, S. H. (1920), *Studies in Parsi History*. Bombay: Shahpurshah Hormasji Hodivala.
Hurmazdān Hurmazd Pārsī (1866), *Mīzān-i Pārsī*, Tehran: n.p.
Iranian Zoroastrian Amelioration Fund (1865–7), *Īrān Deśnā Garib Zarthośtioni Hālat Sudhārvā Sāru Astāpelā Dharam-Khātāni Upaj-nipajno Ahevāl* I: 1858–61, II: 1861–64, III: 1864–66, Muṃbai.
Jeremiás, É. (2006), "Hormoz Hormozdân's Nâme-ye Mizân-e Pârsi (A Grammar Written for "Zoroastrians")," in: A. Panaino & R. Zipoli (ed.), *Proceedings of the 5th Conference of the Societas Iranologica Europæa*, Milan: Mimesis, 411–28.
Karaka, D. (1884), *History of the Parsis*, London: Macmillan.
Kharegat, R. (1935), *A Tourist Guide to Iran*, Bombay: Caxton Press.
Kiash, K. D. (1889), *Ancient Persian Sculptures*, Bombay: Education Society's Press.
Kulke, E. (1974), *The Parsees in India: A Minority as Agent of Social Change*, Munich: Weltforum.
Maneck, S. (1997), *The Death of Ahriman: Culture, Identity, and Theological Change among the Parsis of India*, Bombay: K.R. Cama Oriental Institute.
Marashi, A. (2008), *Nationalizing Iran: Culture, Power, and the State, 1870–1940*. Seattle: University of Washington Press.
Mīrzā, J. (1868), *Nāma-yi Khusrawān*, Tehran: Maṭba'-i Muḥammad Taqī.
Modi, J. J. (1905), *A Few Events in the History of the Parsis and Their Dates*, Bombay: Fort Printing Press.
—— (1926), *Māri Muṃbaini Bahārni Sehel: Yurop ane Irānni Musāfarinā 101 Patro*, Muṃbaī: Jām-e Jamśed Printing Works.
Mullā Fīrūz (1999), *Mathnavī-yi Aḥvāl-i Zindagī-yi Mullā Fīrūz*, ed. Shāyista Akhtar Jāvīd, Bombay: Qalam.
Nadri, G. (2007), "Commercial World of Mancherji Khurshedji and the Dutch East India Company — A Study of Mutual Relationships," *Modern Asian Studies* 41: 315–42.
—— (2009), *Eighteenth-Century Gujarat: The Dynamics of Its Political Economy, 1750–1800*, Leiden: Brill.
Namīrāniyān, K. (1387/2008), *Zartushtīyān-i Īrān pas az Islām tā Imrūz*, Kirmān: Markaz-i Kirmānshināsī.
Nandy, A. (1983), *The Intimate Enemy: Loss and Recovery of Self under Colonialism*, Delhi: Oxford University Press.
Nora, P., ed., (1996–98), *Realms of Memory: Rethinking the French Past*, 3 vols., tr. Arthur Goldhammer, New York: Columbia University Press.

Palsetia, J. (2001), *The Parsis of India: Preservation of Identity in Bombay City*, Leiden: Brill.

Patel, B. B. (1900), "A Brief Outline of Some Controversial Questions That Led to the Advancement of the Study of Religious Literature among the Parsis," in: J. J. Modi (ed.), *The K. R. Cama Memorial Volume*, Bombay: Fort Printing Press, 170–82.

Paymaster, R. B. (1931), *Ahevāl-e Mullā Firoz bin Mullā Kāus Jalāl*, Muṃbaī: Union Press.

—— (1954), *Early History of the Parsees in India*, Bombay: Jam-e Jamshed Press.

Ringer, M. (2009), "Reform Transplanted: Parsi Agents of Change amongst Zoroastrians in Nineteenth-Century Iran," *Iranian Studies* 42: 549–60.

Seervai, K. and B. B. Patel (1899), "Gujarat Parsis," in: J. Campbell (ed.), *Gazetteer of the Bombay Presidency IX, Part 2*, Bombay: Government Central Press, 183–254.

Shāhābādī, Hamīd Rizā (2000–10), *Tārīkh-i Āghāzīn-i Farāmāsūnrī dar Īrān.* Tehran: Ḥawza-yi Hunarī.

Shahmardan Irani, R. (1967), "Mullā Kavus bin Rostam: What led to his departure to Iran and his achievements there?" in: *The Sir J. J. Zarthoshti Madressa Centenary Volume*, Bombay: Trustees of the Parsi Punchayet Funds, 175–84.

—— (1363/1984), *Tārīkh-i Zartushtiyān: Farzānagān-i Zartushtī*, Tehran: Faravahar.

Stausberg, M. (2003), "Māṇekji Limji Hatāriā and the Rediscovery of Ancient Iran," in: C. Cereti and F. Vajifdar (ed.), *Ātaš-e Dorūn — The Fire Within: Jamshid Soroush Soroushian Commemorative Volume*, Bloomington: 1st Books, 439–46.

Tavakoli-Targhi, M. (2001), *Refashioning Iran: Orientalism, Occidentalism, and Historiography*, New York: Palgrave.

Torri, M. (1998), "Mughal Nobles, Indian Merchants and the Beginning of British Conquest in Western India: The Case of Surat 1756–1759," *Modern Asian Studies* 32: 257–315.

Tūsirkānī, Mīrzā Isma'īl Khān (1894), *Farāzistān*, Bombay: Cheetra Prabha Press.

Unvala, M. R. (1922), *Dârâb Hormazyâr's Rivâyat* I–II, Bombay: British India Press.

Vafadari, S. R. (2003), "A Note on Kerman and Dastur Jamasb," in: C. Cereti and F. Vajifdar (ed.), *Ātaš-e Dorūn - The Fire Within: Jamshid Soroush Soroushian Commemorative Volume*, Bloomington: 1st Books, 447–53.

Vitalone, M. (1992), "La controversia sul calendario e la revāyat persiana del 1635," *Annali dell'Istituo Universitario Orientale* 52: 403–22.

—— (1996), *The Persian Revāyat "Ithoter": Zoroastrian Rituals in the Eighteenth Century*, Naples: Istituto universitario orientale, Dipartimento di studi asiatici.

Westergaard, N. L. (1846), "Extract from a Letter Addressed by Professor Westergaard to the Rev. Dr. Wilson, in the Year 1843, Relative to the Gabrs of Persia," *Journal of the Royal Asiatic Society of Great Britain and Ireland* 8: 349–54. [= *Oriental Christian Spectator* 8: 171–5 (1848)].

Williams, A. (2009), *The Zoroastrian Myth of Migration from Iran and Settlement in the Indian Diaspora: Text, Translation and Analysis of the 16th Century Qeṣṣe-ye Sanjān <The Story of Sanjan,'* Leiden: Brill.

Wilson, J. (1848), "The Parsis of Bombay and the Gabars of Persia," *Oriental Christian Spectator* 8: 228–9, 468–9.

Yoshida, Masaharu (1894), 波斯之旅 *[Expedition to Persia]*, Tokyo: Hakubunkan. Persian tr. by Rajabzāda, R. (1994), *Safarnāma-yi Yūshīdā Masāhārū: nakhustīn firistāda-yi Zhāpun ba Īrān dar dawra-yi Qājār.* Mashhad: Āstān-i Quds-i Raẕavī.

Zerubavel, E. (1981), *Hidden Rhythms: Schedules and Calendars in Social Life,* Berkeley: University of California Press.

—— (2003), *Time Maps: Collective Memory and the Social Shape of the Past.* Chicago: University of Chicago Press.

Zhukovskiĭ, V. A. (1885), "О Положенiи Гевровъ въ Персiи" [On the Position of the Gabrs in Persia], *Журналъ Министерства Народнаго Просвѣщенія* 237: 77–94.

Limning the Land

Social Encounters and Historical Meaning in Early Nineteenth-Century Travelogues between Iran and India[1]

Mana Kia

THIS ARTICLE CONSIDERS THE IMPORTANCE of place of origin in two Persian travelogues that span a critical historical moment, the first three decades of the nineteenth century. At this time, the Persianate world was fractured and shrinking. British presence in the South Asian subcontinent was becoming unmistakably dominant, and, though newly unified under the new Qajar state, Iran was embroiled in wars that would bring British and Russian imperial pressures to impinge on its sovereignty. Scholars have shown this period as a critical moment when indigenous discourses began to shift. In Bengal, elites began to adopt the terms of colonial discourse.[2] The most studied example is Raja Rammohan Roy, who first worked for the British as a classically trained Persian *monshī* before making a name for himself as a social reformer. Lata Mani has shown how as the discursive terrain of his exhortations changed, so too did the languages he chose to write in – abandoning Persian first for Bengali, and then also English.[3] These changes in elite discourse in the subcontinent took place as a split in literary aesthetics was being formalized between Irani and Hindustani Persian from the early nineteenth century.[4] In Iran, a new awareness of European scrutiny and Orientalist evaluations of society and culture began to

1. This title is a nod to Firoozeh Kashani-Sabet's work on the role of new notions of geography in the conceptualization of land in modern nationalist imaginings of Iran (Kashani-Sabet 1999, 47-74). However, Kashani-Sabet's focus is exclusively on Iran's interaction with Europe, whereas this article is the beginning of attempts to think about how modern ways of seeing, thinking and being may have entered Iran by way of its interaction with South Asia.

2. For instance see Mani 1998, 42–82. This process is less well understood in Iranian studies, though Afsaneh Najmabadi postulates that mid-nineteenth century shifts in notions of gender and sexuality toward heteronormativity that underwrote Iranian modernity were the result of a European gaze (Najmabadi 2005, 4–5).

3. For more celebratory accounts of Roy than Mani's, see Robertson 1995; and Zastoupil 2010.

4. For more on the disputes that caused the stylistic split, see Faruqi 1998, esp. 17–21; Alam 2003, 177–86; and Smith 2009.

Caravanserai on the road from Isfahan to Shiraz (litho), Flandin, Eugene (1809-76). (Courtesy Bibliothèque des Arts Decoratifs, Paris, France / Archives Charmet / The Bridgeman Art Library.)

pervade Irani Persian encounters with Europe.[5] How do these changes make themselves felt in encounters between Iran and India? This paper argues that differences between two early nineteenth-century travelogues reflect historical changes, but that older Persianate ideas about the spiritual and moral meanings of geography and culture are more significantly constitutive of the texts.

Āqā Aḥmad Behbahānī (1777–1819), a *mojtahed* (jurisconsult) from a long line of prominent religious scholars, was the author of the first travel narrative. Born in Iran, he journeyed to Iraq in 1797 for study and pilgrimage, and then widely within Iran. From 1805 to 1810 he traveled throughout India. After unsuccessful attempts to gain long-term patronage in Hyderabad, Lucknow and Murshidabad, Behbahānī obtained the position of Friday prayer leader at the Shi'i congregational mosque in British-ruled Patna.[6]

5. Tavakoli-Targhi 2001, 35–53 and 54–76. Also see Najmabadi 2005, 4–5.

6. This patronage was extended by the elites of Patna, though after his falling out with the ruling nobles and clerics of Lucknow, he secured British protection in the form of guards, exemptions from customs and taxes, and letters of safe passage. For more on Behbahānī and his text, see Cole 1988, 141–2; Cole 1996; and Alam and Subrahmanyam 2007, 240–2.

Merāt al-aḥvāl-e jahān-nomā was written at the end of his stay in Patna, just before he returned to Iran. Behbahānī encountered India at a time when Mughal power had devolved on to regional centers and the British were among a number of powerful players on this field. Though the text reflects rising British power, Mughal rule and its regional successors still served as worthy exemplars for Qajar rule.

Twenty years later, ʿAlī Mīrzā "Maftūn," a minor poet from Delhi resident in Patna (ʿAẓīmābād), traveled through Iran in 1826–27.[7] In November 1825 Maftūn left for the Hijaz via Calcutta and the Indian Ocean. After performing hajj, he traveled from Jeddah to various ports on the Arab side of the Persian Gulf and then on to Iran, arriving in the port of Bushehr in November 1826. Due to the unsafe roads between Bushehr and Baghdad, he decided to forgo pilgrimage to the Iraqi shrine cities in favor of pilgrimage to the tomb of the eighth Shiʿi Imam in Mashhad, where he returned to India via Transoxiana. His long journey to Mashhad was punctuated by stops in Shiraz, Esfahan and Tehran, as well as smaller towns. Maftūn completed his text soon after he returned to Patna from his travels, but given the level of detail and information about each stage of the journey (*manzel*), he must have taken notes during the trip itself. Maftūn encountered Iran during the reign of Fatḥ ʿAlī Shāh (r. 1797–1834), the second Qajar monarch, just as British power was eclipsing Muslim rule in the subcontinent and Persian was soon to be abolished as the language of power in their domains. Maftūn's text does not seem to have left Patna or even to have been copied beyond the original manuscript, while Behbahānī's text circulated widely in both Iran and India.[8]

Both travelers were Persian-speaking Shiʿa Muslims whose travel was inflected with religious concerns, bringing place of origin into relief as their primary parochial difference. In this context, I examine their representations of encounters with new places and people in their respective texts, and the ways in which expression of strangeness and familiarity of geographical and social contexts were mutually constitutive. Behbahānī narrates places largely according to social encounters, as well as local practices. While physical details of place are important, it is the ethical comportment and moral

7. Maftūn, meaning one who loses all in the throes of love, was his *takhallos* (poetic pen name). There is no known birth or death date for him.

8. Since my analysis looks at how each author expressed himself according to ways each assumed would be intelligible to his audience, differences in the reception and impact of the texts are less important, especially since the lack of circulation of Maftūn's text is likely to be due to the decline of Persian and his more modest social influence. The only known manuscript is HL 272 and HL 273 in the Khuda Bakhsh Oriental Public Library in Patna, India. The published version that I cite below begins on folio 32b of HL 273.

stature of its inhabitants that gives meaning to place. In Maftūn's text, place itself is central, with moral meaning narrated according to the history that inheres in geography and its physical structures. Social encounters and practices usually function as further embellishments of the meaning of place. Such an analysis allows for an appreciation of how a shared culture of Persianate learning could allow two individuals from different places of origin to experience new places and people as familiar to some degree, though the limits of this familiarity are telling of the local inflections of a shared culture.

Directions of Travel and Structures of Meaning

Place of origin, direction of travel and reasons for writing influence the structure of meaning within these texts. For both writers, the larger tradition within which they wrote framed Hindustan as a land of worldly wealth and Iran as part of the Islamic heartlands, though these characteristics could be given different meanings within larger textual narratives. Movements from South Asia toward the Middle East were usually written as pilgrimage to sacrilized heartlands, via Iran, dotted with the scenes of pre-Islamic and Islamic Qur'anic figures, as well as the well-known saints of the far past. The Iraqi shrine cities were adjacent to Iran, and were primary centers of Shiʿi devotion and education. Iran and Turan (Transoxiana) had accrued further meaning as the originary landscape of Persian history and culture, defined through epic literature, universal histories, and commemorative texts that limned the land with famous rulers, invaders, heroes, poets and heretics.[9] Movements from Iran to the subcontinent were usually written as journeys away from this heartland, of which most migrants and travelers from Iran saw themselves a part (the shrine cities of Iraq and Khurasan being as important for Shiʿa Muslims as the Hijaz). Travel there was seen, even under voluntary circumstances, as to a place less spiritually pure (with a largely non-Muslim population) and in possession of more worldly wealth, an ethically ambivalent trait under the best of circumstances.[10] Travel from Iran to India by various groups of people, from elite courtiers to merchants, soldiers and craftsmen, is well-documented, and quite frequent in the centuries

9. This Persianate history is often discussed in the context of studies of Iranian modernity and nationalism, though such works usually refer to it as quasi or entirely mythical. See Tavakoli-Targhi 2001; Marashi 2008; Kashani-Sabet 1999. A closer look at eighteenth-century Irani and Hindustani Persian texts demonstrates that these ideas circulated widely and provided paradigmatic signification for historical events and geographical locations. See Kia, forthcoming.

10. For further discussion, see Sharma 2003; Dale 2003; and Kia 2011, Ch. 1.

leading up to the early nineteenth century.[11] Less known is movement in the opposite direction. In both cases such flows of people were facilitated by the fact that Persian was the language of power and education in India. At the height of the Mughal Empire, seven times more Persian-speakers lived in India than in Iran.[12] Though Persian would be abolished as the language of government in the 1830s, and eventually replaced by Urdu as the language of education in the nineteenth century, in its early decades, travel between Iran and India was still facilitated by the predominance of Persian in literature, administration and elite culture.

In the scholarly literature on travelers from Iran to India, the dominant argument is that the encounter with India was "Orientalism." Juan Cole has outlined this point most explicitly through a specific analysis of Behbahānī's text and extrapolates that it "exhibits a sentiment of cultural and civilizational superiority which pervades eighteenth and nineteenth century [Iranian] Persian writing about India."[13] In the first place, sentiments of superiority are not the same as Edward Said's definition of the term Orientalism, since by Cole's own admission "this sort of writing lacked the power nexus of imperialism," and as importantly, it also lacked the institutionalization of such knowledge into disciplines.[14] Secondly, such sentiments need to be read within context, and against other features of the text that contradict and disrupt such assertions. For example, Cole notes that "inferences by intertextual frames required the audience to have read other Persian works about India, including romances, chronicles and travel accounts."[15] But how can this be understood as a systematic body of knowledge that created a sense of radical difference, since a number of the texts upon which Behbahānī draws are in fact Hindustani Persian? For example, he uses Amīr Khosrow Dehlavī's poetry to extrapolate on the adornments of the four-wheeled chariots used by rulers and nobles in India, and cites extended passages from the *Jahāngīrnāma* to explain the Mughal governing system.[16] Behbahānī's harshest censure is for those whom he perceives

11. Dadvar 1999; Green 2004; Green 2011, ch. 4 (118–54); Khan 1978; Richard 2000; Subrahmanyam 1988; Subrahmanyam 1996; and Tavakoli 2011.

12. Cole 2002, 16–17.

13. Cole 1996, 42. Alam and Subrahmanyam adopt Cole's characterization (2007, 242).

14. Cole 1996, 41. Also see Hamid Dabashi's critique of this use of the term (2007, 272–3 n14).

15. Cole 1996, 43.

16. For Behbahānī's use of Amīr Khosrow, see 1993, 183 and 184–5. For his use of the *Jahāngīrnāma*, see 1993, 187–90 and 191–8. He also mentions other famous texts, such as Gholām Hosayn Khān Ṭabāṭabā'ī's history, *Seyar al-mota'akharīn* (186). For his mention of Shaykh Bahā al-Dīn 'Āmelī's travel narrative on India, see 1993, 202. For a somewhat problematic and incomplete translation, see Behbahānī 1996.

to violate the norms of ethical comportment or for Shiʿa who violate what counts as orthodox Shiʿism in his estimation. The governing principle of this text is therefore not an assumed "Iranianness" that lends Behbahānī a protonationalist interpretive framework of cultural difference. It is rather an older Persianate ideal of ethics, one that he shares with his Hindustani Persian subjects and interlocutors.[17]

The Primacy of Social Encounters in Behbahānī's *Merāt al-aḥvāl-e jahān-nomā*

In his encounters with India, new places are both strange and familiar, but place itself is not the ground upon which such understandings are narrated. Far more central to his representations of difference or familiarity are social encounters, narrated through an ethics of sociability. It is not that Behbahānī does not understand differences between places. For example, he describes his birth "in the town of Kermanshah ... from within the borders of Iran (*az ḥodūd-e Iran*)."[18] Yet, while he demonstrates a sense of a geopolitical place called Iran, rather than encountering "Iranians" in India, Behbahānī meets "Qizilbash": persons whom he identifies with place-name monikers that signal their own or their immediate forefathers' origin or arrival from provinces or cities ruled by the Safavid shahs of Iran.[19] The term Qizilbash (red-capped) evokes the Turkomen tribes that brought the Safavid rulers of Iran to power. But in post-Safavid times, in India, it distinguished Persian-speaking Shiʿa from former Safavid Iranian domains from other Persian-speaking Muslims. There were non-Qizilbash Shiʿa, and non-Muslims, such as Parsis, whom Behbahānī identified as originating from the land of Iran in the distant past. Behbahānī describes Parsis as migrants from Iran who are "all fair-skinned and beautiful" because they have not intermarried with "outsiders" (*bīgāna*), and who "are extremely familiar (*ma'lūf*) with the Qizilbash" in Bombay.[20] Ostensibly pure descendants of the land of Iran, Behbahānī and the Qizilbash seem to understand a degree of consanguinity with these Parsis despite their religious difference. This similarity is not just through genealogical overlaps, but realized through social interaction.

Behbahānī's inclusion of substantial biographical information about the

17. Though I disagree with its main argument, Cole's 1996 article is still a useful source of information about the text. For further discussion of this text, see Kia 2011.

18. Behbahānī 1993, 140. This and all following quotes are my own translations from this published Persian edition.

19. For instance, he refers to "ʿAlī Bayg Khān Kermānī," who "was the head of the Qizilbash community," Behbahānī 1993, 231.

20. Behbahānī 1993, 227.

life and work of his famous forbears as a prelude to his own narrative is indicative of the formative role of social encounters within his text. Indeed, the text is titled *Merāt al-aḥvāl-e jahān-nomā* (The World-Revealing Mirror of Events), which could indicate an autobiographical journey of a life, rather than just a geographically defined travel narrative. The centrality of autobiography in the text is heralded by the long section at the beginning of the text through which he introduces himself through biographical, scholarly, and familial accounts of his biological and intellectual ancestors.[21] His life is produced from its location within a particular social fabric. This foregrounding of himself in the text may have served to act as introduction to a potential patron, the Qajar prince, Mohammad 'Alī Mīrzā Dawlatshāh (1789–1821), to whom the text is dedicated.[22] Features of the narrative, such as the ways in which he recommends emulation of certain Mughal state institutions, including the system of marking time and the postal system, address directly the imagined concerns of this prince.[23] Furthermore, the decided inferiority of Shi'i power in Murshidabad and Awadh reflected well on the new Qajar monarchy as the protector of the faith, particularly in the midst of the first Perso-Russian war. But these sorts of discussions on different practices and polities are presented in the context of knowledge derived from travel, part of the larger body of Behbahānī's learning by which he defines himself. Thus, his narrative is best understood as the autobiographical telling of his journey through life, which encompasses his geographical journeys and is encompassed by his social affiliations.

Behbahānī's notion of friendship, based on shared notions of culturally specific ethical behaviors, expressed a basis for affiliation outside of consanguineous or legal bonds. This is not to say that differences did not matter; instead they held varying degrees of significance. Friends and enemies, kind and repugnant, make frequent appearances in Behbahānī's narrative, but these figures are not constructed along neat lines of religion, social location or place of origin. Behbahānī deems people virtuous and thus socially desirable according to their virtuous comportment. Traitorous Iranians were

21. Volume One focuses on Mollā Mohammad Taqī Majlesī, Behbahānī's ancestor, removed by five generations. From there he moves to Majlesī's son and then to his son-in-law, from whom Behbahānī is directly descended, concluding with accounts of his grandfather and father, Vahīd and Mohammad 'Alī Behbahānī. The accounts revolve around a list of their major works, accomplishments, and chain of familial links, including teachers, in-laws and children (Behbahānī 1993, 68–138).

22. Behbahānī 1993, 66; for more on this oldest son of Fatḥ 'Alī Shāh Qajar, see Amanat 1994.

23. For Behbahānī 's description of time-keeping, see Behbahānī 1993, 206–7; for his description of the postal system see 1993, 208–9.

cursed, and conscientious Hindus lauded.[24] Being Muslim was not enough to be cast in a good light. For a man whose biological and intellectual forefathers were responsible for the dominance of the Usuli method of jurisprudence in Shi'ism, practices and beliefs that fell outside a specific idea of "proper Islam" were ridiculed and derided. But in personal relations, adherence to religious injunctions was not enough, because recognized modes of ethical comportment were also a basis of virtue. Thus, while a man might have good connections, high social standing, and a proper religious reputation, lack of hospitality or humility trumped these positive characteristics.[25]

On the way to India, Behbahani narrates two encounters, one with the antithesis of a desirable friend, and another with a wayward student. After receiving permission to issue legal rulings (*ejāza*) from the famed Sayyed 'Ali Ṭabāṭabā'ī and Mohammad Hosayn Shahrestānī in the Iraqi shrine cities, Behbahānī sets out for Qom.[26] There he teaches junior scholars, studies with senior scholars and collects another *ejāza*. Behbahānī then makes a similar pilgrimage to Mashhad, after which he journeys to Bandar Abbas to sail for India. His pupil, Mollā Esmā'īl, is with him on all these journeys. At Bandar Abbas he meets Sayyed Rezā Sindhī, "who previously had come to Najaf and with exquisite trickery persuaded me to make a trip to India." Sindhī is "inherently wicked" and "accursed" because "he avoids neither fornication, anal intercourse, nor any other of the religiously prohibited behaviors." Behbahānī laments being stuck with the man, especially when Sindhī publicly (and dishonestly) claims to be Behbahānī's patron. The only way to preserve his honor (*ḥefz-e āberū-ye khod*), he explains, is to bite his tongue and pay his own way. Preserving his honor entailed maintaining the fiction that all was as it seemed.[27] It is no coincidence that Behbahānī mentions religiously prohibited anal intercourse and fornication in the same breath as the unethical behaviors of dishonesty and stinginess.

To add insult to injury, Mollā Esmā'īl, whose expenses Behbahānī had been bearing in full, "was separated from me by the temptation of that ac-

24. Behbahānī curses the Qizilbash who betrayed (*namak be-ḥarāmī karda*) his master, Tipu Sultan, to the Nizam of Hyderabad's army, although that army was led by Mīr 'Ālam, whose father was a migrant from Iran and a sayyed (234–5). On his first attempt to travel from Patna to Benares, Behbahānī was robbed. The first person to come to see him after his party limped back to Patna was his student, a Hindu Monshī Rāmchand, whom he praises for his solicitude in the wake of this misfortune (Behbahānī 1993, 282).

25. Behbahānī uses the example of the Navvab of Lucknow, Sa'ādat 'Alī Khān, a devout Shi'a who refused to accept state revenue from religiously prohibited activities such as alcohol consumption and prostitution, but whose character was marred by stinginess (*emsāk*), Behbahānī 1993, 219.

26. Behbahānī 1993, 163.

27. Behbahānī 1993, 174–5.

cursed [Sindhī]." Although they had houses next to one another, "for the duration of two months he [Mollā Esmā'īl] did not greet me (*be-man salām namīkard*)."[28] Upon arriving in Muscat, Behbahānī found another patron and eventually "the accursed Sayyed" departed for Sindh. Mollā Esmā'īl, "remorseful of his deeds, expressed his apology and demonstrated his repentance." Behbahānī accepted his apology and allowed him back as a student.[29] That Behbahānī forgave Mollā Esmā'īl, after his rude behavior and unsavory activities with Sindhī, indicates that perhaps at this early stage in his career Behbahānī needed students in order to secure his status as a religious scholar and teacher. More than anything, though, Behbahānī's forgiveness narrates his own magnanimity.

In a narrative that presents himself and his friend as virtuous individuals, Behbahānī relates the ethical conduct that took place within a desirable friendship in Hyderabad. He describes a welcoming committee meeting him, headed by 'Alī Bayg Khān Kermānī, the head of the Qizilbash community, about three kilometers from the city. The day after he entered the city, his second day in Hyderabad, he was called on by a group of city notables, including Mīr 'Abd al-Latīf Shūshtarī. Shūshtarī also returned the following day with an apology on behalf of his paternal cousin, Mīr 'Abd al-Qāsem Khān (titled Mīr 'Ālam), who had sent the welcoming committee but was himself unable to pay Behbahānī a visit due to the advanced state of his leprosy.[30] Noting his visitors' illustrious ancestry, Behbahānī elaborates on their correspondingly noble (ethical) acts of hospitality by describing his visit to Mīr 'Ālam's house in minute detail. Upon arriving at his house, Behbahānī was greeted and escorted inside by another of Mīr 'Ālam's cousins and then met in the middle of the courtyard by Mīr 'Ālam and a host of notables: "When I reached the edge of the carpet, two people holding Mīr 'Ālam by the underarms brought him to greet [me]." In spite of the severity of Mīr 'Ālam's disease, which had ravaged his face and body, and the general injunction to flee lepers, Behbahānī tells us that he and Mīr 'Ālam sat next to one another and were freely affectionate (*dast va baghal shodīm*).[31] Recounting the honors that Mīr 'Ālam bestowed on him indicated to the reader that Behbahānī was a high-status person of noble lineage and ethical comportment, further demonstrated by his disregard of Mīr 'Ālam's leprosy.

While Mīr 'Ālam became his patron, through whom Behbahānī se-

28. Behbahānī 1993, 175.

29. Behbahānī 1993, 176.

30. Behbahānī 1993, 231. Mīr 'Ālam and Shūshtarī hailed from an illustrious lineage of learned scholars, including their great-grandfather, Sayyed Ne'matollāh Jazā'erī, a famous late Safavid *mollā*. For more on this family, see Momen 1985, 118; and Cole 1988, 22.

31. Behbahānī 1993, 231–2.

cured funds to repair and build fortifications around the Iraqi shrine cities, Shūshtarī is narrated as his closest friend in Hyderabad. Having told us of their close and constant friendship, he describes Shūshtarī as "extremely well spoken and well mannered (*nīkū aṭvār*), generous, humble, and his was the soul of gentility (*mabādī-ye ādāb*)." To demonstrate these characteristics, he remarks that "there was never an occasion at his house or at my house but that he sat opposite me on the *masnad* [raised platform], even though all the officials and notables viewed him with such honor and respect... he had not lost his humility (*kūchak-delī va forū-tanī*)."[32] Inviting a guest to sit next to, rather than facing a host of high-status birth and high rank could signify the host's acknowledgement of a similar status, as well as the humble display of honor bestowed upon a guest through intimacy.

At one point Behbahānī fell sick, and Shūshtarī visited him and received Behbahānī's request that, should he die, Shūshtarī accompany his corpse to the graveyard on foot. But Behbahānī recovered, and it was Shūshtarī who fell ill and died. Behbahānī faithfully attended to his friend's affairs and "in spite of the fact that people flee from the dead and if anyone attends to them [the dead] even a little bit he is considered a corpse-washer (*morda-shū'ī*), I closed his eyes and mouth myself and carried his corpse outside of the house."[33] As they set off for the graveyard, Behbahānī, at the insistence of the attending notables and officials, was about to accompany the bier in a carriage because of pains in his legs that had rendered him virtually unable to walk: "Just when I was about to climb [in the carriage], the request I had made of him [Shūshtarī] that he should accompany my corpse on foot, came to my mind. I took heed of this warning (*'ebrat*) and I accompanied [the bier] on foot." To drive the point home, Behbahānī reports that "for as long as I was in that city, on Friday nights I would visit his grave and read the prayer for [the forgiveness of] the dead (*fātiḥa*)." Behbahānī remained a loyal friend even beyond death through the fulfillment of this ritual, in spite of the fact that this put him in an awkward position vis-à-vis Shūshtarī's adversaries.[34] By depicting the ethical comportment of friendship, embodied in the exchange of physical acts, Behbahānī narrates Shūshtarī as kindred. It is through the forms of these relationships that exchanges of status and patronage are made. In the act of sitting next to him, two powerful citizens of the city embrace the young religious scholar of renowned family who traveled through elite circles in Iran. Behbahānī's description of the honor

32. Behbahānī 1993, 236–7.

33. Behbahānī 1993, 238.

34. Behbahānī 1993, 238. For more on Shūshtarī's family and involvement in Hyderabadi politics, see Dalrymple 2002, 129–39.

and intimacy they show him repays this kindness in the public space of his text. It buttresses his own status, depicts Hyderabad as a place, and animates the journey of Behbahānī's life.

The Primacy of Place in Maftūn's *Zubdat al-akhbār fi sawāniḥ al-afsār*

Just as Iranians came to India in the sixteenth and seventeenth centuries to perfect their poetry, so, in the early nineteenth century, Maftūn represented his travels through Iran as a way to perfect his spiritual state. Never far from spiritual integrity was Persianate cultural perfection, and Maftūn's narration of his trip through Iran alternates between veneration of the tombs of *emāmzādas* (children of the twelve Shi'i Imams) and Persian poets, effusive praise of men of religion and men of letters. It is through these affiliations with the Shi'i and the Persianate that Maftūn's place of origin is framed as a locality, and Iran as an unfamiliar, rather than foreign, place. As the nineteenth century waned, Maftūn's way of affiliating with Iran became increasingly unintelligible, since first languages vested in territorial origins came to dominate the terms of identity. The prestige of Persian was vested in land and Persianate culture could then only be understood as foreign to India.

After the Napoleonic wars, Russia emerged as Britain's main imperial rival in Central Asia. Qajar Iran was caught in the middle of this Great Game. By the early nineteenth century, the former Safavid Empire had been reunited under the rule of Qajar kings, though Iran was engaged with Russia in two wars (1804–13 and 1826–28) over the last of these erstwhile domains in the Caucasus. The result was the loss of not just Georgian and Armenian Christian subjects, and Sunni subjects in Dāghestān, but also, with the loss of half of Azarbaijan, of Shi'a subjects to Russian rule.[35] In India, the Mughal monarchs in Delhi were virtually British prisoners and their political legitimacy was slowly being demoted. The once powerful regional kingdoms of Awadh and Hyderabad, heirs to the Mughal imperial system, were increasingly unable to resist the pressures of British power. The legitimacy of Mughal sovereignty was still acknowledged by Indian princes, who continued to read the *khoṭba* (Friday prayer), strike coins and sign decrees in the Mughal emperor's name, as his vassals. The British government had also observed Mughal ritual forms.[36] But this changed in the 1820s as the British

35. For an account of these wars and their context, see Algar 1969, 45–102; and Kashani-Sabet 1999, 19–23.

36. Burke and Quraishi 1995, 25–29.

government began addressing Akbar Shāh (r. 1806–37) as they addressed the sovereigns of West Asia, as peers rather than overlords.[37] The British, then, were dismantling the formal edifices of Mughal power when Maftūn visited Iran.

As Shi'a, both Maftūn and Behbahānī related to Iran as a part of the Persianate world that concentrated a Shi'i ruler, religious community and centers of learning. Both Maftūn and Behbahānī describe Fatḥ 'Alī Shāh as *pādeshāh-e Islam* (the King of [Shi'i] Islam), invoking a responsibility to protect Muslim subjects, especially from non-Muslim rule. In the geopolitical context of the third decade of the nineteenth century, Maftūn's travel text exhibits some differences from its eighteenth-century predecessors. Whereas previous travelers to Iran and the Ottoman domains from Hindustan could proudly boast of the accomplishments of the Muslim Mughal monarchs in turning Hindustan into a paradisiacal land prospering due to just (Islamic) government and able administration, Maftūn is strangely silent.[38] His effusive praise of past and present Shi'i rulers of Iran and their accomplishments (as seen in cities and across the land) needs to be read in the context of this silence about home. Like Behbahānī, Maftūn's praise is articulated according to an ethics of proper comportment based on religious norms, but not reducible to them. He notes that Karīm Khān (r. 1750–79) was known as *Vakīl* (Regent or protector) because "he sincerely believed that he was not worthy of taking the throne... Inspired by great belief in the Lord of the Age (the Hidden Imam) he considered himself a Regent among the deputies of that choicest part of God's mercy (the Hidden Imam) entrusted with the custody and guardianship of the Shi'a populace and their vassals (*mavālī*)," and the inscriptions of the gold and silver coins of his reign bear witness to his fidelity to that promise (*bar ṣadāqat-e īn qawl shāhed ast*).[39] Such a narration highlights the fulfillment of the promises of Shi'i rule, unencumbered by British dominion.

In the section on Tehran, where Maftūn outlines the ongoing events of the second Perso-Russian war, he reports that Sayyed Mohammad Ṭabāṭabā'ī, the foremost *mojtahed* of the Iraqi shrine cities, based on reports of Muslim persecution under the Russians, forced Fatḥ 'Alī Shāh to declare war in 1826. Maftūn refers to the Russians as "uncouth godless ones (*bī*

37. Burke and Quraishi 1995, 52–3.

38. See for instance, Kashmīrī 1970, 215–7. 'Abd al-Karīm Kashmīrī's *Bayān-e Vāqe'* has a similar itinerary to Maftūn's. Kashmīrī traveled from Delhi with Nadir Shah Afshar's army in 1739 to Iran, and then to visit the Iraqi shrine cities on his way to the Hijaz to perform hajj. He returned to Hindustan via a ship to Bengal in 1742. See further Alam and Subrahmanyam 2007, 247–90; and Kia 2009.

39. Maftūn 2003, 9.

dīnān-e bad-ā'īn)," linking a lack of proper comportment with a lack of proper belief.[40] Ṭabāṭabā'ī issued a fatwa tarring as an unbeliever (*kāfer*) anyone who failed to do their utmost to struggle against the Russian dominion over the Shi'a subjects of former Iranian domains. Maftūn approvingly describes Ṭabāṭabā'ī 's concern and initially gentle attempts to convince the Shah, finally going so far as to travel from Karbala to Tehran to rally support.[41] For Maftūn, the clergy is rightfully protecting the people and forcing the Shah to do the same. This concept of the proper relationship between ulema and ruler, and their creation of an ethical/religious realm for the protection of the people is not inherent to Iran or India, but the ability to realize this ideal relationship is specific to Iran in Maftūn's time.

For Maftūn, the new land he encounters is laden with spiritual and cultural significance, focused around figures and places Hindustani Persians would know from various literary and commemorative texts. It is the physical presence of spiritual and cultural markers through which he narrates Iran. It is not that cities in Hindustan do not have illustrious founders, or are not dotted with the tombs of saints, but they are not integral to pre-Islamic Persian or Qur'anic history, or part of the early history of Islamic heartlands. The city of Shiraz boasted the tombs of the poets Hāfez and Sa'dī, both of which Maftūn visited and described at length.[42] Shiraz was also home to the shrine of Shāh Cherāgh, and other prominent *emāmzādas*, whom Maftūn calls *ma'ṣūmzāda*, or born of purity.[43] This difference in the valence of geography, however, is not the radical alterity that modern notions of native versus foreign evoke.

Shared understandings of geographical valence are the product of a literary culture that contained the tools through which the unfamiliar could be rendered familiar. Maftūn has a sense of India and Iran as distinct but similar places, like the broad road out of Būshehr that resembles, for him, the roads in India.[44] When extolling the natural beauty of Shiraz and its environs, he comments that "its green plains and verdant city are the cause of shame and the hyacinth and narcissus filled hills are the envy (*rashk*) of the agreeable hills of Kashmir."[45] Nothing in Maftūn's biography, little known as it is, indicates that he traveled to Kashmir. There is no reason to assume

40. Maftūn 2003, 117.

41. Maftūn 2003, 117–8. For Maftūn's full description of the wars and these politics, see 2003, 117–28. For an analysis of the declaration of this war as jihad, see Masroori 2004, 263–74.

42. For his visit to Hāfez and then Sa'dī's graves, see Maftūn 2003, 25–30.

43. For instance, Maftūn 2003, 24 and 26.

44. Maftūn 2003, 3.

45. Maftūn 2003, 8–9.

his readers would have done so either. It is more likely that he was familiar with the common literary image of Kashmir as a paradisiacal land, passed down in Hindustani Persian texts, which would have been familiar to his readers as well.[46] By connecting the beauty of a place in Iran with a place in the subcontinent, Iran is reinforced as unfamiliar, but not radically different and thus foreign. But rather than link the beauty of the two places equitably, Maftūn places the beauty of the Shirazi countryside above that of Kashmir, causing it to be a source of envy.

Though political fragmentation, colonial encroachment and a decided Iranianization of the Persian language had occurred in both India and Iran, a Hindustani Persian could still narrate the history of places according to a dual Islamic and pre-Islamic Persian narrative.[47] This dual parallel narrative permeated Irani and Hindustani Persian culture up through the early nineteenth century, as seen in various kinds of texts, from formal historical chronicles, *tazkeras* (commemorative compendiums) or travel narratives like Maftūn's.[48] Maftūn's text is laden with historical context, both the immediate political context of current rulers and ongoing events (like the Perso-Russian war), as well as the near and far past of places. The far past was the history of a place of which no physical marks remained, rather knowledge of this history saturated Persianate literary and visual culture in the form of universal and dynastic histories, literary epics and symbolic representations in miniature painting. Julie Meisami notes that "[t]he role of history in linking present rulers with past ones (whether with those of ancient Iran or early Islamic times) and thereby legitimizing the transfer of power to the current incumbents is clearly crucial" and had been since the early eastern Islamicate regimes embraced Persian as one way to cultivate autonomous authority from the Caliphate.[49]

Maftūn begins his description of Esfahan with a genealogy of its builders,

46. This view is propagated in Mughal texts, and shared by Iranian Persian texts as well. See Kia, forthcoming; and Kashmīrī 1970. Kashmir became the summer residence of Mughal emperors.

47. The narrative of pre-Islamic Persian kings is a prose re-inscription of the epic poem the *Shāhnāma* (Book of Kings). This format of reconciled, parallel Biblio-Qur'anic and pre-Islamic Persian history followed by the birth of the Prophet and the start of the era of Islam in the universal history *Rawzat al-safā* became the template for Mughal and Safavid-period universal histories throughout the early modern period, however differently their post-Timurid accounts might be focused. See Tavakoli-Targhi 2001, 93 and 85; Quinn 2000, 127–36; and Meisami 1993.

48. For an example of this type of mapping of history on to geography in a *tazkera*, see Āzar Begdelī's *Ātashkada*, written in the 1770s in Qom. Also see Kashmīrī's *Bayān* and 'Abdul Latīf Shūshtarī's *Tohfat al-'Ālam*, among many others.

49. Meisami 1993, 250.

locating the city not just as the best city of Iran, and by extension the world, but also as the oldest. He notes that "the flourishing of the city was built by the heirs of Tahmūrath Pīshdādī and Jamshīd and Eskandar and Kayqobād, who was the first Keyāni ruler."[50] This Persianate history also visually limns the physical structures of the cities. In Shiraz, Maftūn provides a detailed description of the governor's palace.[51] He notes that the walls are painted with images of the feats of "lion-hunting heroes and well-known champions (*tahamtanān*), including Rostam, Zāl, Gīv, Gūdarz, Farāmarz, Pashūtan, Bahman, Rohām, Borzū'ī, Sohrāb, and Esfandeyār.[52] The mention of such names is not accompanied by any explanation, suggesting that Maftūn could assume his audience's familiarity with such information. Islamic and pre-Islamic Persian historical narratives run in parallel harmony in most universal histories so that the latter does not conflict with the former. Together they could be evoked to link a new land with familiar meanings slower to change than the meaning of the near past.

Another historically specific aspect of Maftūn's text is the new form of representation that structures Maftūn's text. The minutiae of the state of the roads, every caravanserai and its nearby villages, as well as information about the quality of available water, and kinds of food stuffs in village market places, indicate that at least one possible use for the text was as a practical manual for future pilgrims and travelers. These descriptions also demonstrate that Maftūn's celebration of Iran is not uniform, that he found some places less than spectacular. An instance is Maftūn's description of Mehyār, the final halting place before Esfahan:

> With two hours remaining of the night we set out and arrived at the next halting place near to perishing (*qarīb-e zavāl*). Its main road is level and at the middle of the way is a flowing stream, around which there is a rundown village (*qarīa-ye kharābī*) in which agriculture takes place. There are also several gardens visible. There is a caravanserai fine and firmly built, solid and spacious in the fashion of Shāh 'Abbās's structures, where reservoir water, bread and accompanying victuals (*qāteq*) can be obtained. The headman (*kadkhodā*) is Hajji 'Alī Akbar. Its [the village's] income is 3000 tomans a year. At this time, revenue collection is [in the hands of] Amīr Qāsem Khān and copper coin is the collected currency. The office higher [than that of Amīr Qāsem Khān] belongs to the prince of Esfahan. This halting place is five farsakhs [from the previous one].[53]

50. Maftūn 2003, 55. For more on these figures, see Ferdowsi 2007.
51. For the full description, see Maftūn 2003, 11–4.
52. Maftūn 2003, 13–4; for more on these figures, see Ferdowsi 2007.
53. Maftūn 2003, 54.

The descriptions of cities provide another conundrum, one not so easily chalked up to practical information for the future pilgrim. Various structures within cities, usually those that classically define Islamicate cities – palace, bath, bazaar, mosque and garden – are described in such a way that very nearly create a photographic image of these structures through written description. Certain structures even warrant pages of versified praise, such as the mosque and bathhouse built in Shiraz by Karīm Khān Zand.[54] In addition to structures common to every Muslim urban center, Maftūn describes those that define Iran within the Persianate world—providing painstaking details of the design and inscriptions of *emāmzādas*, tombs of poets and structures built by political figures.[55] He carefully identifies the builder of each, the builder's history, the building's location, its appearance and its features. Previous travel texts, like Behbahānī's, certainly mention and describe important or impressive buildings within cities, but not in such realistic, comprehensive and minute detail down to the type of stone, its color and inscriptions. In fact, Maftūn maps every major city that he travels through from end to end, beginning with each gate, its major thoroughfares, the sectors of the cities, pinpointing the structures he describes in three-dimensional detail on to the map. For instance, after pages of both prose and poetic description of Karīm Khān's mosque and baths, Maftūn notes that "to the east of the mosque is the market square (*chār sū*) of the Vakīl, which without exaggeration has no equal in all the provinces of the seven climes. Length-wise it is approximately just over 1500 paces, and the same in width. In the center is a perfectly laid out, well-cut octagonal fountain (*ḥawż*). In all four directions are substantial (*matīn*) shops, possessing high, full ceilings, singular in height and width, and each property is in such an appointed condition which is not to be found elsewhere." He then goes on to detail which areas of the market square contain which wares, all described in detail.[56] The cities are presented as sites of political power, cultural prestige and religious devotion. These descriptions go on for over twenty pages in Shiraz, Esfahan, Tehran and Mashhad. This limning of the landscape, mapped with such detail, materially recreates Iran, in all its spiritual and cultural glory, as well as providing practical information for the would-be traveler.

Perhaps a reason for this unprecedented virtual tour lies in an earlier shift in representational forms of painting in late eighteenth-century India, where the artistic focus shifted to the architectural monuments of urban

54. Maftūn 2003, 9; for descriptions of Shiraz, see 2003, 11–32; for poetry in honor of the mosque 2003, 15; and in honor of the bathhouse 2003, 16–8.

55. For the shrine of a son of the fourth Imam, see Maftūn 2003, 24.

56. Maftūn 2003, 18.

spaces. Architecture always had a presence in Mughal painting, but mostly as backdrop to provide context of place. Thus buildings were drawn with specifically identifiable features, but these were vaguely articulated due to the largely stylized forms of depiction. Previous travel texts also described cities and their major structures, but these descriptions were not realistic; rather they provided several specificities, couched in vague, stylized terms used for any number of other structures. Beginning in the eighteenth century, architecture in Mughal manuscript traditions would emerge as a central subject of representation in subsequent artistic traditions, in contrast to the earlier prevalence of portraiture and studies of flora and fauna. These textual and pictorial representations of architecture, in more technical and clearly articulated detail, lent character to a place and posed architecture as a more integral sign of the achievements of rulers.[57] This connection is echoed in Maftūn's description of the history of cities in terms of its architecture that was always linked to a patron/ruler. Just as Maftūn connects Karīm Khān to the structures of Shiraz, he limns Esfahan with structures built by the Safavid Shahs, Tehran as built by Fatḥ ʻAlī Shāh and Mashhad as built by centuries of rulers, particularly Nāder Shāh and Shāhrokh Shāh Afshār. These linkages between architectural structures mapped on to urban space and political order serve as a vehicle through which Maftūn narrates the political and cultural impact of history.

Social encounters play a smaller role in the text, buttressing the effect of geographical descriptions. In Tehran, Maftūn and his companions receive visits and invitations from other Hindustani Persian Shiʻa migrants. One of these is Sayyed Akbar ʻAlī Fayzābādī, a prominent physician "who has been in this land (*deyār*) for eighteen years and has chosen to settle down and establish a family (*ta'hel*). He can enter into the society of many great and leading nobles of the city without ceremony and they accord him great honor and respect (*ʻezzat va eqtedār*)."[58] Representations of Hindustani Shiʻa in Iran, described as commanding respect and receiving great honor from prominent local nobles and officials, serve to make Iran more familiar.

Encounters with religious scholars buttress Maftūn's spiritual limning of the land. For example, Maftūn and his eminent Hindustani travel companions arrive in Tehran with letters for local personages, such as the Friday prayer leader of Tehran, Sayyed Mohammad Mahdī. On the first day Maftūn arrived in Tehran he was invited to call upon the Sayyed. He describes him with such honorifics as the "cream (*zobdat*) of the ulema" and effusively lauds his praiseworthy qualities and morals/manners (*awṣāf-e ḥamīda* and

57. Dadlani 2010, 186–9.
58. Maftūn 2003, 108.

akhlaq-e pasandīda). He also notes that the Sayyed is descended from the son-in-law of Mollā Mohammad Bāqer Majlesī, the famed late Safavid Shakyh al-Islam of Esfahan. This information draws a parallel that would be obvious to a Shi'i audience, exalting clerical lineage in a reflection of the nobility of prophetic lineage. After the Sayyed had received and read the letters, he welcomed the travelers. Maftūn comments that, "as much as this noble group (*ṭā'efa-ye sharīfa*) has customs (*rasm*), more than [even] those rituals and polite manners (*akhlāq*) came into practice."[59] For Maftūn, the pinnacle of the Persianate is also the pinnacle of Shi'ism. Throughout his text, those devoted to and correct in religion are also the most noble and virtuous in terms of the ethics of sociability. The idea of Iranian kingship as a Shi'i monarchy, as protector of the faithful and the domains of the faithful, was the idiom through which the land of Iran came to be venerated.[60] We can see this veneration of Iran as a sacred site in Maftūn's extensive descriptions of Iranian cities. In a poem extolling and elaborating on the mosque that Fatḥ 'Alī Shāh had built in the bazaar neighborhood of Tehran, Maftūn calls it the second Ka'ba (*bovad īn masjed-e Fatḥ 'Alī Shāh ka'ba-ye dovvom*).[61]

As a final note, it is important to note that Iran was not automatically a site of pilgrimage for Maftūn. His original intention, like many of his predecessors, was to visit the shrine cities of Iraq. Only when that way was closed to him did he journey toward Mashhad and thus visit the poetic centers of Esfahan, Shiraz and the capital city of Tehran. Other Persian travelers from the subcontinent had been perfectly content to bypass Iran on their return to India, such as Abū Ṭāleb Esfahānī, who visited Kazamayn, Samara, Najaf and Karbala on his return from Europe to India in 1804.[62] In fact, the Hindustani Persians whom Maftūn finds living in Tehran are all described as having taken up residence there on their way to or just after pilgrimage to the Iraqi shrine cities, rather than as having intentionally traveled to Iran to settle. Still, once there, Iran was limned according to well-known religious, poetic and Persianate historical personages and events, according it a kind of spiritual and cultural veneration on the part of a Shi'i Hindustani Persian living under British rule. Over the course of the next decades, room for this veneration would shrink and shift as first colonial and then anti-colonial nationalist narratives vested geographical entities with discrete cultures embodied in exclusive native language(s), until Persian became as foreign to India as the Indian was in Iran.

59. Maftūn 2003, 108.
60. See Babayan 2002.
61. Maftūn 2003, 113.
62. Abū Ṭāleb 2004, 400–35. For the early nineteenth-century English translation of this travelogue, see Abū Ṭāleb 2009.

Encountering Difference

In spite of the ways both Maftūn and Behbahānī render the new as familiar and comprehensible, they also encountered people, places and practices that were alien and incomprehensible to them. Unfamiliar practices were interpreted according to proximity or distance from Muslim lands, or the efficacy of Muslim rule in creating an ideal virtuous society. Behbahānī identifies local customs mostly as deviations from the true faith that stem from adoption of Hindu practices. He notes difference primarily with Hindustani Shi'a, and it is for them that he reserves harsh censure. For instance, Behbahānī describes the local practice of marriage rituals as undermining the gender relations upon which proper social order rests:

> [In this country,] they [Muslims] give a marriage portion (*mahr*) [to a wife] beyond their means: a man who does not possess the capacity to pay even a thousand rupees commits to forty or fifty thousand, up to even twenty or thirty lac rupees. It is for this reason that women in this country rule (*mosallaṭ*) over their husbands, except for a few, who because of their endowed goodness (*khūbī-ye dhāt*) are submissive and strive to please their husbands.[63]

Women rule rather than men, a calamity for the social order produced by erroneous practices. Behbahānī comments that most of these customs, along with many others, are of Hindu origin and were introduced into Muslim practice under the Mughal emperor Akbar. But this disapproval is due to the perception that this intermingling with Hindu practice had in some cases led to the abrogation of Muslim law, such as the supposed abandonment of circumcision among imperial princes.[64] Such disapproval was not uniform toward any local practice. As noted above, Behbahānī admired certain institutions, including the postal system. He also lauded certain social practices, such as adoption and fosterage, and himself adopted a son, for whom he professed "love as for a true son." Rendering it proper to Islam, he notes that it was a custom prevalent in the Hijaz, though unknown in Iran.[65] Thus in some ways Hindustan was superior to Iran in the practice of Islam.

Similarly, Maftūn stopped in Kazarun and had to camp outside the city because of the violent rivalry between the Ne'matīs and Haydarīs, factional affiliations territorially rooted in the various neighborhoods of the city: "There are groups called Ne'matīs and Haydarīs who fight and kill each other. The reason for their generations-long quarrel since olden times has been

63. Behbahānī 1993, 212.
64. Behbahānī 1993, 214.
65. He cites the introduction of Zayd ibn Ḥārisa, Behbahānī 1993, 222–3.

for the purpose of the perfection of their own sect. The astounding thing is that they are together united in the Twelver Shi'i sect." But the reason for this conflict is not a result of the corrupting influence of another faith. Maftūn states that "No other reason for the origin of this war and strife comes to mind, except the deceit of the accursed Devil (*Eblīs*). And no threat or contrivance of any governor or leader has profited the situation at all. Taking heed of this bad activity (*bad-'amalī*), I made camp a little outside the town in the warehouse (*barband*) of Hajji Husayn, which was an enclosure without a ceiling."[66] Since this rivalry was territorially rooted, his residence in any part of the city would have automatically affiliated him with one of the two rival factions. He thus avoids error and involvement in an erroneous practice by staying outside the city proper, in rather uncomfortable circumstances. In Iran, error was caused by the Devil and not by idolaters, as it was in India for Behbahānī. Yet Maftūn's tone of condemnation is somewhat more muted, likely because he is not a *mojtahed*, but also because such error is caused by the exceptional work of the devil, rather than the sustained interaction with a faith perceived as idolatrous.

Although Persianate culture was something in which people both in Iran and India participated, *'ajam* meant more than a Persian-speaker. Muzaffar Alam calls *'ajam* "the non-Arab world of eastern Islam." The high culture dominant in both Mughal and Safavid realms in the early modern period, based on a shared education and literary asthetics, developed through "a dialogue between the Persian language and the Indian cultural ethos...a result of constant interaction between the literary matrices of India, on the one hand and of Iran, Afghanistan and Central Asia on the other."[67] This interaction was also of a social nature, as migration, even in the less frequent and less documented travel from east to west, resulted in an embodied social aspect of this shared cultural ethos. Maftūn, for example, describes being entertained by the various Hindustani Shi'a of Tehran:

> Janāb Mīr Mughal Sāheb, who is of the Sayyeds from within the borders (*khetta-ye*) of Kashmir is unrivaled in his praiseworthy qualities (*awṣāf-e ḥamīda*) and had residence (*qeyām*) in Lucknow. Having arrived in Iran five or six years ago, he undertook noble pilgrimage to the holy cities of Iraq, and chose to settle down here [Tehran] ... he offered us hospitality in the Persian style (*żeyāfat-e 'ajamāna*).[68]

The idea of *'ajam* appears as a distinctive style, something Maftūn attri-

66. Maftūn 2003, 6. For more on these factions, see Perry 2003.
67. Alam 2004, 121.
68. Maftūn 2003, 109.

butes to the form of Kashmīrī's hospitality, while another of his hosts, Janāb Chaudhuri, is described differently as "taking the greatest pains" (*be-kamāl-i takallof*).[69] Maftūn recognizes *'ajamāna* as a particular manner and custom of hospitality, something that Hindustanis can and do practice, making them Persian in Iran.

For Behbahānī, the presence of ethical social behavior and resulting community harmony could change the nature of place itself. He notes, "unlike the residents of the island of Bombay, where everyone is a blood-thirsty enemy (*doshman-e khūnkhvār*) and seeks to ruin each other's business," all of the Qizilbash in Masulipatnam "appeared in unanimity (*mottafeq*) with each other." Because of the "beauty of the unity and morality (*ḥosn-e ettefāq va akhlāq*) [of the inhabitants of Masulipatnam] that port has come to resemble (*nemūna-ye*) Iran."[70] Social interaction here has a direct impact on perceptions of place, transforming the proximity and thus identity of place itself. Such observations are hardly the polarized radical difference of place that defines Said's notion of Orientalism.

Like many learned Persians, Behbahānī's mobility was a constant feature of his existence, even before he set out for India. Behbahānī's text presents his early travels in Iran and Iraq as a search for knowledge. When he arrives in the subcontinent this purpose becomes inverted, as he seeks to impart religious knowledge as a way to gain patronage. In contrast, Maftūn traveled westwards to improve his spiritual state through pilgrimage, a form of gaining knowledge. As a Persian poet, his travels through Iranian literary centers provided a means of cultural self-perfection through the acquisition of another kind of knowledge. These differences were bound up in the shared understanding of the meaning of different lands where West and South Asia had contrasting relationships to sacred space and cultural knowledge. However, access to knowledge and the sacred could be acquired through travel and study. As a text of travel and specifically of pilgrimage, the rhetorical labor of Maftūn's narrative can be read as a forum where he displays his religious and poetic knowledge, for his audience at home, confirmed through the cultural and spiritual luminaries of the Hijaz and Iran. Traveling out of their respective domains, yet still within the Persianate world, albeit somewhat fractured by the early nineteenth century, Behbahānī and Maftūn reveal place of origin as a category of difference still tied to pre-colonial meanings where difference was not absolute, and could contain certain similarities forged according to a shared understanding of virtue and ethical comportment.

69. Maftūn 2003, 109; the phrase also means offering many dishes.
70. Behbahānī 1993, 252–3.

Works Cited

Abū Ṭāleb ibn Mohammad Esfahānī (1383/2004), *Masīr-e Ṭālebī yā, safarnāma-ye Mīrzā Abū Ṭāleb Khān*, 4th ed, ed. Hosayn Khadīvjam, Tehran: Sāzmān-i Enteshārāt va Āmūzesh-i Enqelāb-i Eslāmī.
—— (2009), *Travels of Mirza Abu Taleb Khan in Asia, Africa, and Europe, during the years 1799, 1800, 1801, 1802, and 1803*, tr. Charles Stewart, ed. Daniel O'Quinn, Peterborough, Ont.: Broadview Press.
Alam, Muzaffar (2003), "The Culture and Politics of Persian in Precolonial Hindustan," in: Sheldon Pollock (ed.), *Literary Cultures in History: Reconstructions from South Asia*, Berkeley: University of California Press, 131–98.
—— (2004), *The Languages of Political Islam: India, 1200–1800*, Chicago: University of Chicago Press.
Alam, Muzaffar, and Sanjay Subrahmanyam (2007), *Indo-Persian Travels in the Age of Discoveries, 1400–1800*, Cambridge: Cambridge University Press.
Algar, Hamid (1969), *Religion and State in Qajar Iran, 1785–1906: The Role of the Ulama in the Qajar Period*, Berkeley: University of California Press.
Amanat, Abbas (1994), "Dawlatšāh, Mohammad-'Alī Mīr-zā," *EIr*, VII: 147–9.
Babayan, Kathryn (2002), *Mystics, Monarchs and Messiahs: Cultural Landscapes of Early Modern Iran*, Cambridge: Center for Middle Eastern Studies.
Behbahānī, Āqā Ahmad ibn Mohammad 'Alī (1372/1993), *Mer'āt al-ahvāl-e jahān-nomā*, ed. 'Alī Davvānī, Tehran: Amīr Kabīr.
—— (1996), *India in the Early 19th Century: An Iranian's Travel Account, Translation of Mir'at al-ahval-i jahan numa*, tr. A. F. Haider, Patna: Khuda Bakhsh Oriental Public Library.
Burke, S. M. and Salim al-Din Quraishi (1995), *Bahadur Shah: The Last Mogul Emperor of India*, Lahore: Sang-e-Meel.
Cole, Juan R. I. (1988), *Roots of North Indian Shi'ism in Iran and Iraq: Religion and State in Awadh, 1722–1859*, Berkeley: University of California Press.
—— (1996), "Mirror of the World: Iranian 'Orientalism' and Early 19th-Century India," *Critique: Critical Middle Eastern Studies* 5: 41–60.
—— (2002), "Iranian Culture and South Asia, 1500–1900," in: Nikki R. Keddie and Rudi Matthee (ed.), *Iran and the Surrounding World: Interactions in Culture and Cultural Politics*, Seattle: University of Washington Press, 15–35.
Dabashi, Hamid (2007), *Iran: A People Interrupted*, New York: New Press.
Dadlani, Chanchal (2010), "The 'Palais Indiens' Collection of 1774: Representing Mughal Architecture in Late Eighteenth-Century India," *Ars Orientalis* 39: 175–97.

Dadvar, Abolghasem (1999), *Iranians in Mughal Politics and Society, 1606–1658,* New Delhi: Gyan Pub. House.
Dale, Stephen Frederic (2003), "A Safavid Poet in the Heart of Darkness: The Indian Poems of Ashraf Mazandarani," *Iranian Studies* 36: 197–212.
Dalrymple, William (2002), *White Mughals: Love and Betrayal in Eighteenth-Century India,* London: HarperCollins.
Faruqi, Shamur Rahman (1998), "Unprivileged Power: The Strange Case of Persian (and Urdu) in Nineteenth Century India," *The Annual of Urdu Studies* 13: 3–30.
Ferdowsi, Abolqasem (2007), *Shahnameh: The Persian Book of Kings*, tr. Dick Davis, New York: Penguin.
Green, Nile (2004), "A Persian Sufi in British India: The Travels of Mīrzā Hasan Safī ʿAlī Shāh, 1251/1835–1316/1899," *Iran* 42: 201–18.
—— (2011), *Bombay Islam: The Religious Economy of the West Indian Ocean, 1840–1915.* New York: Cambridge University Press.
Kashani-Sabet, Firoozeh (1999), *Frontier Fictions: Shaping the Iranian Nation, 1804–1946*, Princeton: Princeton University Press.
Kashmīrī, 'Abd al-Karīm (1970), *Bayān-e vāqe': sarguzasht-e ahvāl-e Nāder Shāh va safarhā-ye musannef Khvāja 'Abd al-Karīm ibn Khvājah 'Āqebat Mahmūd Kashmīrī*, ed. K. B. Nasim, Lahore: University of Punjab.
Khan, Yar Muhammad (1978), *Iranian Influence in Mughal India.* Lahore: Yar Muhammad Khan.
Kia, Mana (2011), "Contours of Persianate Community, 1722–1835," Ph.D. dissertation, Harvard University.
—— (forthcoming), "Imagining Iran before Nationalism: Geocultural Meanings of Land in Azar's Atashkadeh," in: Kamran Aghaie and Afshin Marashi (ed.), *Rethinking Iranian Nationalism*, Austin: University of Texas Press.
—— (2009), "Accounting for Difference: A Comparative Look at the Autobiographical Travel Narratives of Muhammad 'Ali Hazin Lahiji and 'Abd al-Karim Kashmiri," *Journal of Persianate Studies* 2: 210–36.
Maftūn, Hajji 'Alī Mīrzā (2003), *Zubdat al-akhbār fī savāniḥ al-asfār: safarnāma-yi Irān, qarn-i nūzdahum-i mīlādī*, ed. Zakira Sharif Qasemi, New Delhi: Islamic Wonders Bureau.
Mani, Lata (1998), *Contentious Traditions: The Debate on Sati in Colonial India,* Berkeley: University of California Press.
Marashi, Afshin (2008), *Nationalizing Iran: Culture, Power, and the State, 1870–1940,* Seattle: University of Washington Press.
Masroori, Cyrus (2004), "Russian Imperialism and Jihad: Early 19th-Century Persian Texts on Just War," *Journal of Church and State* 46 (Spring): 263–74.

Meisami, Julie S. (1993), "The Past in the Service of the Present: Two Views of History in Medieval Persia," *Poetics Today* 14: 247–75.
Momen, Moojan (1985), *An Introduction to Shi'i Islam: The History and Doctrines of Twelver Shi'ism*, New Haven: Yale University Press.
Najmabadi, Afsaneh (2005), *Women with Mustaches and Men without Beards: Gender and Sexual Anxieties of Iranian Modernity*, Berkeley: University of California Press.
Perry, John R. (2003), "Ḥaydari and Neʿmati," *EIr*, online ed.
Quinn, Sholeh A. (2000), *Historical Writing During the Reign of Shah 'Abbas: Ideology, Imitation and Legitimacy in Safavid Chronicles*, Salt Lake City: University of Utah Press.
Richard, Francis (2000), "Some Sixteenth-Century Deccani Persian Manuscripts in the Bibliothèque nationale de France," in: Muzaffar Alam et al. (ed.), *The Making of Indo-Persian Culture: Indian and French Studies*, New Delhi: Manohar, 239–49.
Robertson, Bruce Carlisle (1995), *Raja Rammohan Ray: The Father of Modern India*, Delhi: Oxford University Press.
Sharma, Sunil (2003), "The Land of Darkness: Images of India in the Works of Some Safavid Poets," *Studies on Persianate Societies* 1: 97–110.
Smith, Matthew C. (2009), "Literary Connections: Bahār's Sabkshenāsi and the Bāzgasht-e Adabi," *Journal of Persianate Studies* 2: 194–209.
Subrahmanyam, Sanjay (1988), "Persians, Pilgrims and Portuguese: The Travails of Masulipatnam Shipping in the Western Indian Ocean, 1590–1665," *Modern Asian Studies* 22: 503–30.
—— (1996), "Iranians Abroad: Intra-Asian Elite Migration and Early Modern State Formation," in: Sanjay Subrahmanyam (ed.), *Merchant Networks in the Early Modern World*, Aldershot, UK: Variorum, 72–95.
Tavakoli-Targhi, Mohamad (2001), *Refashioning Iran: Orientalism, Occidentalism and Historiography*, London: Palgrave.
—— (2011), "Early Persianate Modernity," in: Sheldon Pollock (ed.), *Forms of Knowledge in Early Modern Asia: Explorations in the Intellectual History of India and Tibet, 1500–1800*, Durham: Duke University Press, 257–87.
Zastoupil, Lynn (2010), *Rammohun Roy and the Making of Victorian Britain*. New York: Palgrave Macmillan.

Portrait of Mahdi Hasan Fath Nawaz Jang. (Courtesy Omar Khalidi.)

An Indian Passage to Europe

The Travels of Mahdi Hasan Khan Fath Nawaz Jang

Omar Khalidi

TRAVEL LITERATURE IS A LARGE SUBFIELD in Western literary history, particularly in the study of cultural contacts and the making of images and stereotypes. Because of the sheer quantity and easier availability of materials, however, most research in travel literature focuses on the Western perspective of the "Other."[1] Studies of representations of Europeans by Indians and Middle Easterners during the eighteenth and the nineteenth centuries, the era of colonial hegemony, are few and far between. Unlike the Middle Eastern countries that were in contact with Europeans from early on, it was not until the seventeenth century that Indians came into closer contact with Europe through the trading companies on the western and eastern seaboard.

Between the years 1600–1857, about twenty thousand Indians of many different social classes traveled to Britain, according to one researcher,[2] a majority being lascars, coolies, and nannies.[3] Perhaps a larger number of Europeans traveled in the reverse direction. Compared with the large number of memoirs written by European colonists or visitors to India during this period, only a handful of Indian accounts of Britain and Europe have come to light, since most Indians going westward during the period were subaltern, poor, and illiterate. In the eighteenth to the mid-nineteenth centuries, Persian was the language of communication amongst the elite in much of India. Among the travelogues that have come to light are those of Mirzā I'tisāmuddīn, who traveled in 1766–9;[4] Munshī Ismā'īl, who journeyed in 1771–3;[5] Mīr Muhammad Husain ibn 'Abd al-'Azīm Isfahānī-Londonī, physi-

1. The easier availability of Western accounts as opposed to those of others has tended to eclipse the observation of Indian and Islamic travelers to the West; see Alam and Subrahmanyam 2003, 4.

2. Fisher 2004; Das 1924.

3. Visram 1986; Ansari 2004.

4. For various translations of his travelogue, see the general bibliography. University of Madras Professor Abu Hashim Sayyid Yushaa (d. 1983) owned or had access to a manuscript of the *Shigarfnāma*, but sadly did not live to publish it, see Umri 1974, 573.

5. Digby 1989, 49–65.

cian-poet of Murshidabad, who traveled in 1774–7 to England and beyond.[6] Many returned home, but some decided to stay once they reached England. Among them was Dean Mahomed (1759–1851) who, unlike earlier travelers of aristocratic and middle-class, came from humble circumstances.[7] In 1794, Mirza Ahmad Khan, a prince of Bharuch, Gujarat, went to Paris, where he learnt French and translated into Persian the *La Déclaration des droits de l'homme et du citoyen*, a fundamental document of French constitutional history adopted in 1789 by constituent assembly.[8]

At the close of the eighteenth century, Mirzā Abū Tālib Khān, a nobleman from Lucknow, accompanied an English friend home in 1799 and spent some time traveling around.[9] Nawab Iqbāl ad-Daula and Padshāh Begum ("Queen Mother") of Oudh (Awadh) traveled to England in 1838 and 1857–8 respectively.[10] According to one literary source, Mawlavī Ahmad Allāh, better known as a freedom fighter of the 1857 Mutiny against the East India Company, went to Europe and England in the early 1800s.[11] In the nineteenth century, before the formal end of the Mughals in 1857, three travelogues are noteworthy. One is by Yūsuf Khān Kambalposh, a Hyderabadi migrant to Lucknow who sailed to Europe from Calcutta in 1836.[12] The second is by Lutfullāh of Malwa, who traveled in 1844.[13] In 1856, Masīhuddīn Khān, an envoy of Vājid 'Alī Shāh (r. 1847–56), the king of Oudh (Awadh), left for London and returned home after a few years.[14]

The post-1857 era of Indian history increased Indian travel to Britain. Among others, two travelers were Sayyid Ahmad Khan of the Aligarh-based

6. Ansari 1998.

7. Fisher 1996. Rammohan Roy, founder of the Brahmo Samaj, came to England in 1831 to plead the case for increasing the purse of the Mughal emperor Akbar II (r. 1806–37), and, like Dean Mahomed, stayed on.

8. Hasan 1970.

9. For various translations of his travelogue, see the general bibliography. For biographical information on the author, see Kabir 1961.

10. See Chapter Four, "Indian Visitors to England," Llewellyn-Jones 2000, 86–124.

11. Tayib Lucknowi, *Tavārīkh-i Ahmadī*, a *masnavī* composed in 1863, five years after the death of Ahmadullāh in 1858, according to Fārūqī 1973, 51–4. The poem was first printed in 1925, long after the author died in 1902.

12. Ikram Chaghatai 2004, the editor of this travelogue, claims to have found the original Persian text and restored the original Urdu title; see the book review of this edition by Intizar Hussain in *Dawn* 04 July 2004, electronic edition. According to Chagahtai, the travelogue was written in Persian, but never published; the author then wrote or translated it into Urdu, which was first published by Delhi College's Maktabat al-'Ulūm in 1847, reprinted in Lucknow in 1873. Tahsin Firaqi had earlier published the same Urdu translation of *'Ajāyibāt-i Firang* in 1983 in a new edition with notes.

13. Lutfullah 2007.

14. Biographical information in 'Alavī Kakorvī 1999, 399–403, and the travelogue in Masih Uddin Khan 1969.

educational movement among Indian Muslims,[15] and by Mīr Lā'iq 'Alī Khān Salar Jang II, a *dīvān* (prime minister, hereafter divan) of Hyderabad, Deccan, in the late nineteenth century.[16] American historian Michael Fisher has so far found about twenty pre-1857 Indian travelogues to Britain, though more may be discovered.[17] Even though meager compared to the number of travelers, their writings constitute an important part of early modern history of South Asia for, in the words of Mohamad Tavakoli-Targhi, "Persian [and Indian] travelers, by constituting Europe as a differentiated site of analysis and gaze, produced a significant body of knowledge about European history, politics, culture, science, and economy ... The dialogic interaction of European and Persianate knowledge set in motion the dynamic process of modern cultural (trans)formations."[18] One such traveler was Mahdi Hasan Khan, a resident of Lucknow, who after a meteoric rise in Hyderabad earned the title of Fath Nawaz Jang from the Nizam's government.

The Life and Career of Fath Nawaz Jang

Following the financial and administrative collapse of the Nizam's Dominion in 1853, the able divan of Hyderabad, Salar Jang I, undertook to reform the bureaucratic system, particularly the revenue departments. Within a few years, a large increase in the state funds was achieved. Since the Deccani ruling class was neither interested in the reforms nor could, due to the lack of modern education and experience, provide the necessary personnel for the administration, Salar Jang I had to look for outsiders from the British Indian provinces in upper India, Madras, and Bombay to employ in the higher posts in the newly created departments and institutions. The most famous of these men were Sayyid Mahdi Ali, later Nawab Muhsin al-Mulk; Mushtaq Husain, later Nawab Wiqar al-Mulk; "Deputy" Nazir Ahmad; Sayyid Husain Bilgrami, entitled Imad al-Mulk; Chiragh Ali, later titled Azam Yar Jang; and Agha Mirza Baig, entitled Sarwar al-Mulk. Among these outsiders, those less known than the ones cited, was Mahdi Hasan Khan. He rose to be the Mīr-i Majlis-i 'Adālat al-'Ālīya, or the chief justice of the high court.

15. Sayyid Ahmad Khan 1961.

16. Salar Jang 2008.

17. Personal communication, May 17, 2004. For an overview, see Abdul Qadir 1930, 83–96. For a bibliography of travelogues, see the introduction by Tahsin Firaqi in the Urdu translation of Yusuf Khan Kambalposh 1983, as well as Ballhatchet 1985–6, 158–179; and Llewellyn-Jones 1990, and the expanded version in Llewellyn-Jones 2000. For an overview of travelogues in Persian, see Storey 1927, 1138–62. Tej Rai 1903 contains the 1887 travels of the nobleman Prime Minister Āsmān Jāh to Europe; for the Italian part of the journey, see Aqil 1995, 261–9.

18. Tavakoli-Targhi 2001, 44. For an overview of the subject, also see Khan 1998; and Rayachaudhuri 2002.

Mahdi Hasan Khan was born in circa 1852 in Fathpur, a historically notable *qasba* some thirty miles from Lucknow, now in district Barabanki.[19] He came from a prosperous and cultured Shia family of Awadh. His father Shaikh Lutf-i Husain was a revenue contractor for the Awadh nawabs. Education at home and at Canning College (the precursor of Lucknow University) prepared him for a career in revenue service and law in the newly created United Provinces, where he became a *tahsīldār* and a magistrate. In 1873, he met and married Ellen Gertrude Donnelly, daughter of an Irish resident of Lucknow.[20] Miss Donnelly is described in the local English newspaper *The Pioneer* as "a young lady of irreproachable character."[21] She embraced Islam, "under the auspices of a Mahomedan Raja of Oudh."[22]

During his tenure as magistrate, Mahdi Hasan Khan left Lucknow for Hyderabad. Like many of his contemporaries in upper India, he came to Hyderabad with a recommendation from Sayyid Ahmad Khan of Aligarh for employment.[23] He arrived in Hyderabad on 9 February 1883, the day after Salar Jang I died.[24] Nonetheless he was able to secure a job in the Nizāmat 'Adālat-i Dīvānī. During the tenure of Salar Jang II as divan, he was appointed as the chief revenue and judicial officer of the area around Hyderabad city.[25] Shortly afterwards he received rapid promotions: a member and secretary of the Majlis-i 'Adālat al-'Ālīya, then its acting chief, and finally confirmed as the chief justice, an office he held between 1884–89.[26] During the Nauroz celebration in 1886, the Nizam conferred upon him the title of Fath Nawaz Jang. A little later he became the Home Secretary, an important post. Evidently, he was quite popular among the elite in the capital, both among the Indians and the British. He was elected the first secretary of the Nizam Club, founded in 1884, and remained in that post until 1892, as noted on the roster of the board of officials in the Club. The founding of the Club was itself an innovation in the hide-bound Hyderabadi society of the time. It was also a counterpoint to the British-dominated Secunderabad Club in the cantonment.

In early 1888 he was deputed by the Nizam's Dominion to travel to London

19. The year of his birth is determined by his age, given as 15 years on 3 July 1867 in the admission register of Canning College, Lucknow, see Prasad 1893, xiv of the Appendix. The Fathpur of Mahdi Hasan is different from the more famous Fathpur-Sikri, near Agra.

20. Ellen Gertrude Donnelly's deposition to the court in Hyderabad as noted in Prasad 1893, 439.

21. *Pioneer*, 11 January 1871, as cited in Oldenburg 2001, 245.

22. Oldenburg 2001, 245.

23. Mahvī 1946. I am grateful to Babar Siddiqi, grandson of Mahvī, for providing the extract from this rare book.

24. Serverul Mulk 1932, 253, 284.

25. Rao 1909, 361.

26. Rao 1909, 362.

in connection with a case regarding Hyderabad (Deccan) Mining Company. He came back to Hyderabad on 9 January 1889.[27] He was commended for his work there. In fact while still in London, he was appointed the Director of the Nizam's Guaranteed State Railways.[28] During the stay in London, he carefully noted down his observations of English society and institutions in the Victorian era. The wealth of details as seen through an Indian eye has been seldom matched by anyone of his country during this time. His observations were first partly published in a journal in England.[29] Later the observations were issued as a book, meant "for private circulation."[30] His Aligarh friend, Aziz Mirza, translated and published the book. Aziz Mirza, a Hyderabad official and a fine author himself, rendered the English original in a highly readable and idiomatic Urdu, as *Gulgasht-i Firang*, making the translation almost an original work.[31] Besides his London travel diary, Mahdi Hasan translated *A Memoir of Salar Jang*, written by Sayyid Husain Bilgrami and published as *Muraqqa'-i 'Ibrat.*[32] Even before arriving in Hyderabad, he contributed as many as seven articles to *Tahzīb al-akhlāq*, the journal edited by Sayyid Ahmad Khan.[33] In October 1883, he wrote to Sayyid Ahmad Khan proposing a memorial for Sayyid Babr 'Ali Anīs and Mirzā Salāmat 'Alī Dabīr, the two classical Urdu poets of *marsīya* (elegy to Imam Husain, the grandson of Prophet Muhammad). He volunteered with a donation of a hundred rupees as a start.[34] His minor writings—departmental reports and a letter to *The Times*, London, about Muslim apathy toward the Indian National Congress—are documented elsewhere.[35]

Hyderabad politics in the nineteenth century centered around the Nizam's relations with the British Resident on the one hand and the relations of the Residency with the nobility and the divan on the other. Intrigues by various individuals and factions in the nobility also played their part in

27. Akbar 'Alī Baig 1987, 145.
28. Mahdi Hasan 1890, 101.
29. Hobhouse 1890a, 61–73; 1890b, 139–58, as cited by Burton 1998, 232.
30. Mahdi Hasan 1890.
31. Mahdi Hasan 1889. The Azad Library of Aligarh Muslim University owns a copy, and the facsimile is being reproduced from that copy, thanks to its Chief Librarian Dr. Shakil Ahmad Khan. The book cost three rupees when published, a large sum by the standard of the time. It may have precluded large circulation as noted by Prof. C. M. Naim in a personal communication to the present writer. Prof. Baig presented a photocopy to me in Hyderabad on December 29, 2004, just before his death in January 2005.
32. Mahdi Hasan 1910.
33. Mahdi Hasan 1987, 45. I am thankful to Dr. Shakil Ahmad Khan for sending a copy of this index to me.
34. Mahdi Hasan 1967, 289–90. I am grateful to David Lelyveld for pointing me to this work.
35. Khalidi 1985.

the politics of the era. In 1888, the Diwan happened to be Nawab Asman Jah; the parties and interests opposed to him started to attack the officials and men under him. They began with Mahdi Hasan Khan.

An anonymous pamphlet entitled *A Shocking Social Scandal,* casting aspersions on the character of Ellen Gertrude Donnelly, the Irish wife of Mahdi Hasan Khan, began circulating among the Hyderabad nobility.[36] The pamphleteer harshly criticized her husband for knowingly presenting his wife, despite her alleged character, to Queen Victoria during a levee held in London during Mahdi Hasan Khan's visit to London.[37] The pamphlet had the desired effect. Mahdi Hasan Khan was suspended from service on 22 September 1892. In defense, Mahdi Hasan Khan filed a defamation suit against S. M. Mitra, an impoverished journalist affiliated to *The Hyderabad Record*, based in the Residency area, outside the Nizam's jurisdiction in the capital. Mitra was accused of being the author and publisher of the pamphlet. A costly and lengthy court case followed. O.V. Bosanquet, the Justice of the Peace and the Superintendent of the Residency Bazaars, acquitted Mitra of the alleged offense in a judgment delivered on 19 April 1893. However, at the same time the judge declined to go into the truth or falsehood of the accusation made against Mahdi Hasan Khan and his wife.[38] Mahdi Hasan Khan's reputation was nonetheless ruined as he was dismissed from the Nizam's service on 25 April 1893. An unknown Urdu poet punning on his dismissal wrote a doggerel lampooning Mahdi Hasan:[39]

> kyā ʻizzat va jāh va māl kho kar niklā / nāmī thā magar nām dubo kar niklā
> ek mem kī ulfat men is sāl afsos / kyā Mahdī Hasan zalīl ho kar niklā

> What honor, greatness and wealth Mahdi Hasan lost.
> He was famed but sank his own reputation.
> For the love of a *mem* this year,
> Mahdi Hasan was dismissed and dishonored.

Another poem about Mahdi Hasan Khan's dismissal from service is attributed to Masʻūd ʻAlī Mahvī, a Hyderabad official and our author's compatriot:

36. Husain 1892. I am grateful to Dr. Hasanuddin Ahmad for sharing a longhand copy with me. Upon enquiry, no one by the name of Mirza Bakir Husain, the alleged author of the pamphlet, was discovered in Lucknow; see full court proceedings in Prasad 1893; Rao 1909, 262. Husain claimed to have studied at Canning College, but makes too many errors in writing, including referring to Ellen Gertrude Donnelly as *Lady* Mahdi Hasan, a term usually designated for the wives of knighted men. Mahdi Hasan never claimed to have received a knighthood. I am grateful to Prof. C. M. Naim for pointing out the errors in the pamphlet.

37. Prasad 1893,

38. Prasad 1893,

39. Khalidi 1993, 53–4.

mahram-i rāz īn pamphlet bi-nivisht / guft īn mem nīst, randī hast
chūn rasīd īn bi-gosh-i Fath Navāz / istighasā kunān zi jā bar jast

The "knower-of-secrets" wrote this pamphlet
declaring: "Not a lady at all, she is a prostitute."
When these words reached Fath Nawaz,
he leapt from his chair and filed a suit.[40]

Two days after removal from service, Mahdi Hasan Khan left Hyderabad and returned to Lucknow with his wife. They had no children. Despite the scandalous court case and no children, he did not divorce her as would have been common in that time and class. In the absence of anything else, we must conclude that they had a strong marriage and remained devoted to each other. Back in his hometown, he began a legal practice in partnership with Sayyid Ahmad Khan's son Sayyid Mahmud. Some years later, he is described as a trustee of the Mahomedan Anglo-Oriental College at Aligarh in 1898, the forerunner of the Aligarh Muslim University.[41] According to Mahvī, Mahdi Hasan converted to Qadiyanism in his final years.[42] He passed away on 20 January 1904 in Lucknow.[43] His dead body was brought to Fathpur, near Lucknow for burial in the Pakki Phulwadi cemetery.[44] Thus ended the life of Mahdi Hasan, a remarkable story of the meteoric rise and fall of a talented writer and civil servant. Not much else is known about the short life of Mahdi Hasan—barely fifty-two when he died—beyond what is gathered here.[45]

The Travelogue

Hyderabad State emerged after the eighteenth-century contest for power between the European trading companies and Indian military elites as a princely state with a high degree of internal autonomy, but firmly under

40. The present writer found the poem in an article by Abbasi 1956, 936. However, Babar Siddiqi, Mahvī's grandson, denies that his grandfather would have written this poem. Personal communication, February 23, 1998. The Urdu word *mem*, derived from English "madam," refers to a European lady in colonial India. I am grateful to Professor C. M. Naim for help with the translation.

41. Beck 1991, 130.

42. Mahvī 1946.

43. According to file number L5/94, 1904 Private Secretary's Office of the Nizam's Government, in A.P. State Archives (APSA). I am grateful to Sayyid Shakil Ahmad Anwar, a former archivist at APSA, for locating this file for me. Thanks also to David Lelyveld for alerting me to this file, which led to its fresh examination by Anwar.

44. Mahvī 1946.

45. His own portrait is found in Mudiraj 1934, 572. References to Mahdi Hasan are also found in Nadwi 1925, 255–62, 333–4, as well as in Sarvar al-Mulk 1932a and Server el-Mulk 1932b, 253–84.

the control of the British Raj based in Calcutta. After nearly five decades of internal chaos and financial doom, it gained peace and some economic and educational development under the leadership of Salar Jang I, who became the divan in 1853. He turned to the British for economic development and bureaucratic modernization. The discovery in 1872 of significant coal deposits in the Singareni area near Warangal and the Godavari River spurred industrialization and railway development in the Nizam's Dominions.[46] In the early 1880s, some Hyderabadi and British officials sought to combine the railway and mining concessions, since the prospect of profitable freight would be an incentive to British investors in the expansion of the Nizam's Guaranteed State Railway. It was in this connection that Fath Nawaz Jang traveled to England in early 1888. He began his travel diary even before he left Hyderabad on 4 February 1888 for Bombay. After a short stay in Bombay, he embarked on the journey on board the *Sutlej* on 10 February. In addition to the final destination, London, his travels took him to parts of Egypt, France, Switzerland and Italy. The last entry in his diary is dated 24 October 1888, written while in Naples, Italy. The total duration of his overseas visit is over eight months.

Mahdi Hasan Khan's Observations and Perceptions: General Remarks

During this time Fath Nawaz Jang observed Egyptian, British, French, Swiss, and Italian societies, sometime from close quarters. Besides his official engagements he found time to visit and write about politicians,[47] political institutions and system, the class system, the attributes of modernity such as time management, Englishwomen and their status, the compartmentalization of private and public life, academia, museums, financial institutions, theaters, sports, clubs, and the technological and scientific progress of Europe. In his own words, "I have not looked at things from the ordinary point of view, and hence I mention the smallest details, however trifling. In my opinion, that was the only way in which I could convey to the minds of my readers the ideas and feelings that I experienced. I am quite conscious of the fact that for an insignificant person like myself to write a diary is presumptuous,[48] and yet I think it of advantage of those of my countrymen

46. Sethia 1986; for later developments, see Khalidi 1991.

47. Fath Nawaz Jang's meeting with British Prime Minister William E. Gladstone (1809–98) was reported as "Gladstone Friendly to Turkey," *The New York Times*, 21 February 1888, an article in which he is described as the Nizam's agent.

48. His characterization as such can only be attributed to the culture of *kasr nafsī*, self-effacement so prevalent among some Indian Muslims of his class.

who have never been to England for me to lay my life there open before them, and thus give them an opportunity of sharing with me my feelings for England and the English people."[49] Christianity, whether of the Anglican denomination in England or Catholicism in Italy, does not seem to have interested Mahdi Hasan at all, making it perhaps the only aspect of European life that escaped his scrutiny. To what can we attribute his lack of interest in European religious life? He may have been familiar with the basic beliefs of Christian theology in India both as a Muslim and, perhaps, also because his wife was born in a Christian family. It may also be due to familiarity with missionaries, fairly numerous then as now in India. One more puzzling aspect of Mahdi Hasan's travelogue is his near silence on his wife. She is mentioned three times in the dairy, first when she came to see him off at Bombay, then when he notes not hearing from her on 18 February 1888, and when she evidently joined him in London by April 11, when they go together to an "At Home." How was this interracial marriage received in Victorian England? Was it approved, disapproved, or simply treated with indifference? Regrettably we shall never know firsthand, as Mahdi Hasan simply did not write about it.

As an associate of Sayyid Ahmad Khan and his Aligarh movement for the educational and material advancement of Indian Muslims, Mahdi Hasan Khan traveled to England with introductions to the relatives and colleagues of English officials in India, particularly those connected with Aligarh, such as Theodore Beck,[50] whose sister received him in London.[51] He generally moved in the high society of Victorian England, and thus formed an opinion based on his interactions with that class. Mahdi Hassan appears acutely conscious of being a Muslim. Boarding the ship, he remarked in his diary: "It pained me very much to notice that the only Mahomedan faces on board were those of the lascars or menial servants of the ship. The history of the rise and fall of nations is deeply interesting; the Mahomedans in their time were the rulers of the earth and sea."[52]

Progress of Science and Technology

A major theme of his diary notations is made up of his remarks on the material progress of the European nations, and its absence in India, particularly

49. Mahdi Hasan 1890, 4.

50. Beck 1991, 130.

51. Mahdi Hasan 1890, 54. He identifies her as Miss B.! The University of Minnesota copy of the book bears the name of a Joseph Beck, the father of Theodore Beck, a principal of the Mahomedan Anglo-Oriental College. I am grateful to David Lelyveld for information on the Becks.

52. Mahdi Hasan 1890, 21.

among his co-religionists. While on board the *Sutlej*, he notes the amazing development in the science of navigation.[53] The Royal Mint, the Royal Arsenal, the printing establishment of the *Times*, the telephones and the telegraph, the textile mills of Manchester,[54] and the foundries of Sheffield similarly astonished him.[55] When he arrived in Cairo, Egypt, en route to England, Mahdi Hasan visited both a modern school and a traditional madrasa attached to the al-Azhar mosque. When "we entered the mosque ... I saw a painful sight. There are about 10, 000 Mahomedan students from all parts of the world ... The education is of the oldest style, and any attempt on the part of the government to alter the character of the teaching meets with obstinate resistance ... The lessons ... are mostly in theology ... I was grieved at the ruin of these co-religionists of mine and at the waste of public money in achieving it. I should say that Mr. Wilfrid Blunt ought to be made principal of this university."[56] From the madrasa, he went to see a school: "I went around the school and was delighted with what I saw. Some two or three hundred boys receive instruction in every branch of mechanics, they are taught from the book every day for a few hours, and after that they work ... many of them find employment in railway workshops or private shops. Most of the other educational institutions here are rotten, and show very little progress."[57] Though Mahdi Hasan never enrolled at any of the English universities, his interest in modern scientific education led him to the universities of Oxford and Cambridge.[58]

While in London, Mahdi Hasan went to a theater to see Richard Wagner's romantic opera *Lohengrin*.[59] Although the opera was in German, he was able to follow the story: "In a most effective way we were shown the triumph of Virtue and Knowledge over Vice and Ignorance. But one people, the Indians, were conspicuous by their absence from this field of triumph; and their absence spoke eloquently to the fact that the unfortunate natives of India have as yet no share in the development of science and civilization."[60] Coming as he did from the relatively slow pace of time in Lucknow and Hyderabad, the energy and pace of Londoners sharply struck him: "London is the city of business; everyone appears busy; the pedestrians walk fast as if racing with

53. Mahdi Hasan 1890, 21–2.

54. Mahdi Hasan 1890, 135–6.

55. Mahdi Hasan 1890, 15–6.

56. Mahdi Hasan 1890, 34–5; Wilfrid Scawen Blunt (1840–1922), an Islamophile British writer, was a great advocate of modernization among Muslims everywhere; see Blunt 1909.

57. Mahdi Hasan 1890, 36.

58. Mahdi Hasan 1890, 63, 111.

59. See the essay by Sunil Sharma in this volume for a female traveler's description of the same opera.

60. Mahdi Hasan 1890, 52.

time itself. Time is very valuable here, as it ought to be everywhere ..."[61] and "It appears that time in London is divided into three portions—from nine to six is business time, from six to midnight the time for pleasure and dissipation, and the rest is for sleeping."[62]

Political Orientation

During and after the 1857 "Mutiny", Indian Muslim elites for the most part remained loyal to the British, exemplified by the cases of Nizams of Hyderabad and the Aligarh movement led by Sayyid Ahmad Khan. As one closely associated with Aligarh, it is unsurprising that Mahdi Hasan demonstrates loyalty to the British and, at times, extreme Anglophilia. For example, while still in Cairo, he agreed with the favorable opinion of the colonial authorities as expressed to him by the Egyptian elite: "I am more and more convinced that the destiny of the Mahomedan world is interwoven with England. If Mahomedans ever again prove able to take a high place in the assembly of the world it will be through the generosity of England."[63] During the course of a conversation about Queen Victoria, he asserts, "All the blessings that India ever received have been conferred during the reign of this lady, and we all love her, and almost worship her."[64] To his surprise, not only did his English companions not share his sentiments, but they also complained about the wasteful public expenditure on the royal life style.[65] On April 30, he attended the levee for the Queen held by the Prince of Wales and appears to have been overwhelmed by feelings of loyalty: "I forgot all the Anglicized feelings which have been forced upon me by the circumstances of the last fifteen years of my life and felt inclined as if by the force of some spell, to revert to the Oriental custom, to throw myself at the feet of that noble Prince, and to kiss his hand."[66] When presented to the Queen, "I was so confused with extreme affection rather than fear that, after making a humble obeisance and stooping very low, I hardly caught sight of Her Majesty at all: I saw her nodding to me with such a gracious smile that tears of joy and love came to my eyes so that I could see neither her nor the Princesses, and passed on."[67] Consonant with these pro-British sentiments, he wrote a forceful letter to the *Times*, explaining his and the Muslim community's opposition to

61. Mahdi Hasan 1890. 57.
62. Mahdi Hasan 1890, 74.
63. Mahdi Hasan 1890, 39. Sayyid Ahmad Khan in his *Musāfirān-i London* compares Indian culture negatively with that of the English.
64. Mahdi Hasan 1890, 51.
65. Mahdi Hasan 1890, 51.
66. Mahdi Hasan 1890, 98.
67. Mahdi Hasan 1890, 104.

the newly-formed Indian National Congress's "radical principles of government." He saw these principles as unfit for India and his community, which he claimed "have a strong predilection for that form of rule which is known as despotism."[68]

His visit to the Parliament left a favorable impression of the British political system,[69] the culture of open, fearless debate, discussion, consensus, and collective decision-making.[70] Regarding politics, his positive assessment of the parliament was reinforced by the feelings of school children, when he visited a school. What impressed him most was the acute awareness even among school children that people collectively govern the nation: "In one of the classes, the teacher asked who governed the country, and the boys said, 'We govern the country.' Then they were asked how, and they replied, 'By sending representatives to the House of Commons, which governs and legislates' ... [T]he extent of their information, and the interest which they took in politics at so tender an age, astonished me. An Indian boy of fifteen is an utter fool, so far as politics are concerned."[71] No foreign visitor to England could overlook the class system and its dynamics, just as no visitor to India in the past or present can ignore the caste system. Mahdi Hasan was thus no exception: "In England, class divisions are very strictly observed; the royalty is a class by itself, and in spite of the spread of Radical views, is as much worshipped by the English people as by us."[72] He adds, "Next comes the nobility, the main support of the Throne and the gems of England; and then the middle class; representing the power, intellect, and wealth of the country."[73] Later he writes, "The aristocracy is here a class apart, but nobody cares for them; the powerful people are the commoners. Ability and intellect alone can make a great man. A man, by the aid of ability or eloquence, may achieve the highest rank among the rulers of the empire. And it is a peculiarity that he who rules the empire today may tomorrow be in the position of a very ordinary gentleman."[74] And "Last, but not least in importance, comes the lower or working class. Each class in England is quite independent of the others, and hence the general content and happiness."[75]

68. Mahdi Hasan 1890, 109; the letter is dated March 30, 1888.
69. Mahdi Hasan 1890, 12–13.
70. Mahdi Hasan 1890, 58–9.
71. Mahdi Hasan 1890, 69.
72. Mahdi Hasan 1890, 10.
73. Mahdi Hasan 1890, 10
74. Mahdi Hasan 1890, 88–9.
75. Mahdi Hasan 1890, 10.

British Financial Institutions

Since becoming the director of the Nizam's Guaranteed State Railway, Mahdi Hasan naturally showed interest in London's world of high finance. To acquaint himself with the business environment of Britain he visited financial institutions. At the Bank of England, he was shown around the operations where he observes, "Here honest machines, without any human help, are engaged in weighing the sovereigns. There are long tubes filled with thousands of sovereigns, each sovereign in turn is mechanically pushed forward, weighed, and slipped into a box on the right hand; if there is the least deficiency in weight, the machine turns it off to a box on the left. The process is carried on by the machines with the greatest coolness and regularity."[76] Next he visited the Stock Exchange: "It is a large building, and no one but the members is admitted. Almost all brokers and jobbers, whose offices are round the building, are members. After eleven o'clock the place is full, and the noise and excitement arising from mutual transactions is intense. If you want to buy some stock, you go to a broker, and he buys it for you from the jobbers. The whole affair is a paper business. A jobber will sell fifty thousand pounds worth of stock at a given rate, while he has not a pennyworth in his possession. Then it becomes his duty to procure the stock somehow or other. To spread the idea that there is a great demand for a certain stock, and to enhance the price of it, is called to "bull" the stock, and the contrary operation is called to "bear." The whole business is complicated and the language too technical for an outsider to understand."[77] His next stop is at the Royal Exchange, "where twice a week in the afternoon, people assemble and settle their accounts. But besides that there is a clearing house, by means of which millions of money changes hands every day without the trouble and risk attendant on the transfer of gold from place to place."[78] Given his primary assignment in London regarding the Hyderabad Railways, he met the officials and bankers associated with the project, including a former British Resident Sir Richard Meade. During these meetings, the politics of various factions in Hyderabad came to light.[79]

British Society and Women's Rights

Apart from matters of business, finance, government and politics, Mahdi

76. Mahdi Hasan 1890, 129–30.
77. Mahdi Hasan 1890, 130.
78. Mahdi Hasan 1890, 130.
79. Mahdi Hasan 1890. 88, 100–1, 105, 107.

Hasan Khan kept a sharp gaze on the English society of the time. He described the "English people, their physique, their social, intellectual and moral qualities."[80] According to Mahdi Hasan, "The English people are exceedingly polite when you go to see them; they are open-hearted, and their hospitality is genuine. People of greater intimacy are invited for dinners and people who are rich give a few big "At Homes."[81] According to him, "We have much to learn from the English in the art of social enjoyment. It pains me to think that if there were twenty Mahomedans on board beside myself, they would not make the least effort to enhance their mutual social pleasures. The reason of this is that the inequality and imperfection of education in India has left us on such different levels, and with such different tastes and modes of thinking that we are unable to enjoy one another's company."[82]

Mahdi Hasan Khan's modern education at Canning College, his association with the modernist Aligarh movement, and marriage to an Irishwoman, all may have contributed to his views on the place of women in Indian and Islamic societies, which may seem somewhat contradictory or at least ambivalent in the twenty-first century. Early on in the diary, he informs the readers that he is "in favor of complete freedom for women. I do not see any reason why women should not enjoy all the liberties of men when they are as advanced in intellectual capacity ... I recognize that a complete equality between men and women is impossible, for women have one solicitude in the world which men have not ... I mean their reputation ... There is no harm, therefore, in women's innocent enjoyment of man's society, but a certain decorum is to be maintained even in this."[83] Comparing the condition of women in India to those in Egypt, he noted while in Cairo, "The thing that most pleased me here was that Mahomedan ladies are not so strictly deprived of enjoyment as in India, where it is a social crime for women of respectable families to go for a drive or to the theater, or in short to any place where there are men."[84] Despite the constraints on the freedom of women, he observes "that the Mahomedan law concerning marriage and the rights of women is more reasonable and more compatible with the principles of utility than the English law, which in certain cases makes marriage an institution not favorable to domestic happiness.[85] Marriage according to English law is indissoluble, unless there be exposed in open court a scandal of such

80. Mahdi Hasan 1890, 8.
81. Mahdi Hasan 1890, 9.
82. Mahdi Hasan 1890, 23.
83. Mahdi Hasan 1890, 25.
84. Mahdi Hasan 1890, 31.
85. In this respect, he seems to echo the views expressed earlier by Mirza Abu Talib Khan; see Fisher 2000.

a nature as to ruin the husband or wife in public estimation. There is no reason why the parties to contract should not be allowed to agree to break it. The common tie of affection in children, and the long habit of living together, which in itself is sufficient to produce affection, is a sufficient check on any frequent resort to divorce when the woman has passed the best years of her life and could not easily find a new home. The best proof of this is that the Mahomedan law sanctions such divorce, yet it happens rarely. Marriage is dissoluble by Mahomedan law, if both the parties agree ..."[86]

Mahdi Hasan's ambivalence toward women is best illustrated in his encounter with a woman on a bus. Many Indian visitors to Victorian London were uncomfortable at the sight of women in the streets, as exemplified by the observations and experiences of Behramji Malabari, who visited London in 1890: "The crowds of women in the streets, walking rapidly past, pushing and elbowing every one who stands in the way, all intent on business or pleasure, are a sight not likely to be forgotten..."[87] Then while on an omnibus, Malabari observes, "I am [sitting] in between two of the prettiest and quietest women [who have rushed in the bus] feeling a strange discomfort. As the bus hobbles along I feel my fair neighbors knocking against me every moment. They do not seem to mind it at all. It is a matter of course ... Evil to him who evil thinks ..."[88] Like Malabari, Mahdi Hasan too misunderstood the proximity of female passengers. He was convinced that he was being solicited by a woman he met on a bus, until he confronted the lady in question and she, according to his own account, expressed horror at the thought of being mistaken for a prostitute.[89] It is ironic that upon his return to India, he became a victim of a scandal centering on allegations against his wife for giving sexual favors to high officials in return for her husband's promotion. Since his wife stoutly denied the allegations and her husband stood by her, we must conclude that Mahdi Hasan Khan remained faithful to his wife and ideals.

Clubs and Places of Entertainment

Turning to the world of entertainment, Mahdi Hasan found time to explore English and European theaters and clubs.[90] He was quite struck by their number and variety: "There are thousands of clubs in London. Every Englishman has got his club, which is generally his address. There he finds his

86. Mahdi Hasan 1890, 76.
87. Burton 1998, 169.
88. Burton 1998, 169.
89. Mahdi Hasan 1890, 83–4.
90. Mahdi Hasan 1890, 61–2, 81.

letters; there he receives and entertains his friends. On many gentlemen's cards on the left side may be found their private address and on their right side their club address. There are clubs in London to suit every taste—political clubs, literary clubs, clubs for men of science, clubs composed entirely of mercantile people, clubs for artists, and so on. People are seldom to be seen in their private houses."[91] Mahdi Hasan himself seems to have been an early enthusiast for clubs in Hyderabad, as he was chosen as the Nizam Club's first secretary in 1884. One of the early symbols of Westernization in the city, the Nizam Club was the first in Hyderabad, preceded only by the British-controlled Secunderabad Club, the first to be established in the Dominions.

Unsurprisingly, Mahdi Hasan made the rounds of London's tourist landmarks such as the Aquarium, the British Museum and the South Kensington Museum (now the Victoria and Albert Museum).[92] He noted, "In 1877 there were as many as ninety thousand visitors in some months, and never less than thirty thousand. This shows the love of art in the English people. We have museums in India, but ninety-nine percent of my countrymen never go to see them. Years of ignorance have expelled the spirit of inquiry and exploration."[93] At the British Museum, it is noteworthy that he paid particular attention to the "mass of scientific treasures accumulated here by the English people."[94] In other words he was paying attention more to the science and technology rather than the antiquities of the ancient civilizations assembled in the museum, which shows his progressive bent of mind. Finally, Mahdi Hasan, in an observation at once astute to his time but also somewhat unfairly stereotypical of Indians, noted, "All natural passions and emotions are common to us and Englishmen, but in them even these are more systematic, civilized and genuine. We no doubt love each other, but we do not express it in their warm and impressive way."[95]

Conclusion

The diary of Mahdi Hasan reveals him as a keen observer of Indian and foreign societies, a man with progressive views on material advancement, education, and women's rights. At the same time, he is clearly an Anglophile in the tradition of Sayyid Ahmad Khan's North Indian Aligarh movement's political orientation, reinforced by high office in the Nizam's Hyderabad, the southern stronghold of loyalty to the British Empire. His visits to the-

91. Mahdi Hasan 1890, 65, 78, 92.
92. Mahdi Hasan 1890, 86.
93. Mahdi Hasan 1890, 88.
94. Mahdi Hasan 1890, 129.
95. Mahdi Hasan 1890, 56.

aters, clubs and sports clearly identify him as a man about town. The detail with which he observed the English society of his time makes him an outstanding observer of Victorian England. In writing this detailed account of his trip, Mahdi Hasan reveals much about himself and by extension about the thinking and orientation of the Muslim elite of Hyderabad and Lucknow of his time, just as he does about the English men, women, and institutions with which he came in contact.

Works Cited

Abbasi, Mahmud Ahmad (1956), "Maulvī Da'ūd 'Abbāsī Amrohāvi," *Nuqūsh*, Lahore, Shakhsīyat number, 2.

Abdul Qadir, A. F. M. (1930), "Early Muslim Visitors of Europe from India," *Proceedings of the All India Oriental Conference*, 6: 83–96.

Aqil, Moinuddin (1995), "Italy and Hyderabad," *Area and Culture Studies* 51: 261–9.

Akbar 'Alī Baig, Mirzā (1987), *Muhammad 'Azīz Mirzā: Hayāt aur kārnāma*, Hyderabad: Idara-yi Shi'r va Hikmat.

Alam, Muzaffar and Sanjay Subrahmanyam (2003–4), "Beijing to the Bosphorus: Notes on the Travel Account," *India International Center Quarterly* 30, 3 and 4: 89–107.

'Alavī Kakorvī, Hāfiz Muhammad 'Alī Haidar (1999), *Mashāhīr-i Kakorī*, Patna: Khuda Bakhsh Oriental Public Library.

Ansari, Humayun (2004), *The Infidel Within: History of Muslims in Britain Since 1800*, London: Hurst.

Ansari, S. M. Razaullah (1998), "Modern Science in Indo-Persian Writings," in: Mohammad Aslam Khan, Ravinder Gargesh, and Chander Shekhar (ed.), *Indo-Persian Cultural Perspectives: Prof. Bhagwat Saroop Memorial Volume*, Delhi: Saud Ahmad Dehlavi, 143–67.

Ballhatchet, Kenneth (1985–6), "Indian Perceptions of the West," in: Bernard Lewis, Edmund Leites, and Margaret Case (ed.), *As Others See Us: Mutual Perceptions, East and West, Comparative Civilizations Review* 13/14: 158–79.

Beck, Theodore (1991), *Theodore Beck Papers from the Sir Syed Academy Archives*, ed. K. A. Nizami, Aligarh: Sir Syed Academy.

Bilgrami, Sayyid Husayn (1910), *Muraqqa'-i 'Ibrat*, Hyderabad: Kanz al-Ulum.

Blunt, Wilfrid Scawen (1909), *India under Ripon: A Private Diary*, London: Unwin.

Burton, Antoinette (1998), *At the Heart of the Empire: Indians and the Colonial Encounter in Late-Victorian Britain*, Berkeley: University of California Press.

Das, Harihar (1924), "Early Indian Visitors to England," *Calcutta Review* 3rd series, 13: 83–114.

Digby, Simon (1989), "An Eighteenth Century Narrative of a Journey from Bengal to England: Munshi Ismail's "New History," in: Christopher Shackle (ed.), *Muslim South Asia: Studies in Honor of Ralph Russell*, London: School of Oriental and African Studies, 49–65.

Fārūqī, Muhammad Abrār Husain (1973), *Majmū'a-yi adab va tavārīkh: ya'nī, mīrāt-i Ahmadī sharh-i masnavī Tavārīkh-i Aḥmadī*, Gopamau, Hardoi: Kutubkhāna-yi Farūqī.

Fisher, Michael (1996), *The First Indian Author of English*, New Delhi: Oxford University Press.

—— (2000), "Representing 'His' Women: Mirza Abu Talib Khan's 1801 'Vindication of the Liberties of Asiatic Women," *The Indian Economic and Social History Review* 37/2: 215–7.

—— (2004), *Counterflows to Colonialism: Indian Travelers and Visitors in Britain*, New Delhi: Permanent Black.

Hasan, Mohibbul (1970), "An Indian Prince and the French Revolution," *Iran Society Silver Jubilee Souvenir, 1944-69*, Calcutta: Iran Society.

Hobhouse, Mary (1890a), "London Sketches by an Indian Pen," *Indian Magazine and Review* (February): 61–73.

—— (1890b), "Further Sketches by an Indian Pen," (March): 139–58.

Husain, Mirza Bakir (1892), *A Shocking Social Scandal: An Appeal to the Ladies of Hyderabad*, Aminabad, Lucknow: Mirza Bakir Husain.

Kabir, Humayun (1961), *Mirza Abu Talib Khan*, Patna: The Russell Lecture, Patna College.

Khalidi, Omar (1985), *Haydarabad State under the Nizams, 1724–1948: A Bibliography of Monographic and Periodical Literature*, Wichita, Kansas: Hyderabad Historical Society.

—— (1991), *Memoirs of Cyril Jones: People, Society and Railways in Hyderabad*, New Delhi: Manohar.

—— (1993), *Madah va Qadah-i Deccan*, ed. Omar Khalidi and Muin al-Din Aqil, Hyderabad: Majlis-i Tarikh-i Deccan.

Khan, Gulfishan (1998), *Indian Muslim Perceptions of the West during the Eighteenth Century*, Karachi: Oxford University Press.

Llewellyn-Jones, Rosie (1990), "Indian Travelers in Nineteenth Century England," *Indo-British Review* 18/1: 137–141.

—— (2000), *Engaging Scoundrels: True Tales of Lucknow*, New Delhi: Oxford University Press.

Lutfullah (2007), *Seamless Boundaries: Lutfullah's Narrative beyond East and West*, ed. Mushirul Hasan, New Delhi: Oxford University Press.

Mahdi Hasan, Nawaz Jang (1987), *Ishārīya-yi Mandarajāt-i Tahzīb al-Akhlāq*, ed. Muhamad Ziyauddin Ansari, Aligarh: Mawlana Azad Library, Aligarh Muslim University.
—— (1889), *Gulgasht-i Firang*, tr. Aziz Mirza, Agra: Mufid-i Aam.
—— (1890), *Extracts from the Diary of the Nawab Mehdi Hasan Khan Fattah Nawaz Jung*, London: Talbot Bros.
—— (1967), *Selected Documents from the Aligarh Archives in Maulana Azad Library*, ed. Yusuf Husain, Bombay: Asia Publishing House.
—— (2006), *An Indian Passage to Europe: The Travels of Fath Nawaz Jang*, ed. Omar Khalidi, Karachi : Oxford University Press.
Mahvī, Mas'ūd 'Alī (1946), *Makhdūmzādgan-i Fathpur*, Hyderabad.
Mudiraj, K. Krishnaswamy (1934), *Pictorial Hyderabad* II, Hyderabad: Chandrakant Press.
Masih Uddin Khan, Mohammad (1969), *British Aggression in Avadh*, ed. Safi Ahmed, Meerut: Meenakshi Prakashan.
Nadwi, Muhammad Ikramullah Khan (1925), *Viqār-i hayāt*, Aligarh: Muslim University Press.
Oldenburg, Veena Talwar (2001), *The Making of Colonial Lucknow, 1856–1877*, in: *The Lucknow Omnibus*, New Delhi: Oxford University Press.
Prasad, Babu Ishwari (1893), *The Hyderabad Sensational Case: Complete & Detailed Proceedings of the Pamphlet Case*, Lucknow: P. Varma Bros.
Rao, Manik Rao Vithhal (1909), *Būstān-i Āsafiya*, I, Hyderabad: Anvarul Islam.
Rayachaudhuri, Tapan (2002), *Europe Reconsidered: Perceptions of the West in Nineteenth-Century Bengal*, 2nd ed., New Delhi: Oxford University Press.
Sayyid Ahmad Khan (1961), *Musāfirān-i London*, ed. Shaykh Muhammad Ismail Panipati, Lahore: Majlis-i Taraqqi-yi Adab.
Salar Jang II, Mīr Lā'iq 'Alī Khān, (2008), *Vaqāyi'-i musāfirat-i Navvāb-i mustatāb-i ashraf-i arfa'-i vālā Mīr Lāyiq 'Alī Khān*, ed. Omar Khalidi and Sunil Sharma, Tehran: Nashr-i Kitāb.
Sarvar al-Mulk (1932), *Kārnāma-yi sarvarī*, Aligarh: Muslim University Press.
Server el-Mulk (1932), *My Life*, London: Arthur Stockwell.
Sethia, Tara (1986), *The Railways and Mining Enterprises in Hyderabad under the British Raj*, Ph.D. dissertation, University of California, Los Angeles.
Storey, C.A. (1927), *Persian Literature: A Bio-bibliographical Survey*, London: Luzac, I/1, 1138–62.
Tavakoli-Targhi, M (2001), *Refashioning Iran: Orientalism, Occidentalism and Historiography*, New York: Palgrave.
Tej Rai (1903), *Sahīfa-yi Āsmān Jāhī*, Hyderabad: Matba' Sāhib-i Dakkin.
Umri, Muhammad Yousuf Kokan (1974), *Arabic and Persian in Carnatic, 1710–1960*, Madras: Muhammad Yousuf Kokan.

Visram, Rozina (1986), *Ayahs, Lascars, and Princes: Indians in Britain, 1700–1947*, London: Pluto Press.

Yūsuf Khān Kambalposh (1983), *'Ajāyibāt-i Firang*, ed. Tahsin Firaqi, Lahore: Makkah Books.

——, (2004), *Tārīkh-i Yūsufī*, ed. Ikram Chaghatai, Lahore: Sang-i Mil.

Around the World in Twenty-Nine Days

The Travels, Translations, and Temptations of an Afghan Dragoman

Thomas Wide

Introduction

While Afghanistan has long resided in the western imagination as a barren and isolated space, a land of "rocks, sand, deserts, ice and snow,"[1] recent scholarly attention has started to deconstruct this view of the country, focusing on "mobility" and "transnationalism" as lenses for understanding Afghanistan in its regional and trans-regional context.[2] Sources in Urdu and Pashto have provided useful means for grappling with the contours and limits of Afghanistan's inter-connectivity, focusing on the role of exiles, foreign travelers, and cross-border travels in the creation of nation.[3] This chapter aims to add to this burgeoning study of Afghan travel and transnationalism by focusing on a Persian travel-account, written by the Afghan intellectual and statesman Mahmud Tarzi and published in 1915, of a trip he made through the Ottoman Empire as a young man accompanying his father on the hajj in 1891.[4] As Roberta Micallef and Sunil Sharma note in their introduction to this volume, modern travel accounts of Muslims to other parts of the Islamic world have been little studied, and this Afghan travelogue is no exception.[5] In keeping with the tenor of this volume, the chapter is interested less in travel-writing as complicit with, or an extension of, various imperial projects; rather, it focuses on the way Muslim intellectuals, in this case an Afghan exile in the Ottoman Empire, made sense, and opportunity, of a world in rapid transformation and the role of

1. Marquis Wellesley's letter to Lord Ellenborough 4th July 1842, quoted in Low 1883, 382.

2. See, for example, the work of Monsutti 2004, Nichols 2008, Green 2011.

3. Caron 2009, Green 2011.

4. Tarzi 1915. Thanks to Wasim Amiri, of Joy Sher, Kabul, for finding me a copy of this rare work.

5. See the introduction to this volume, 5. With the exception of two pages of an appendix in Schinasi 1975, and a recent article on Mahmud Tarzi by Arbabzadeh 2012, this extremely important work has received no scholarly attention.

travel writing in this process. Part of that "making sense" was a reliance on older cultural patterns and connections; in line with the broader aims of this volume, the chapter hopes to suggest ways in which this Afghan traveler drew on traditional Persianate literary and cultural motifs at the same time as he incorporated and adapted influences from Turkish, Arabic, Urdu and European traditions. As the chapter suggests, Tarzi was, like the travelogue he produced, a thoroughly hybrid entity as aware of a Persianate and Islamic heritage as he was of the transformations of a new age (*'aṣr-i jadīd*) that he felt both a product of and witness to. If the chapter aims to focus on the human impact of such transformations through a specific reading of a single text and traveler, its secondary aim is to illustrate larger global transformations taking place in the world during the late nineteenth century and early twentieth century, transformations both physical and conceptual, which were brought about by the development of globalized industrial communications. While this type of combination of material and conceptual history has been written for the Atlantic, European and broadly "Muslim" contexts, this chapter attempts to situate Afghanistan in that larger story.[6] It thus marks an attempt to write peripheral regions such as Afghanistan back into global history. The text bears witness not only to one Afghan's journey, but also to larger movements and communities of Afghan travelers scattered across the Ottoman Empire. In tracing the encounters between Tarzi and such groups, this chapter suggests how such meetings provoked reflections on larger issues of identity and homeland (*waṭan*). Tarzi's work thus not only documents the global movement of peoples through new industrialized spaces, but also the conceptual impact of such travels: how transformations in travel brought about new conceptions of the world, particularly changed notions of time and space, which had concomitant effects on conceptions of history and geography. Fortunately for the scholar today, these new conceptions were enshrined by various steam-powered travelers in "the quintessential Muslim document of the industrial era,"[7] the printed travelogue. It is to one such steam-powered traveler, Mahmud Tarzi, and his steam-powered travelogue, that we now turn.

Mahmud Khan, Meet Mahmud Bey: An Afghan-Ottoman in Exile

While it has become customary to analyze travelogues of the late nineteenth and early twentieth century through the post-colonial lens of "alteritism,"

6. See Green, forthcoming.
7. Green, forthcoming, 5.

that is, the study of the encounter between "Self" and "Other," a study of individuals such as Mahmud Tarzi suggest that "hybridity" is a more useful concept and lens for understanding the emergence of a new type of transcultural traveler and travelogue during the period.[8] Like many Muslim intellectuals of the period, Tarzi was a political exile, briefly in Karachi and then for over two decades in the Ottoman Empire. Tarzi's family was one of a large number of high-status Afghan families exiled by the Afghan Amir, Abdur Rahman (r. 1880–1901) during his consolidation of power during the late nineteenth century, and which were scattered across British India, Iran, Central Asia and the Ottoman Empire.[9] Following an amnesty granted by Abdur Rahman's son, the modernizing monarch Habibullah Khan (r. 1901–19), many of these Afghan exiles returned to play central roles in the development of the ideologies and institutions of Afghan nationalism in the twentieth century.[10] None were more successful in this respect than Tarzi, a charming and erudite conversationalist who quickly gained the confidence of the young Amir, and who forged strong familial links to the royal family through the marriage of one of his daughters to the future Amir, Amanullah Khan, and another to Amanullah's brother, 'Inayatullah. Tarzi would go on to edit Afghanistan's first newspaper, *Sirāj al-Akhbār*, and later become Afghanistan's first Foreign Minister after Afghanistan's independence in 1919.

Despite his later proudly expressed Afghan identity, Tarzi spent twenty-five years of his life in a world removed from his Afghan and Indo-Persian heritage, where he took on the clothing and cultural mores of a young Ottoman *efendi*. Fluent in Turkish, well versed in Arabic, able in French, Tarzi thus belied little trace of his Afghan heritage. Little trace that is, except for his father, Ghulam Muhammad Tarzi (1830–1900), an exiled nephew of the former Afghan ruler Dost Muhammad Khan (r. 1826–63), who was a constant figure in the young Tarzi's life and with whom Tarzi conversed in Persian and Pashto. The difference in the acculturation between the two men is clear from their photographs, printed at the start of Tarzi's travelogue. On the left hand side of the page, Mahmud appears as something of an Ottoman dandy, in suit, bowtie, fez, and neatly turned moustache. On the right hand side, Ghulam Muhammad is dressed in the traditional clothes of an Afghan *khan*—long robes, a flowing white beard, large turban, prayer beads in his hand.[11] The two men are just one generation removed and yet appear as if

8. For a recent study which focuses on Tarzi's "hybridity", see Arbabzadeh 2012.

9. For an accounts of Tarzi's early life in his own words, see Tarzi 2011; part of this text has been translated into English, Tarzi 1998; for secondary literature on his life, see Schinasi 1979, Ch. 2.

10. Wide, forthcoming.

11. Tarzi 1915, 14–15.

Portraits of Mahmud and Ghulam Muhammad Tarzi, as depicted in *Siyāḥatnāma-yi sih qiṭʿa-yi rū-yi zamīn dar bīst o no rūz* (1915). (Courtesy Thomas Wide.)

from different worlds. This sartorial differentiation had an immediate impact on how the men were perceived as they travelled; while Mahmud was addressed with the Turkish appellation *Beyefendi* by the people they met, his father was mostly given the Persian honorific *Ḥażrat Ṣāḥib*.[12] With his father not speaking any Turkish and only a smattering of Arabic, Mahmud acted as his father's interpreter and guide on their travels, a kind of personal *dragoman* who claimed a salary of thirty pounds a month for his work.[13] Mahmud Tarzi's clothes, appellation as *Bey* not *Khan*, and his professional role allowed Tarzi to play with his identity as it suited him; at times, he disguised his relation to his father in order to take advantage of the greater freedom and access he could gain by being viewed as an Istanbuli or Damascene. In par-

12. Tarzi 1915, 212.
13. Tarzi 1915, 176.

ticular, it ensured that his actions would not in any way negatively effect his father's reputation while they travelled. Thus during his first dinner at the captain's table on his way from Beirut to Istanbul, Tarzi hid his Afghan roots, describing himself as from "the environs of Istanbul" (*aṭrāf-i Istanbul*), which for an Afghan originally from Kandahar seems a little economical with the truth.[14] At other times Tarzi emphasized his *afghāniyat* (Afghan-ness) as it suited him, such as in his meetings with fellow Afghans abroad discussed later on in this chapter.

Printing Afghan Modernism: The 'Inayat Press

Although Tarzi's travelogue has been little studied in Afghan or western scholarship, it remains an extremely important, even revolutionary, text. Not only is it the first travelogue ever printed in Afghanistan, but it is also one of the most radical Afghan texts of the early twentieth century, in terms of both its formal innovations and its thematic scope.[15] Of particular note are its frank and first person depictions of gender and sexual relations. At the same time, it is valuable for the scholar in providing a window on to the impact of the development of print culture and travel book circulation throughout the Muslim world, even in countries deemed "peripheral" such as Afghanistan.[16] For the story of the text is also the story of the development of Afghan printing—and one printing press in particular, the 'Inayat Press. This press was set up by the Afghan prince 'Inayatullah in 1913, with the support and encouragement of his father-in-law Mahmud Tarzi.[17] The press became a kind of Afghan equivalent to the Hogarth Press, the outlet for the dissemination of literary modernist works in Britain set up by Virginia Woolf and her husband Leonard in 1917.[18] Like the Hogarth Press, the 'Inayat Press was funded with private money, was resolutely anti-commercial, printed a small group of writers from a particular social circle, and printed self-consciously "new" works of translation and fiction.[19] However, unlike the Hogarth Press, the 'Inayat Press was a state-backed project, which viewed the development of new types of literature as key to the uplift (*taraqqī*) of its country. At the heart of this self-conscious literary modernism

14. Tarzi 1915, 73.

15. A fragment of another travel-account by Tarzi of an earlier trip to Istanbul also exists. See Tarzi 1913, 82–104.

16. For an account of Muslim travelers and printing during the period, see Green 2009.

17. For a history of printing in Afghanistan, see Rahin 2007.

18. For a history of this press, see Willis 1992.

19. For a programmatic statement of 'Inayatullah's aims for the press, and its uncommercial nature, see introduction to Tarzi 1913, 3.

in Afghanistan was an interest in "travel," as activity and object of literary discussion,[20] and it is telling that the first books translated and published by the 'Inayat Press were translations by Mahmud Tarzi of four novels of fantastical technological travels by the French author Jules Verne.[21] These translations were not directly from the French, but rather mediated through Ottoman Turkish translations made by the Ottoman publisher and writer Ahmad Ihsan Tokgöz (1868–1942). For Tarzi, the value of Verne's work lay in its practical role in showing its Afghan audience a sight of the "age of progress" (*zamān-i taraqqī*) taking place all around Afghanistan, and in educating its readers in science and geography at the same time as it entertained them. Modern technological travel, and the accounts of such travel in novels and travelogues, was thus to be praised and encouraged as a means for educating and transforming the country.[22] It is in this context that Tarzi published an account of his own globe-trotting adventures.

"I am no Phileas Fogg": Travelling Fictions in Tarzi's Travelogue

Despite Tarzi's evident interest in the work of Jules Verne, he is at pains in his introduction to stress that his work is quite different from that of the French author:

> I'm not writing a novel (*rumān*), but a travel-account (*siyāḥatnāma*). I am no "Phileas Fogg" who travels all around the world in eighty days, nor am I a "Captain Nemo" who time and time again journeys under the seas. This journey (*siyāḥat*) is not one of those extraordinary journeys but rather a plain, simple, and limited (*maḥdūd*) journey.

It is hard to take these words at face value. Even his title "An Account of a Journey on Three Continents in Twenty-Nine Days" seems to be comparing itself (competing with?) Phileas Fogg's free-wheeling global travels in Verne's most famous novel, "Around the World in Eighty Days."[23] His statement that his work is a "travel-account" and not a "novel" is also to be treated with caution. The narrative structure of the work, as well as its tone and content, suggest that the work is a composite one containing an account of his travels (probably relying on his old travel diaries)[24] combined with fic-

20. For a discussion of this concern with "travel" in Afghan modernism, see Green 2012.
21. Verne 1912, 1913, 1914a, 1914b.
22. For Tarzi's thoughts on the value of travel, see Tarzi 1915, 9–10.
23. Jules Verne 1873/1912.
24. That these travel-diaries existed is supported by frequent internal references to Tarzi's writing of a diary. Tarzi claims that the diaries were brought with him to Afghanistan and later copied out with the help of a *mīrzā* (scribe) in Afghanistan, Tarzi 1915, 8.

tional episodes influenced by a wide variety of sources. The fact that the text was not published until twenty-four years after his actual journey strengthens the case for some creative reworking of his travel diaries to create a decidedly hybrid text. Although the journey ostensibly describes Tarzi's accompanying of his father on the hajj, on the narrative level the overarching narrative arc is that of a *bildungsroman* in which the young fallible narrator is transformed by the events he narrates.[25] In Tarzi's text, the primary transformation is from that of irresolute and inexperienced young man to someone surer of his own identity and place in the world. Embedded inside this narrative framework are various melodramatic episodes of adventure and romance, which suggest more the influence of European nineteenth-century popular fiction than experienced event. This chimes with Tarzi's interest in, and promotion of, such French novelists as Xavier de Montepin and Victor Hugo, whom he translated into Persian (from Turkish translations) and published in books and in his newspaper.[26]

Embedded narratives in the text often emerge out of conversations he has with fellow-passengers, allowing for Tarzi the author to narrate romantic tales while maintaining authorial distance. For example, there is the Hungarian actress "Camilia," whom Tarzi meets on board a French steamer on his way to Alexandria. One evening Camilia confides in Tarzi the story of her relationship with a Palestinian man named "Barlan" whom she met while studying in Vienna.[27] Her story is a classic melodramatic tale of thwarted love, whereby the two young lovers are forced apart by family differences: Camilia's mother demands she honour her professional commitments as an actress, while Barlan's father orders his son to return home. Tarzi himself, in a rather unlikely fashion, is given two letters by Camilia, one in a red packet, the other in a yellow packet. Tarzi is tasked to go and find Barlan and to discover if he has remained true to Camilia or has re-married. If Barlan is still loyal to Camilia, Tarzi is to give him the red packet; if he has re-married, Tarzi is to give him the yellow packet. Tarzi then prints the contents of these two letters, as if he had read them himself.[28] The whole episode seems highly improbable, and its outcome is never revealed by Tarzi in the travelogue or even mentioned after Camilia's disembarkation at Alexandria. One can only conclude that the episode is inserted by Tarzi to add excitement and colour to the narrative, as well as showcasing the "new style" (*ṭarz-i jadīd*) of literature he advocated in Afghanistan.

25. For the relation of hajj literature to other new forms of modern literature, see Metcalf 1990, 87.

26. For de Montepin, see for example the first three issues of the newspaper *Sirāj al-Akhbār*; translations of Victor Hugo appear in Tarzi 1913, 60.

27. The story is recounted at Tarzi 1915, 567–579.

28. Tarzi 1915, 576.

Such artistry and artificiality extends to Tarzi's pacing of his narrative. Here, the shift between events is almost always marked with "just at that moment ..." or "just then ..." in order to bind disparate elements of the narrative into a coherent and flowing whole.[29] This neat "novelizing" of his travels also extends to his characterization of the principal actors of the work, and one cannot help but feel the influence of Verne once more. The relation between the young Tarzi and his faithful retainer Abu Muhyi al-Din brings to mind Phileas Fogg and his manservant Passepartout, who have an occasionally tense but nevertheless inter-dependent relationship while on their travels. Like Passepartout, Abu Muhyi al-Din is a model of resourcefulness, getting his hands on ingredients while out at sea by paying off the ship's cook, and producing huge Afghan meals out of nowhere for Tarzi's father when the old man has grown weary of the food *à la franca* provided onboard.[30] Like Passepartout, too, Abu Muhyi al-Din also serves as a source of comic relief, whether reeling from seasickness[31] or, like Passepartout, getting left behind during the journey.[32] As Fussell has argued for English travel-writers of the early twentieth century, it seems Tarzi's experience of travel, certainly as he narrates it, has been shaped by what he has read as much as by what he has seen.[33]

These European inter-texts in Turkish translation all point to the mediating function which Ottoman print culture played in shaping Tarzi's literary worldview. His travelogue explicitly comments on this print culture, with descriptions of Tarzi's visits to his favourite bookshops and bazaars in Istanbul.[34] It was not just European works in Turkish translation that Tarzi found in those bookshops, but also Turkish-language works composed by Ottoman travelers and thinkers. Tarzi's text clearly bears the mark of Turkish-language travelogues of the time, particularly the work of Ahmad Midhat (1844–1912), the energetic Ottoman litterrateur and intellectual who wrote travelogues that blended a personal narrative coloured by novelistic passages, dialogue, and character development with historical and geographical information.[35] Tarzi saw Midhat as something of a role model, writing a long eulogy to Midhat following his death in the Afghan newspaper he edited, *Sirāj al-Akhbār.*[36] The two men shared similar literary and political interests,

29. See, for example, Tarzi 1915, 139.
30. Tarzi 1915, 120.
31. Tarzi (1915), 83.
32. Tarzi 1915, 215.
33. Fussell 1980.
34. Tarzi 1915, 310.
35. Findley 1998, 23.
36. *Sirāj al-Akhbār* Year 2, vol.19, 13–14; also Schinasi 1979, 184.

and both wrote quickly and prolifically on a wide variety of subjects including the educative role that "travel" (*safar, siyāḥat*) could play in promoting "progress" (*taraqqī*).[37] Moreover, Tarzi's eulogy in print makes clear that he had read many of Midhat's works, including the Turkish-language account, *Avrupa'da bir Cevelan*, which Midhat wrote about a trip he made to Europe.[38] Published just two years prior to Tarzi's journey, it is not impossible that Tarzi bought a copy during his stop in Istanbul, and even took it back with him to Afghanistan.

In such multilingual and inter-connected places as the port-cities of the Ottoman Empire, this translation (in its Latin sense of *trans* + *latus* i.e. "carrying across") of objects, ideas, and people, was common, and muddies any idea we may have of a coherent "Persianate cultural space" from which Tarzi's Persianate travelogue emerged; the boundaries were always extremely porous amongst such multilingual intellectuals and travelers as Mahmud Tarzi. This three-fold exchange of objects, ideas, and people between the Ottoman Empire and Afghanistan is neatly illustrated in the use of photographs, drawings, and maps throughout Tarzi's travelogue. This type of illustrated travelogue had become increasingly popular in the Ottoman Empire, as pioneered by the Ottoman translator and printer Ahmad Ihsan Tokgöz, previously mentioned as the translator of Verne into Ottoman Turkish.[39] On the practical side of things, however, it was the physical travels of exiled Ottoman and Indo-Muslim printers that led to lithographic printing in Afghanistan in the early twentieth century, a development that in turn allowed for the printing of images in books. One of these men, Mehmet Fazlı, would write the first illustrated Ottoman travelogue about Afghanistan, which was published by Ahmad Ihsan Tokgöz.[40] It was the work of such transnational journeymen that allowed for Tarzi's travelogue to be printed with images in Afghanistan in 1915. The images themselves had travelled considerable distances, either being copied from various books that Tarzi had imported from Turkey to Kabul or bought by him in the photo shops which dotted the waterfronts of the port-cities through which he had passed.[41] From such transnational artistic and practical collaborations of a small network of multilingual journeymen intellectuals did Afghan printing emerge.

37. For a programmatic statement by Midhat (translated into English) of his views on travel and travel-writing see Herzog and Motika 2000, 141–151.

38. Midhat 1889–90; the book is referenced in *Sirāj al-Akhbār* Year 2, vol.19, 13.

39. For the role of photography in Ottoman travelogues, see Herzog and Motika 2000, 177–8.

40. Mehmet Fazlı 1909; for other Ottoman travelogues which mention Afghanistan, see Wasti 1991.

41. For a description of his buying of such photos in Port Sa'id, see Tarzi 1915, 648.

This translation of genres, narratives, and media (whether text, photographs, drawings, maps) from multiple sites even extended to Tarzi's incorporation of the texts of visiting cards,[42] address cards,[43] telegrams,[44] and love letters,[45] which he attempted to mimic on the pages of his work using special borders and layout. This was a technique that Tarzi was to continue to employ right up to his final published work, his 1933 collection of poetry *Zhūlīda/Pizhmurda*, which contained poetry in the form of travelogues, letters (complete with envelope-shaped borders), and translations of Arabic-language songs that he had heard on the gramophone.[46] Although Tarzi would go on to an important journalistic and political career in Afghanistan in later life, it seems he would never give up his role as cultural dragoman.

Just as the text was a hybrid of various disparate genres and formal elements, its style was also equally composite. Primarily Tarzi oscillated between two modes, a literary mode in which he framed the narrative of his travels and an informational mode in which he described the various places he visited. In informational mode, Tarzi was clearly following once more the Ottoman-Turkish model of Ahmad Midhat, who would pepper his travelogues with facts and figures cribbed from encyclopedias.[47] On this model, after a description of his travels in each city Tarzi's text contains a separate section called "The General and Specific Geographical and Historical Conditions of..." Thus we are told of Damascus: "*Shām* [i.e. Damascus] is a city that is heavily populated, full of water, trees, and fruit. It has a population of 250,000 people ... it is situated at a latitude of 33.20 degrees and a longitude of 33.57 degrees. It is 2,400 feet above sea level."[48] This kind of detail is followed by geographical descriptions of major areas, a description of the current state of each city's administration and development (schools, hospitals, banks, post-offices), and finally a sketch of each city's history. The more practical considerations of travel—the number of steamships, timetables, ticket prices - are also frequently mentioned. Thus while in Beirut, Tarzi tells his readers that one can take a French or Russian steamer to Istanbul, the Russian steamer costing thirty pounds for two first class tickets, and two pounds for an engine-level ticket.[49] While in Istanbul, Tarzi explained how a "check" (*chek*) works to an Afghan audience that had no institutionalized

42. Tarzi 1915, 207.
43. Tarzi 1915, 100.
44. Tarzi 1915, 215.
45. Tarzi 1915, 576.
46. Tarzi 1933.
47. Findley 1998, 20.
48. Tarzi 1915, 16.
49. Tarzi 1915, 58.

banking system to draw on.[50] These informational, "guide-book"-style sections may also reflect the influence of Urdu literature of the late nineteenth/early twentieth century; it is an often-neglected element of Tarzi's cultural background that he was an Urdu speaker who had spent a significant period of his exiled youth in Karachi.[51] With the proximity and scale of Urdu printing just across the border in British India, Tarzi may well have been aware of, and had some affinity with, the type of practical travelogue increasingly common in Urdu literature of the early twentieth century.[52]

When he was out of informational mode and writing in literary mode, however, Tarzi drew frequently not on Turkish or Urdu sources but on earlier pre-colonial Persianate models (often themselves stemming from the Arabic tradition), which stressed the delights and wonders of travel abroad for an audience unlikely ever to make the journey themselves. However, such delights were now set by Tarzi to the context of a modern world in rapid transformation. The text thus contains long purple patches of descriptive prose on the beauty of cities, people, and natural landscapes (*shahrāshūb*),[53] although these now incorporate descriptions of the infrastructure of modern travel, a world of paved roads and tramway tracks.[54] He frequently employs the trope of the "weird and wonderful" (*'ajīb o gharīb*), another central element of the Arabic and Persianate pre-colonial travelogue.[55] Such descriptions have, however, been translated to late nineteenth-century industrial port-cities, where such wonders are now underwritten and powered by modern technologies. In place of descriptions of the strange tribal customs or burial practices of foreign peoples, the *'ajā'ib* to be marveled at are now how fast people can get their hair washed and cut in Beiruti barber shops or the waxwork models which look identical to real people in the waxwork museum in Istanbul;[56] the *gharā'ib* are now *gharā'ib madanīya*[57] ("civilized wonders") and include the current vogue amongst European and American gentlemen for taking mistresses in foreign cities.[58] New forms of enchantment emerge from Tarzi's experiences of such modern technologies and mores: in place of fantastical creatures or bizarre natural landscapes is

50. Tarzi 1915, 252.

51. For Tarzi's command of Urdu, see Katrak 1929, 4; for Afghan literature's connection to Urdu, see Green 2011.

52. See the contributions by Khalidi, Sharma and Majchrowicz in this volume for such Urdu travelogues.

53. See for example his account of the Greek coast, Tarzi 1915, 175–6.

54. Tarzi 1915, 45.

55. See the Introduction to this volume, 7.

56. Tarzi 1915, 51.

57. Tarzi 1915, 334.

58. Tarzi 1915, 95.

an equally fantastical world of electricity and steam-power, as yet almost unheard of in Afghanistan. Repeatedly the lights in steamboats, streets, and restaurants are described as making the night "like day,"[59] and public gardens are lit up by gas and electric lamps so that people imagine they are "in another world."[60] In Istanbul, Tarzi fuses such Persianate travel writing motifs of wonder with Jules Verne-esque futuristic travels: he goes into raptures of delight while on the *Tünel* funicular train which travels hundreds of metres underground between Kadiköy and Beyoğlu—his very own journey to the centre of the earth.[61]

The Places In Between: Tarzi's Port-City Travels

From the generic, formal, and stylistic considerations of the text, this chapter now turns to the content of the text itself. What can it tell us about the nature and extent of interactions between people from different parts of the world, and what larger forces and flows does it draw out? The work ostensibly describes a journey that Tarzi makes in accompanying his father on the hajj from Damascus to Port Sa'id. On the way, the father and son stop off in Istanbul to pay their respects to the Ottoman Sultan, Abdul Hamid II, who had made Ghulam Muhammad Tarzi an official guest (*mihmān-i khāṣṣ*) of the Ottoman state, and to spend some time at one of Sultan's official guest-houses. Such seemingly religious journeys are the common subject of Muslim travelogues;[62] what is so striking about this one, however, is how little interest Tarzi has in the religious dimension of the journey. Rather than a landscape growing increasingly religious as he approaches Mecca, Tarzi finds an ambiguous and disorienting world in which simple distinctions between Islamic and non-Islamic space have collapsed. While Damascus may have existed in his imagination as an essentially Muslim city, in reality Tarzi finds a land of European-style houses jostling side by side with mosques.[63] This collapsing of polarities is then inscribed in the photographs chosen to illustrate the city, where a shot of the roofline of Marjah in Damascus shows the Sultan Selim Mosque alongside a western-style hospital.[64] Moreover, the detailed informational description of Damascus's institutions presents a modern city of big military hospitals, telegraph offices, and girls' schools.[65] The streets

59. Tarzi 1915, 53, 216.
60. Tarzi 1915, 34.
61. Tarzi 1915, 272.
62. For one such study of *ḥajj* literature in the South Asian context, see Metcalf 1990.
63. Tarzi 1915, 21.
64. Tarzi 1915, 28.
65. Tarzi 1915, 32.

of Beyoğlu in Istanbul look like nothing as much as a "Paris boulevard."[66] In such hybrid spaces, the Tarzis combined activities that would have been both alien and familiar to an Afghan audience: in Lebanese Tripoli, they visit a coffee-house (*qahwakhāna*, an institution unknown in Afghanistan at that time) for an afternoon coffee, walk over to the local mosque to pray, and then get on a tram back to the steamship — traditional religious worship powered by foreign caffeine and modern transport.[67] This collapsing of the distinction between sacred and non-sacred space reflects the nature of the port-cities and train-stations that the steam-powered *Ḥajji* was compelled to pass through: Beirut, Athens, Salonika, Istanbul, Port Sa'id, Jaffa. These were standardized routes, on lines that were based on commercial and imperial interests rather than religious precepts. Tarzi notes the shift, stating that no longer was Damascus the "gateway to Mecca" (*darwāza-yi ḥaramayn al-sharafayn)* for the caravans of hajj pilgrims who would pass through; the Hejaz railway had put an end to that.[68] The port-cities themselves are described as very much "places in between," characterized by a polyglot cast of guides, officials, boatmen, hawkers, travel agents. Rather than the great Islamic monuments of the past, the first view of these port harbors was a disorienting blend of brightly lit electric lights, multilingual poly-ethnic boatmen,[69] and the embodiment of the modern bureaucratic state: policemen, passport officials, health officers.[70]

This de-sacralization of the landscape of the hajj is reflected in the fact that accounts of the hajj were frequently known in Persianate texts as *ḥajjnāmas*, while Tarzi's text is quite consciously a *siyāḥatnāma*. The difference is telling: Tarzi is a *sayyāḥ* (tourist) rather than a *ḥajjī*. This self-representation as a secular tourist not a religious pilgrim reflects the rise of a new class of trans-regional Muslim tourist/traveler, making use of the new travel opportunities provided by industrialized travel and communications. The *sayyāḥ* has a certain identity, which seems largely performative, that is, the *sayyāḥ* is marked out by what he/she does and where he/she does it. Indeed, on one level the whole travelogue can be read as a continual performance of the role of the "steamboat *sayyāḥ*", from the foreign "cologne" (*qūlūnyā*) he puts on before going out,[71] to the calling cards Tarzi orders for

66. Tarzi 1915, 320.
67. Tarzi 1915, 76.
68. Tarzi 1915, 23.
69. See for example Tarzi's arrival at Pera, Tarzi 1915, 123.
70. For encounters with the police, see Tarzi 1915, 74, 101–2; for passport officials see Tarzi 1915, 64; for health inspectors see Tarzi 1915, 592.
71. Tarzi 1915, 56.

his father in Beirut to give to guests he meets on board,[72] to the telegraphs he sends back to his family in Damascus,[73] to the pleasantries he exchanges (in a variety of languages) in post-prandial strolls on the top deck.[74] The *sayyāḥ* draws on a reservoir of knowledge which he uses to navigate his way through such novel spaces as the transition from steamboat to port-city, the captain's dining room, the travel agency, relying on his linguistic ability and experiential savvy to make his way without being fleeced, embarrassed, or lost. Throughout the travelogue, Tarzi sets himself up as just such a knowledgeable and experienced *sayyāḥ*, arranging the small boats (*qā'iq*) which take his father and himself to the shore,[75] smoothing their way through customs posts,[76] returning to hotels he remembered as good from previous visits,[77] and then ensuring he gets hold of the rooms with the best views.[78] Ever the forward-thinker, Tarzi even remembers to put a hundred Ottoman lira in the Ottoman Bank in Damascus which he can then draw in Istanbul when his funds run low.[79]

The identity of the *sayyāḥ* was inextricably connected to the space in which he moved, and the travelogue describes in great detail a set of social spaces yet unheard of in Afghanistan. The port-cities abound in modern internationalized entertainment venues such as the theatre, the music hall, the casino. After his father retired to bed, Tarzi often headed out into the night to take advantage of the temptations and delights on offer. These new entertainment spaces provided new social encounters, most striking of all being the opportunity for relations with foreign women. In his accounts of such places, Tarzi's mode of writing is very much that of Mohamad Tavakoli-Targhi's early nineteenth-century "Persian *voy(ag)eurs*," for whom European women were a constant source of fascination.[80] There are page-length descriptions of almost every European woman that Tarzi meets, and such wondrous accounts extend to troupes of European music-hall girls he sees in Beirut and Istanbul, all dressed identically, whom the spectator can invite to join at his table, as long as he is prepared to pay.[81] In this hybrid world, Muslim women, too, provide temptations of their own, and Tarzi re-

72. Tarzi 1915, 207.
73. Tarzi 1915, 215.
74. Tarzi 1915, 86.
75. Tarzi 1915, 74.
76. Tarzi 1915, 63.
77. Tarzi 1915, 52.
78. Tarzi 1915, 53.
79. Tarzi 1915, 249.
80. Tavakoli-Targhi 2001, 54–5; see also Sharma's chapter in this volume, 110.
81. Tarzi 1915, 57.

peatedly describes the attractive and enflaming manner in which Istanbuli women wear their veils (*chādarī*), even reprinting several photos of such women to confirm his point.[82] Moreover, the travelogue contains numerous episodes in which Tarzi not only observes women, but interacts and even has relationships with them. Throughout the work Tarzi presents himself as an inveterate romantic, falling in love with alarming speed and just as quick to profess it.[83] Such temptations and delights produce frenzied dreams in the young man—his flirting with a fellow-traveler, an Istanbuli called "Mary," leads him to intense reveries he can only describe as *ajīb o gharīb*.[84] These relationships were usually unconsummated, and brought to an end by the different destinations of his fellow amatory travelers. The exception is Tarzi's last night in Alexandria, where Tarzi is taken to the house of a former courtesan of the Khedive Ismail of Egypt, a Circassian lady known as *Set Mahpartaw*. Tarzi is quickly seduced by her charm and before he knows it he finds himself in her boudoir, surrounded by paintings of "naked women with fairy faces" (*parī-ṣūrat*).[85] Tarzi spends the night with the lady, and the next morning rises early to catch his boat. Ever the practical *sayyāḥ*, however, he notes that his amorous liaison did not stop him from remembering his ticket for the steamship to Port Sa'id.[86] Such frank descriptions of the sexual mores of the men and women of these port-cities, particularly told from the perspective of a first-person narrator who indulges in them, was a striking innovation in early twentieth-century Afghan literature. It was all the more striking since, as is mentioned in the travelogue, he had recently married, and was thus indulging in adulterous behaviour.[87] It is hard to see how Tarzi could have got away with such scenes if it had not been for the fact that he enjoyed the royal patronage of Prince 'Inayatullah. Indeed, 'Inayatullah in his introduction to the work explicitly mentions his disapproval of the description of such "romantic and poetic events" (*wuqū'āt-i 'āshiqāna-yi shā'irāna*), but nevertheless allows it to pass on the grounds that the harm of such descriptions is outweighed by the benefits that such travelogues had in educating and informing.[88] Under such royal patronage, and on the pretext of its educative value, Tarzi thus managed to introduce subversively a new frankness and realism into Afghan literature.

Through such descriptions of the relations of multilingual men and

82. Tarzi 1915, 307–309.
83. Tarzi 1915, 631.
84. Tarzi 1915, 231.
85. Tarzi 1915, 632.
86. Tarzi 1915, 634.
87. Tarzi 1915, 146, 150.
88. Tarzi 1915, 5.

women whom Tarzi encounters on his travels, the text creates not just "places in between" but people and languages "in between" that move through and animate those places. This extends not just to the port-cities, but to the means of transport that connects those cities, the steamship. It is telling how much of the narrative of Tarzi's travelogue is set on board ship, the very act and means of modern travel thus earning as much interest in Tarzi's eyes as the places he visited. New communal spaces on board such as the captain's dining-room, the smoking room, the deck for strolling and taking in the view, provided new opportunities for socialization just as fluid and binary-collapsing as the casinos, dancehalls, and salons of Istanbul and Port Sa'id. Miles out at sea, men and women from different parts of the world mingled together freely, spending their time reading, smoking, playing the piano (this final pursuit leaving Tarzi dazzled at the lady passengers' virtuosity.)[89]

Aside from fostering a whole new set of social spaces and encounters for the *sayyāḥ*, the steamship also provided new perceptions of time and space. The standardized time of global industrial communications and the necessity of adhering to its dictates to ensure a smooth journey are reflected in Tarzi's precise, relentless detailing of the passage of time and space as he makes his way from Damascus to Port Sa'id. Tarzi is told by an acquaintance in Istanbul that "time is money" (*waqt naqd ast*) in the contemporary age—and Tarzi seems to agree.[90] Like the obsessively time-conscious Phileas Fogg, Tarzi marks each new day with a description of the exact time he got up, as well as a description of his morning washing routine—a suitably hybrid combination of the Islamic ablution *wużū'* with the French *toilette.*[91] The steamships Tarzi travels on enforce these universal temporal and spatial frameworks: the regular mealtimes are announced by a dinner gong standardizing the passengers' eating times; the ships all travel at set speeds on set timetables so that the exact time of arrival and departure can be recorded and predicted. Tarzi's travelogue, however, like other accounts of travelers of the period, illustrates a man still learning to come to terms with such new patterns of measurement, Tarzi sometimes measuring distances and speeds in "kilometers," at other times in "miles." [92] Through such new measurements, Tarzi is able to measure the progress of the ship, which now travels at set speeds "per hour" and is no longer subject to the natural time-

89. Tarzi 1915, 70.
90. Tarzi 1915, 329.
91. See, for example, Tarzi 1915, 150.
92. See, for example, Tabātabā'ī Tabrīzī 2007, analysed in Green, forthcoming a, 7.

frame of seasons and winds.[93] Indeed, the rhythms of the ship are such that they influence Tarzi's narrative, the dinner gong repeatedly acting as Tarzi's alarm clock, or the marking of the end of one episode and the beginning of another.[94] At the same time, however, Tarzi illustrates how older time-frames manage to co-exist with these new orders, particularly through the character of his father. For Ghulam Muhammad Tarzi, the day is still structured around an Islamic timeframe based on the five daily prayers. Ghulam Muhammad also refuses to eat according to the ship's timetable, shunning the ship's international cuisine for a proper Afghan *pilau*, prepared by Abu Muhyi al-Din, at his own leisure.[95]

Alongside new configurations of time and space, the steamship created a whole new set of classification systems, and even class relations. All the rooms on board are numbered, and seating at the captain's table is carried out according to one's room number.[96] Travelers are newly categorized by whether they travel "first class," "second class," or "third class,"[97] and Tarzi even makes a hobby of watching from first class the spectacle of people in "general class" fighting for seats on the lower deck.[98] While first-class travel is marked by the refined pursuits of international *haute cuisine* and piano recitals, those on the lower deck while away the journey in the more traditional past-times of story-telling and *ghazal* singing.[99] These class distinctions crossed national boundaries and could create a sense of community between people as disparate as French countesses, Ottoman telegraph officials, Istanbuli jewelers, French professors, and the odd Afghan *sardār.* At the same time, Muslims from similar parts of the world or even the same country might be separated from each other and their ease of interaction curtailed depending on how much they paid for a ticket: steamships could separate and divide as easily as they could bring together.

Nevertheless, new opportunities emerged for Muslims from different parts of the world to meet and converse; Tarzi finds himself sharing communal space on board ship with Turks working in the Damascus treasury, a Sayyid from Kashgar in northwest China travelling on the hajj, an Arab Muslim family on their way to Tripoli to try and free a family member from

93. Tarzi comments on the steamship's ability to travel in storms; Tarzi 1915, 69.

94. Tarzi 1915, 70.

95. Tarzi 1915, 120.

96. Tarzi 1915, 71.

97. For similar class-consciousness in late nineteenth-century Ottoman travelogues, see Herzog and Motika 2000, 173–4.

98. Tarzi 1915, 162.

99. Tarzi 1915, 173.

prison.[100] During the trip there are times when Tarzi explicitly professes a certain Muslim solidarity in opposition to non-Muslim peoples and practices. Tarzi is critical, for example, of some Italian missionaries he meets on board, whom he represents as bigoted in their attitudes towards Muslims.[101] Again, however, the "encounter" of Muslim and non-Muslim in the text leads to a collapse of oppositions as often as it leads to a strengthening of "Self" and "Other" polarities. Tarzi notes how respectfully the Europeans treat his father while they travel, particularly the European women.[102] At times, these European women even show a concern that the Tarzis are following the precepts of their religion; seeing the Tarzis taking tea on the deck, the women wonder if the two Muslims are drinking brandy, until Tarzi's father sends them over some cups (and a selection of Damascene biscuits) to allay their suspicions.[103] Moreover, the line between Muslim and non-Muslim is portrayed as easily crossed; the Tarzis become good friends with a French monk on board ship who is so well-versed in Islamic thought and sympathetic to Islam that, by the end of the journey, he decides to convert, changing his name from "Charles" to "Muḥammad Dīn."[104] Even when Tarzi discusses non-Muslim characters and customs, he resists easy polarities; Tarzi notes how a Frenchman can't be treated in the same way as an Englishman, since the French are quick to anger and the British much more reserved.[105] Indeed, Tarzi is at his most critical—and "alteritist"—in his description of a fellow-Muslim traveler, a Meccan returning home from Istanbul who labels as "prostitutes" (*zanān-i fāḥisha*) a group of charming Hungarian actresses whom Tarzi had befriended.[106] Tarzi rejects such harsh judgments, and characterizes the Meccan as bigoted and ignorant.[107] In the place of such strict religious judgments, Tarzi rather preaches a language of *insāniyat* ("humanism"), much more in keeping with the characters and spaces of his steamship adventures. Repeatedly Tarzi refers to the value of *insāniyat* to explain praiseworthy actions, be it tending to a man wounded in a bad storm,[108] treating an Arab lady from Jerusalem with kindness,[109] helping Camilia in delivering her letters,[110] or handing out food to the poor below

100. Tarzi 1915, 83; for the Turkish official and Kashgar Sayyid, Tarzi 1915, 83, 90; for the Arab family, Tarzi 1915, 547.
101. Tarzi 1915, 92.
102. Tarzi 1915 84.
103. Tarzi 1915, 86.
104. Tarzi 1915, 544.
105. Tarzi 1915, 86.
106. Tarzi 1915, 536.
107. Tarzi 1915, 539.
108. Tarzi 1915, 533.
109. Tarzi 1915, 88.
110. Tarzi 1915, 574.

deck.[111] This universal value of *insāniyat* collapsed all differences between people, focusing instead on a commonality of shared humanity, a humanity which crossed gender, religion, language — even class of ticket.

From Perception to Conception: A Steam-Powered Transformation

In a recent essay, Nile Green has illustrated how the kind of experiences of modern industrialized travel described above brought about "new conceptual configurations of space and time, geography and history" amongst Muslim travelers.[112] At the heart of these configurations was a "new model of historical time in which the terminology of "progress" (*taraqqī*) took center stage."[113] This new model was "predicated on the comparison of the relative present state of different peoples and places," a comparison "only rendered possible by the ability of Muslims to move between and experientially 'measure' the progress in the different spaces in question."[114] This analysis of the transformative effect that travel had on Muslim travelers' conception of their individual and collective selves seems borne out by Tarzi's text. For underlying Tarzi's travels is an essentially comparative framework, in which the cities he visits are described relatively on the measure of *taraqqī*—a standardized measure which reflects the quantity and quality of such institutions and features as hospitals, schools, post-services, transport links. It is this theme of *taraqqī* and the ushering in of a "new age" (*'aṣr-i jadīd*), which Tarzi was to push home relentlessly in hundreds of articles and publications that he wrote in Afghanistan during the first three decades of the twentieth century.[115] And it is here, in his travels through a world made increasingly comparable through the collapse of distance and time that the development of that ideology of progress, based on a new conception of time, is most clearly visible.

Tarzi's growing awareness of this standardized historical timeframe emerges from various experiences on his travels which are recorded in his travel-account. Of particular note are the encounters he has with French archaeologists and his visits to ancient sites such as the Parthenon.[116] Such experiences lead to an awareness of a timeframe not based on the Islamic *hijrī* calendar but the Christian framework of AD and BC (*mīlādī*) stretch-

111. Tarzi 1915, 517.
112. Green, forthcoming, 2.
113. Green, forthcoming, 15.
114. Green, forthcoming, 15–16.
115. For an account of Tarzi's reformist vision for Afghanistan, see Ahmadi 2008, ch. 2.
116. For French professional and amateur archaeologists, see Tarzi 1915, 113, 561; for his trip to the Parthenon, see Tarzi 1915, 130.

ing back far beyond the birth of the prophet.[117] Tarzi's travel-account gives a glimpse of the impact that such new temporal frameworks were having on other Muslim intellectuals; in Istanbul he meets an Ottoman minister and historian, Cevdet Pasha, who describes the new disciplines of archaeology and geography transforming their understanding of history.[118] This extended temporal framework had a concomitant impact on his understanding of geography, collapsing the distinction between *Dār al-Islām* and *Dār al-Ḥarb* as Tarzi experientially discovered a pre-Islamic or non-Islamic past in seemingly "Islamic" spaces: even the Umayyad mosque, one of the holiest of Islamic sites, is described by Tarzi as formerly a Greek temple.[119] This temporal framework is then reinforced by the perception of a collapsing of distance brought about by the experience of travel in new modes of transport: in Istanbul the experience of navigating the great physical and conceptual divide of Europe and Asia is reduced to a brief boat-ride.[120] Such historical reflection was not confined to visits to ancient sites either; Tarzi also visits museums,[121] libraries,[122] and even waxwork museums (*mujassamakhāna*) where he is able to gaze on the comparanda of the historical past, all housed conveniently under a single roof - historical distance collapsed to a few yards of space.[123]

Such comparative travels lead not only to a reconfiguration of Tarzi's conceptions of time, space, and the idea of "progress," but also to a deconstruction, refashioning, and recreation of Tarzi's "Afghan-ness" (*afghāniyat*), that is, his identity as an Afghan. Tarzi's deracination and movement through hybrid spaces, which have been such a feature of this analysis, paradoxically provided Tarzi the means to see more clearly his *afghāniyat* when he came across it.[124] Considering that Tarzi was to become the ideologue of Afghan nationalism *par excellence* in the early twentieth century, it is illuminating to see how the hybrid spaces of the port cities and steamships provided a laboratory for the deconstructing, refashioning and remaking of Tarzi's own Afghan identity, and even the idea of Afghanistan itself. There were two main ways that this *afghāniyat* was brought into relief. Firstly, the figure of his father, Ghulam Muhammad, is represented by Tarzi as the unchanging guardian of Afghan and Islamic values, allowing Tarzi to experiment and lose

117. For example, Tarzi 1915, 130.
118. Tarzi 1915, 223–4.
119. Tarzi 1915, 26.
120. Tarzi 1915, 191, 196.
121. Tarzi 1915, 277–8.
122. Tarzi 1915, 283.
123. Tarzi 1915, 289–91.
124. For his use of the term, see Tarzi 1915, 146.

himself in a world of ambiguous in-between-ness, while remaining always on hand to reassure and reconfirm his son's essential *afghāniyat*. For example, at dinner one night on board a Russian steamer, one of the captains of the ship suggests that Afghanistan is not a truly independent country. Tarzi is extremely angry by this slur, but at the same time racked with doubt: is Afghanistan really not an independent country? What does that mean for his own Afghan identity if Afghanistan is merely a vassal? Tarzi spends a sleepless night in paroxysms of existential doubt.[125] The next morning, however, Tarzi's father reassures him that Afghanistan is indeed an independent nation, unlike those "nawabs and rajahs of India," and that it is incumbent upon Mahmud to love his homeland (*waṭan*).[126] Although shaken, Tarzi is finally left with a renewed sense of national identity and pride.[127]

The second primary means for Tarzi to reflect on his *afghāniyat* are his encounters with fellow Afghan travelers. In Jaffa, Tarzi comes across a small community of Afghan expatriates while he is looking for an old acquaintance of his father's, an Afghan named "Mulla Jullundur." The episode is illustrative of the kind of simultaneous undermining and bolstering of national identities brought about by encounters between compatriots in expatriate spaces. Tarzi writes:

> I saw an Afghan (*nafar-i afghānī*) in a hut; I approached him and addressed him in the Afghani language (*bi -zabān-i afghānī*, that is, Pashto):
>
> "Brother! Do you know where Mulla Jullundur lives?"
>
> The Afghan, who from his appearance seemed to be an Achakzai or Kakar, and a recent arrival here, looked at my appearance and glasses with surprise, and called to another friend who was inside the room, saying in Afghani:
>
> "Hey! Come and see what this Turk is saying, I don't understand!"
>
> I said: "I'm a Pashtun and I'm speaking to you in Afghani, how do you not understand?"
>
> He said: "Who knew that such four-eyed (*chārchashma*) Pashtuns even existed?"[128]

Here, one gets a glimpse of how Tarzi was perceived by other Afghan trav-

125. Tarzi 1915, 143.
126. Tarzi 1915, 149.
127. For this whole episode, see Tarzi 1915, 141–50.
128. Tarzi 1915, 654. When Tarzi translates this Pashto sentence into Persian, it is notable that he translates the word "Pashtun" as "Afghan" thus merging the two identities together. There is not the space here to discuss this important linguistic and conceptual issue, but for a discussion of slippage between terms during the period, see Wide 2012.

elers of the period, as a man whose clothes and manner are so different that he is not even considered an Afghan, a man who even when he speaks their native language remains unintelligible. At the same time, Tarzi, too, is struck by the differences between himself and his fellow Afghans. At one point he meets a Kabuli traveler who speaks Persian with a thick Kabuli accent. Tarzi is so struck by the man's idiolect that he attempts to imitate it on the page, spelling "Afghanistan" as "Awghānistān", for example, to capture the marked difference in his speech.[129] Such encounters complicate any simple idea Tarzi might have had of the role of language in defining national identity. At the same time, these encounters between far-flung Afghans in such "places in between" stimulate a self-reflection on Afghanistan's existential status and its relative stage of development: Mulla Jullundur speaks of the plight of the 15,000 Afghans he claims are living abroad, as well as discussing the problems these communities face due to Afghanistan's lack of a diplomatic service or any representation abroad;[130] other Afghans debate with Tarzi the need for education in the homeland.[131] Chiming with the experiences of travelers with expatriate communities discussed elsewhere in this volume,[132] the Afghan expatriate communities Tarzi describes provide key encounters and spaces for the negotiation of individual, collective, and national identities.

Conclusion

As this chapter has suggested, Mahmud Tarzi stands as a case study and example of an increasingly common figure during the period — the steam-powered intellectual — whose travels brought about fundamental transformations in their thought. At the same time, the account of his travels stands as testament to wider patterns of interaction and integration between parts of the world that were formerly distinct. For Afghanistan this was an engagement always at one step removed—without a port-city or railway terminus, and before the advent of road-travel in the early twentieth century, Afghanistan would always be "a house without a window" in the words of one Turkish traveler Tarzi meets on his travels.[133] A more traditional journey by foot, horse, camel, or inflated goatskin, would thus always be required to get beyond the country's borders and to reach a trans-regional

129. Tarzi 1915, 656.
130. Tarzi 1915, 654.
131. Tarzi 1915, 657.
132. See the Introduction to this volume and Sharma's chapter.
133. Tarzi 1915, 297.

transport hub in British India, Iran, or Central Asia. Nevertheless, forced exile, economic entrepreneurship, and religious devotion ensured that increasing numbers of Afghans in the late nineteenth century took part in the great transformations of the age. Sharing ideas, experiences, and frequently cabin-space, these individuals are testament to the "opening up" of Afghanistan to the world. The travels and travelogue of the Afghan exile Mahmud Tarzi are thus a product of, and profound reflection on, transformations in the world that were both intensely personal and truly global in scale.

Works Cited

Ahmadi, Wali (2008), *Modern Literature of Afghanistan: Anomalous Visions of History and Form*, New York: Routledge.

Arbabzadeh, Nushin (2012), "Modernizing, Nationalizing, Internationalizing: How Mahmud Tarzi's Hybrid Identity Transformed Afghan Literature," in: Nile Green and Nushin Arbabzadeh (ed.), *Afghanistan Into Ink*, London: Hurst.

Caron, James (2009), *Cultural Histories of Pashtun Nationalism, Public Participation, and Social Inequality in Monarchic Afghanistan, 1905–1960*, Ph.D dissertation, University of Pennsylvania.

Fazlı, Mehmet (1909), *Resimli Afghan siaheti*, Istanbul: Matba'a-yi Ahmad Ihsan.

Findley, Carter Vaughn (1998), "An Ottoman Occidentalist in Europe: Ahmed Midhat Meets Madame Gulnar, 1889," *The American Historical Review*, 103/ 1: 15–49.

Fussell, Paul (1980), *Abroad: British Literary Travelling between the Wars*, Oxford: Oxford University Press.

Green, Nile (2009), "Journeymen, Middlemen: Travel, Trans-Culture and Technology in the Origins of Muslim Printing," *International Journal of Middle East Studies* 41: 203–24.

—— (2011), "The Trans-Border Traffic of Afghan Modernism: Afghanistan and the Indian 'Urdusphere', *Comparative Studies in Society and History* 53/ 3: 479–508.

—— (2012), "The Afghan Afterlife of Phileas Fogg: Space and Time in the Literature of Afghan Travel," in: Nile Green and Nushin Arbabzadeh (ed.), *Afghanistan Into Ink*, London: Hurst.

—— (forthcoming), "Spacetime and the Muslim Journey West, 1860–1930."

Herzog, Christoph and Raoul Motika (2000), "Orientalism "*alla turca*": Late 19th /Early 20th Century Ottoman Voyages into the Muslim Outback," *Die Welt des Islams* 40/2 (July): 139–95.

Katrak, Sohrab (1929), *Through Amanullah's Afghanistan*, Lahore: 'Sind Observer' & Mercantile Steam Press Limited.
Low, Charles (1883), *Major General Frederick S. Roberts*, London: W. H. Allen.
Metcalf, Barbara D. (1990), "The Pilgrimage Remembered: South Asian accounts of the hajj," in: Dale F. Eickelman and James Piscatori (ed.), *Muslim Travellers: Pilgrimage, Migration, and the Religious Imagination*, Berkeley: University of California Press, 85–110.
Midhat, Ahmad (1889–90), *Avrupa-da bir cevelan*, Istanbul: Tercuman-i Hakikat Matbaası.
Monsutti, Alessandro (2004), *Guerres et migrations: réseaux sociaux et stratégies économiques des Hazaras d'Afghanistan*, Neuchâtel: Institut d'ethnologie.
Nichols, Robert (2008), *A History of Pashtun Migration*, Karachi: Oxford University Press.
Rahīn, 'Abdul Rasūl (2007), *Tārīkh-i maṭbū'āt-i Afghānistān*, Stockholm: Shūrā-yi Farhangī-yi Afghānistān.
Schinasi, May (1979), *Afghanistan at the Beginning of the Twentieth Century*, Naples: Istituto Universitario Orientale.
Tabrīzī, Muḥammad Rizā Tabātabā'ī (2007), *Hidāyat al-Hujjāj: Safarnāma-yi Makka*, Qum: Nashr-i Muwarrikh.
Ṭārzī, Maḥmūd (1913), *Az har dahān sukhānī va az har chaman samanī*, Kabul: 'Ināyat Press.
—— (1915), *Siyāḥatnāma-yi sih qiṭ'a-yi rū-yi zamīn dar bīst o no rūz: Āsiyā, Ūrūpā, Afrīqā*, 3 vols., Kabul: 'Ināyat Press.
—— (1933), *Zhūlīda/Pizhmurda*, Istanbul: s.n.
—— (1998), *Reminiscences: A Short History of an Era (1869–1881)*, tr. & ed. Wahid Tarzi, New York: Afghanistan Forum.
—— (2011), *Khātirāt*, ed. Rawān Farhādī, Kabul: Maiwand.
Tavakoli-Targhi, Mohamad (2001), *Refashioning Iran: Orientalism, Occidentalism, and Historiography, New York: Palgrave.*
Verne, Jules (1912), *Seyāḥat bar dawr dawr-i kurrah-yi zamīn bi hashtād rūz* [Le Tour du monde en quatre-vingts jours, 1873], Kabul: 'Ināyat Press.
—— (1913), *Siyāḥat dar jaww-i hawā* [Robur-le-Conquerant, 1886], Kabul: 'Ināyat Press.
—— (1914a), *Jazīra-yi pinhān* [L'Île mystérieuse, 1874], Kabul: 'Ināyat Press.
—— (1914b), *Bīst hazār farsakh-i siyāḥat dar zīr-i baḥr* [Vingt mille lieues sous les mers, 1869], Kabul: 'Ināyat Press.
Wasti, Syed Tanvir (1991), "Two Muslim Travelogues: To and From Istanbul," *Middle Eastern Studies, 27/* 3: 427–56.
Wide, Thomas (forthcoming), "The Travelling State: Afghanistan 1890–1939," D. Phil dissertation, Oxford University.

—— (2012), "Demarcating Pashto," in: Nile Green and Nushin Arbabzadeh (ed.), *Afghanistan Into Ink*, London: Hurst.
Willis, J. H. (1992), *Leonard and Virginia Woolf as Publishers: The Hogarth Press, 1917–1941*, Charlottesville, Virginia: University Press of Virginia.

Delight and Disgust

Gendered Encounters in the Travelogues of the Fyzee Sisters[1]

Sunil Sharma

THE EARLIEST INDIAN MUSLIM TRAVELERS to Europe who authored accounts of their journeys, starting in the second half of the eighteenth century, wrote in Persian and, in keeping with the characteristics of the classical *'ajā'ib* literary genre (catalogue of wonders or curiosities) in Arabic, expressed the emotions of delight and pleasure in encountering new places and people.[2] Their reaction often took the form of exaggerated wonder at new places and people and hyperbolic descriptions of modern and different ways of life. In particular, European women were a constant object of these travelers' gaze, about which Mohamad Tavakoli-Targhi writes, "The early Persian travelers described Europe as "heaven on Earth" (*bihisht-i ru-yi zamin*) ... and the attraction of Europe masqueraded the attraction to "houri-like" (*hurvash*), "fairy-countenanced" (*hur-paykar*), and "fairy-mannered" (*firishtah khuy*) women of Europe. Appearances of unveiled women in public parks, playhouses, operas, dances, and masquerades impressed the Persian *voy(ag)eurs* who were unaccustomed to the public display of female beauty. For them, the only cultural equivalent to the public display of male-female intimacy was the imaginary Muslim heaven."[3] This mode of writing was replaced in the second half of the nineteenth century by a more dry and insipid style devoid of any emotion that, although still focused on the amazing progress and beauty of Europe and, increasingly, also cities in the Ottoman Empire that were regular stops on their journey, seemed to have given up the generic characteristics of the traditional Islamicate or Persianate travelogue.

1. Versions of this paper were presented to the History of Emotions Group at the Max-Planck-Institut für Bildungsforschung, Berlin, May 2010, and at the workshop of the Women's Autobiography in Islamic Societies in New Delhi, December 2010. The comments received from my colleagues have substantially enriched the paper.

2. See Mottahedeh 1997, for a study of this genre and the emotions of astonishment and wonder in Arabic literature. Celebrating the beautiful places and inhabitants of a city was also a feature of medieval and early modern Indo-Persian poetry; see Sharma 2004.

3. Tavakoli-Targhi 2001, 54–5; also see Tavakoli-Targhi 2002.

Casey Blanton writes about the development of the Western works of the genre at this same time, "A narrative that combined inner and outer voyages was not only possible but even predictable. This shift has two consequences for travel writing: the emotions, thoughts, and personal quirks of the narrator become more accessible and more dominant with the narrative and the world itself, its plants, animals, and people, also become a source of knowledge for their own sake."[4] Indo-Persian and Urdu travelogues seemed to follow a somewhat different trajectory than those by Western travelers with respect to the degree in which the author's text is also a narrative about his internal development. In Javed Majeed's view, "[I]n late-eighteenth- and nineteenth-century Indian travelogues, autobiographical detail tends to be incidental to the narrative of travel rather than fused with or elaborated through it, thereby demonstrating the dominance of travel as an empirical narrative over the interiority of the traveller and other possible trajectories of his life before and after his travels."[5] But it would appear that this is not necessarily the case with women's travel writing. In the case of Muslim male writers, this shift away from poetic to documentary can perhaps be explained by the redefinition of the relationship between Indians with their world in the aftermath of the 1857 Mutiny that destroyed Mughal power and established British rule, and also by the emergence of Urdu as the lingua franca in large parts of India as a language with a new register for modern life, largely free from the rhetorical baggage of classical Persian. When we study travel narratives by Muslim women in the post-1857 period, however, it appears that their use of the travelogue literary genre, as well as their engagement with their subject, is still linked to traditional forms of expression, perhaps because they took up travel writing later than their male counterparts and under different social circumstances. In this essay I would like to discuss the travel diaries[6] of two sisters who, on the one hand, wrote in a traditional way, especially in reacting to new places and people, and, at the same time, employed subversive strategies in their comments on masculine values in various cultures to express their emotions within the boundaries of what was deemed proper in narratives by women.

The travel diaries of the two Fyzee sisters from Bombay, Atiya (1877-1967) and Nazli (1874-1969), are remarkable for being the first accounts by Indian Muslim women in Europe, although as in the case of other women's writings of the early twentieth century most of the original Urdu texts are

4. Blanton 2002, 11–2.

5. Majeed 2007, 51–5.

6. The overlapping signification of the terms for the literary genre, *safarnāma* (travelogue) and *roznāmcha* (diary) correspond to the degree of interiority in the texts.

The Fyzee sisters and others on their 1908 European tour, as depicted in *Sair-yi Yurop* (1909?). (Courtesy Sunil Sharma.)

largely unpublished to this day and therefore not included in any larger historical or cultural study of Urdu literature.[7] The Fyzee sisters were part of the extended Tyabji clan of Bombay and like many other members of this family were well educated and progressive. All three sisters, the eldest being Zehra (1866-1940), were actively involved in Muslim women's education and journalism, often contributing essays to Urdu women's journals such as *Khātūn, 'Ismat* and *Tahzīb-un-nisvān*. Written in consecutive years, 1906-07, by Atiya about her stay in London and Germany, and 1908 by Nazli Begum about her travels in London, the European continent and the Ottoman Empire, the autobiographical contents of these two travel diaries provide detailed descriptions about public and domestic life in Europe and the Middle East, their entry into the various networks of Indians, meetings with former colonial administrators, gentry, and even rulers. In addition, the rhapsodic descriptions of textiles, jewellery and flowers, that go on for pages, feminize these accounts and mark them as being different from their male counterparts. When it comes to human beauty and attention to the body, their gaze is mostly reserved for women, the authors being very conscious of writing for an audience of respectable Muslim women, even as their sister, Zehra, edited their prose for publication. Although the narrative of their travelogues

7. See the appendix to this chapter for a list, by no means comprehensive, of known early travelogues by Indian women in various languages.

often masks the upheavals of their emotional lives, the subtext suggests that the world of men and issues of masculinity were very much on their minds, and especially since both were on the brink of permanent changes in their lives with regard to their marital status. How then do we read these two texts through a gendered matrix that reflects the psychological and emotional turmoil of the sisters? Regarding travelogues of the late nineteenth century, and arguably this is applicable to those of the early twentieth century, Javed Majeed states, "While these reflect on the different gender arrangements in British and Indian societies, they rarely question gender categories themselves, or the boundaries of their own gendered identities."[8] Again, we find that the travelogues by the Fyzee sisters share certain characteristics of the earlier body of texts authored by men, but in other aspects, such as those connected with gender and emotion, they are subversive and do implicitly question gender categories.

As one would expect, in her travel diary, *Zamāna-yi tahsīl* (Time for Education),[9] Atiya described her formal classes, teachers, visits to numerous institutions of learning and museums. But more than that, a rather significant source of acquiring knowledge is the company of the right kind of people. On 3 April 1907 she wrote about a small social gathering, "A person can learn so much by talking to scholars. It is an excellent and beneficial lesson to listen to the conversation of those people whose minds are filled with a variety of information. We cannot acquire such important information just from books; it is necessary to have scholarly company to make this possible."[10] Atiya was also at pains to maintain a distinct identity for herself when it came to sartorial matters, something that was true throughout all her life. On 10 November 1906 she wrote, "I have been meaning to write for a while that I have continued wearing my Indian clothes and do not intend to ever give them up. When I go out I cover my head, et cetera, with a gauze cloth. Everything is covered except the face. And our Fyzee charshaf on our body, gloved hands, umbrella, good walking shoes on the feet—altogether it seems to be a complete simple outfit. And everyone appreciates the fact greatly that I have kept my ways in the English world and am setting a good example."[11] Significantly, this elaborate act of covering up functioned at multiple levels in order to present an edited version of herself to the world.

Despite the modification of her dress, various facets of Atiya's identity as

8. Majeed 2007, 228.

9. This work first appeared serially in the weekly journal, *Tahzīb-un-nisvān* (Women's Culture) with a time lag of about three months. It was published as a monograph in 1922. For an English translation of the work, see Fyzee 2010a; the Urdu original was recently published, Fyzee 2010b.

10. Fyzee 2010a, 185.

11. Fyzee 2010a, 151.

an Indian, and specifically as an Indian Muslim woman, were questioned and transformed in the course of her daily life, especially due to her interactions with other Indians of all backgrounds, who represented a wide spectrum of social and communal groups, from students to the elite, from those either living or passing through London. On the other hand, the Indian Muslims she met were either members of her extended family or those connected with the world of learning, from whom she learned about the Indo-Muslim past and the classical Persian heritage. Among prominent Indian Muslim men on the London scene at this time whom Atiya came into contact with were her cousins, the justice of peace Camruddin and Alma Latif (later in the Punjab civil service), Mukhtar Ahmed Ansari (later involved with the Indian National Congress and All-India Muslim League), Syed Ali Bilgrami (lecturer at Cambridge), and, of course, Muhammad Iqbal (1877-1938), Persian-Urdu poet and rising star of the nascent Indo-Muslim nationalist movement. To her surprise, at a lecture at the Imperial Institute in London in December 1906, the scholar and translator of the Qur'an Yusuf Ali included her among capable women in the history of Muslim civilization, in the company of renowned figures from Indian history such as Sultana Razia, Gulbadan Begum, Zebunnisa, Nur Jahan, and Begum Shah Jahan of Bhopal![12] Thus, Atiya was conscious of being held up as a model for her compatriots, especially Muslim women. In her narrative, men are always hovering somewhere in the background, and the ones she met are described briefly as capable and worthy, distinguished by their service to the empire or accomplished in one or another field of learning or the arts.

Atiya met Iqbal in April 1907 at the end of her stay in London when he was a student at Cambridge, and then again in August in Heidelberg when she was on her way back to India. It has been argued that her encounter with Iqbal brought on a serious case of lovesickness in the thirty-year-old unmarried Atiya, leading her to withdraw from the teacher training program in which she was enrolled and return to India to a more secure world where she was in control of her emotional life.[13] Reading her travel diary, the passing references to a few meetings with Iqbal veil the subject of her sexual awakening and the extent of their attachment is only revealed in an English book she wrote forty years later, albeit with a selective memory at work and other historical circumstances dictating her version of the story. In her earlier narrative, Atiya made no bones about the fact that the singular purpose of her trip was to be educated so that she could share the benefits of

12. Fyzee 2010a, 162

13. Further details on Atiya's life and her relationships with men are discussed in Lambert-Hurley and Sharma 2010, 49–62.

her education with her sisters back home, but all kinds of experiences while she was acquiring that education could be of use to her *Tahzībī* sisters.

In her letters to her *Tahzībī* sisters Atiya rather disingenuously mentions meeting Muhammad Iqbal twice, once casually in London at a party on 22 April 1907, when she observes that he "is a very learned scholar and also a philosopher and poet," and again in Germany after her departure from England. At this time Iqbal was already a minor celebrity, as Atiya was in different circles, both back in India and abroad. Atiya's later memoir on Iqbal reveals that there was a lot more to their first encounter:

> For the first of April, 1907, Miss Beck sent me a "special invitation"—to use her own expression—to meet a very clever man by the name of Mohammed Iqbal, who was specially coming from Cambridge to meet me. This caused me a little amusement as I had never heard of Iqbal before, and as I was used to getting such invitations from various Indians in London, it did not rouse more than passing curiosity. Miss Beck who looked after the welfare of Indian students in London and bestowed upon them a great deal of motherly care, had to be obeyed. At the dinner table I found Iqbal a scholar of Persian, Arabic and Sanscrit, a ready wit and ever alert in taking advantage of one's weak point, and hurling cynical remarks at his audience. Miss Beck had impressed on me the fact before he arrived that he had particularly wanted to see me and being straightforward and outspoken, I asked him the reason why. His deep-set eyes did not reveal if he meant to be sarcastic or complimentary when he said, "You have become very famous in India and London through your travel diary, and for this reason I was anxious to meet you."[14]

Although she never admits it, Atiya must have succumbed to Iqbal's legendary charm, as did other women in Europe.

From Atiya's later English narrative we also learn that there were several subsequent meetings in June and July 1907. Atiya describes their meetings as an "intellectual treat" or full of "intellectual fireworks" where they would read and discuss books on philosophy together; he told her that "by reading and discussing in this manner my ideas expand and convictions become firm"[15] and elsewhere, "By discussing with others, a new world opens, and it is with this method that I acquired all that I know."[16] That summer Iqbal left for Germany to complete his studies there and, in a seemingly unrelated move, Atiya soon decided to cut short her stay in London and withdraw from her college programme. But the reader of her Urdu travelogue would not

14. Fyzee 2010a, 273–4.
15. Fyzee 2010a, 275.
16. Fyzee 2010a, 277.

have been prepared for the abrupt interruption in the narrative caused by Atiya's decision to quit her studies. On 5 August 1907 her revelation comes out of the blue for her readers:

> *Inshallah* I will depart from London on the twentieth and, after stopping in a couple of places, I will board the ship *Arabia* in Marseilles and reach Bombay on the 27th or 28th. I am sorry that I am leaving without fulfilling my responsibility but I was constrained by my health. The doctors have said explicitly that if I stay longer I will waste away, for at times I have a fever of 104–5 degrees and I have become extremely weak and afflicted with headaches. I tried to complete the two years in some way, but it was impossible and finally I informed the India Office of the situation. They heard my resignation with extreme sorrow and made preparations for the return trip. Certainly after becoming free from college, there has been some difference in my health, but even then there is no assurance. I am grateful to the government that they did not seek payment for anything, but rather expressed great sympathy. Anyway I hope that I will be able to help my sisters with whatever I have learned, such is my heart's desire.
>
> I did not want to mention my health problems before in this travelogue because I knew that my kind sisters who had expressed their good wishes and joy before I left Bombay would be disappointed. I had thought that everything would be fine again and I would return successful. We think one thing and fate plans another. At last, the time has come to say farewell to London.[17]

Not surprisingly Atiya booked a passage for India with a stopover in Germany. In Heidelberg she spent a couple of joyful weeks at the student pension where Iqbal was staying, getting to know him better, watching him being humbled by his teachers, but also revelling in his genius. She observes more than once that Iqbal "looked as if he was just waking up from a dream" and was unlike the way he was in England. They went on various outings, picnics, boating, singing and dancing, and as a result her health improved tremendously. This last part of her travels is also briefly noted in her Urdu narrative.

In the end, although we must read Atiya's 1906–7 Urdu travelogue alongside her 1947 English account of her meetings with Iqbal, it is clear that there is no public/private dichotomy in them; both works are a deliberate construction of events meant to be interpreted by different audiences at different points of time. For the *Tahzībī* sisters Atiya was the unfortunate student whose studies had been interrupted by her ill health; she could never be a woman who had fallen in love with a young married man in Europe.

17. Fyzee 2010a, 209.

Atiya pursued Iqbal in India as well but, in the end, he refused to be drawn into her cosmopolitan world in Bombay.

A year after Atiya returned to India, her sister Nazli Begum, the wife of His Highness Sidi Sir Ahmad Khan, Nawab of Janjira, a small but prominent princely state in western India, embarked on a grand tour of Europe and the Middle East with an entourage that included her husband, Atiya, their brother Ali Azhar, and a couple of courtiers and servants. Forced into an arranged marriage at the age of twelve, the thirty-four-year old Nazli was more restrained than Atiya and her writing reveals a temperament that is tinged with sadness.[18] Even as this group made the grand tour of the major cities of Europe and the Ottoman Empire, Nazli's marriage was starting to disintegrate, mainly due to their being childless. Nazli's travel diary, *Sair-i Yurop* (European Tour),[19] like her sister's work, was largely silent about such personal matters, dwelling on every other subject that one expected to find in a travelogue of the period: descriptions of historical buildings, endless visits to museums, meetings with royalty, comments on the technological advancement and cleanliness of the West, the exhilaration of being in the Ottoman Empire—the "centre" of the Islamic world at that time, along with accounts of women's clothes and jewellery. Being part of a large official entourage, Nazli was less adventurous than Atiya in her interactions with people, and rarely ventured out of drawing rooms, hotels, and museums.

The most arresting account in Nazli Begum's travelogue is during a visit to the opera in Paris on 25 July 1908 to see Richard Wagner's opera *Lohengrin.* The choice of operas is ironic in the light of her strained relationship with her husband, for it is a tragic story from Wolfram von Eschenbach's Parzvial cycle in which the young bride Elsa is abandoned by her knight-saviour.[20] Describing this strange spectacle to her readers, she wrote, "If one watches operas then the whole story is clear. I am afraid that I understood very little. ... Even in a state of ignorance I enjoyed it and hope that after seeing it more I will understand its real virtue. This can be achieved by listening to it a lot."[21] But her interest, as is usually the case, is centred on the people around her:

> A wealthy man's wife was seated near us. Her dress was extremely tasteful and praiseworthy. There was a man sitting with her who was young and aristocratic. I want to describe this man's sense of fashion, perhaps you

18. For a biographical sketch of Nazli Begum, see Lambert-Hurley and Sharma 2010, 25–7.

19. This work was also written in the form of diary/letters and published privately in ca. 1909. Nazli Begum suggests that this account also appeared in a women's journal but I have not traced this version yet. My English translation of this text is unpublished.

20. See the essay by Omar Khalidi in this volume for a male traveler's description of the same opera.

21. Nazli Begum 1909, 182.

> will enjoy it. He was wearing a silken waistcoat with gems for buttons, large diamond rings on both pinkies, kohl in the eyes, high-heeled patent leather women's courtly shoes with tassels, black tight stockings of fine gauze, and with shoulder-length hair. It was exactly like the get-up of Chhammi Jan of *Fasāna-yi Āzād*.[22] I was turned off by the feminine mannerism and my dislike (*nafrat*) was so intense that I felt nauseous. At once I put some betelnut, cardamom and cloves in my mouth and then felt a bit better. May God give men manly thoughts and also make their deportment manly, otherwise one feels revulsion and hatred. And the icing on the cake was that he was bathed in perfume whose scent was such that one wanted to severely upbraid him. His almond-coloured handkerchief had clearly been soaked in perfume. On top of all the make-up was his American accent that made him even more repulsive. It was clear that he was very wealthy and it was perhaps his first trip to Paris. Walking someone else's walk he has forgotten his own.[23]

Nazli Begum's focus on a person's physical body and outward finery was not unusual, but this was the first instance in her work of a man being the object of such close scrutiny. Faced with the flamboyant decadence, strong scent, and blurring of sartorial gender markers, Nazli Begum was thrown into a state of confusion and disgust that induces nausea, as if in simulation of morning sickness. Why was her reaction so extremely hostile? After all, she would have been familiar with eunuchs (*hijrās*) in India, and being from a cosmopolitan family she would have come across all sorts of people in her life. The effeminate American dandy symbolized the worst example of Western excess for Nazli Begum, and perhaps of the erosion of masculine values. If Western men behaved in this way, there was no hope for Indians.[24]

For Nazli Begum, as she somewhat wistfully muses, Parisian society is a paradise full of enchanting creatures. The dainty sartorial standards, however, are also seen as a cause of the feminizing of the male, as she observes a month previously on 26 June 1908:

> [The French] are people of peculiar temperaments. There are so many beautiful faces. Three out of five women are truly comely. Doubtless they

22. An Urdu picaresque novel published in 1880 by Ratan Nāth Sarshār that depicted sketches of the *demimonde* of Lucknow.

23. Nazli Begum 1909, 182–3.

24. The figure of the dandy and the historical and literary phenomenon of dandyism, especially in the context of the Americans and French, are studied in Feldman, 1–24. Feldman's comment that the dandy "is the figure who casts into doubt, even while he underscores, the very binary oppositions by which his culture lives" (4) is pertinent in the context of Nazli's reaction. The author explains that even as they are fascinated by women, dandies also felt fear and hatred towards them. Here, of course, the loathing is reversed.

> are full of artifice without which they cannot live. But such artifice that it makes a human so beautiful! Isn't this a skill too? The clothes of the less fortunate and poor women here are also worthy of praise, and the shoes, etc. They are very tasteful people. The fashion of men nowadays is such that they wear *angarkhā*-like coats with fitted trousers, and appear to walk moving their waists like Jaipuris. One cannot help laughing at such a sight.[25]

What was merely amusing in the streets of Paris became an unsettling experience at the opera. In the discourse of colonial rule, the trope of the colonized subject as a feminine being stripped of his manhood was commonplace,[26] but here the tables seemed to have been turned. Feminizing the West, as represented by the influence of French fashion on an American individual, allowed Nazli to assume a superior moral stance and dwell on the deleterious effect of Western culture on Indian masculine ideals. Men who were removed from the loving care of family in India and the watchful eye of the British Empire, whose men were manly in comparison to other Westerners, were in danger of becoming dissipated and losing their essential qualities.

A serious cause of anxiety for Nazli Begum is the effect of living on the continent on her fellow country-men. This diary entry on 20 July 1908, a few days before her visit to the opera, appears to be based on personal observation and rumination over the issue:

> One hears strange stories about Indians. In London perhaps they show restraint, but in a paradisial place like Paris they lose control of themselves. It is sad and regrettable that they are infected by every kind of Western influence that is very injurious and harmful for their lives. They are forced to come to Europe to acquire knowledge and skills. But the company—if they are fortunate then they meet good people, otherwise God help them.[27]

She linked the cause of the moral corruption of Indian men to the backward situation of Indian women back home:

> The greatest and real cause for this is connected to the education of women. If thinking about it on this line they would build educational institutions for women in India, the minds of men would not be scattered to this degree, because the sincere attachment to the home with good thoughts would bring them back to their homeland. They would not be

25. Nazli Begum 1909, 110–1.

26. For more on this topic see Nandy 1983; Moore-Gilbert 1996, 214–5, discusses this in the context of fiction writing with a thoughtful critique of Edward Said.

27. Nazli Begum 1909, 171–2.

> tempted to fall into any evil. Those parents who think their daughters' education is not a worthy thing are ruining the foundation of India with the thorns they have sown. When a boy returns from Europe under its influence what does he see in his house? Complete disorder and dark ignorance –, then why would his heart be attached to such a home? And why would he blindly love his own people? It is impossible, rather it is clear that he becomes more contemptuous of them and falls into excesses. The parents are ready to cry and also to curse Europe. But they remain ignorant of the real cause of the ruin. Boys from noble families are reduced to nothing and the reason is only the inattention to women's education and nothing else. Each girl who is ruined represents the tottering of India's firmness, not just the loss of her family. Today Europe is the centre of education and not sending is also not possible. Then it is better that cultured partners for them are born in India, so that a man's life can pass with propriety and attachment. I have said what I had to. Dear sister, I cannot express how such matters cause sorrow to the heart. May God effect that a better system be there for this. Otherwise in the future ruination will show an even more horrifying aspect.[28]

One wonders whether Nazli Begum spoke in such an impassioned way from seeing the effects of dissipation on someone close to her.

In London Nazli Begum had witnessed that Indian men were kept in check due to the salubrious influence of the empire that trained them to inculcate good habits. A month earlier on 10 June 1908, she wrote regarding a visit to a long-time expatriate in the city:

> Mr. Romesh Chunder Dutt had invited us four for lunch. It is a very small but very comfortable house. A delicious lunch was served that everyone ate with relish. After lunch he showed us his books. He has pasted his friends' letters so nicely. He has a collection of forty years. I was amazed at how he had the leisure for this kind of activity after the required college work, and to keep doing it one must have an energetic temperament, otherwise to go on with it is difficult. With respect to age he is sixty years old and fit. We only know how to complain about having no free time. We start complaining about the smallest out of the ordinary task. But such men have time for everything. There are various kinds of books ongoing like this. In one he has pasted clippings from one newspaper. He has been interested in this since a young age and it is praiseworthy that he has kept it up all his life. He never lets too much pile up. This is his secret. What an enthusiastic man he is! If he comes across a beautiful picture, that too is pasted into the collection.[29]

28. Nazli Begum 1909, 172.
29. Nazli Begum 1909, 69.

Dutt (1848–1909), one time Professor of Indian History at University College, London, was a prominent economist and political figure who frequently traveled between India and England.[30] Nazli Begum's admiration and sympathy towards this solitary but solid person who occupies his leisure time so productively contrasts with her despair with respect to wayward Indian men.

After leaving Europe, the Fyzee sisters sojourned in Istanbul for a few weeks at a time of political turbulence. The Young Turk revolution of 1908 was in full swing and although she does not mention it, Nazli Begum delighted in being in the seat of the caliphate. The Turkophilia of the Fyzee sisters also stemmed from the fact that the city of Istanbul was their city of birth, where their father had been a merchant. The Ottoman sultan was revered by Indian Muslims and during this trip Nazli's husband had the honour of an audience with Sultan 'Abdul Hamid II (r. 1876–1909), while Atiya and Nazli received special medals from the court. For this part of her trip, and then in Cairo, Nazli Begum's narrative focused to a great extent on women's domestic lives or topics such as the history and culture of Muslims. But in this world of stricter divisions of male and female than in Europe, another kind of male emerged as an appealing figure to them: the pre-pubescent boy who was of an age when he is still allowed in women's spaces, and who has a long history in Persianate literature and culture as the symbol of the beloved.

On her first voyage to England, Atiya had encountered many interesting individuals on the steamer *Moldavia*, but none charmed her as much as a young boy on 12 September 1906:

> Several passengers came from Port Said. From among them I had the opportunity in the morning to converse with a small boy, and was perplexed by his two companions, wondering to which ethnic group they belonged and who they were. I asked that boy to which community he belonged, where he had come from and where he was going, and he immediately said, "I am a Turk, I am from Egypt and I am going to England for education." Then he told me his own and his father's names, but in such a manner with his tongue rolling as is usual with Turks. If one is not used to it, it is difficult to comprehend. I joyfully asked, "Are you really a Turk?" He said, "I swear I am a Muslim." I then asked if he had brothers and sisters, and he cheekily said he had nine brothers, *al-hamdulilah*, and happily was free of sisters!! A wonderful boy. These people have such a fair colouring. One can right away tell that he is the son of an important man. He promised that he would meet me regularly in London. He spoke at length about the grand Sultan and education, as if he had an intelligent and experienced mind of an adult. He said, "The Sultan cannot do much

30. He also wrote about his earlier travels in Europe; Dutt 1896.

for the country because he is of a sickly temperament; when we wish to acquire higher education we have to go to England and France because it is not possible to study to that level in Istanbul."[31]

Atiya's pleasure in the boy's company enlivens her narrative. She saw a kindred spirit in this spirited boy since, like her, he was also undergoing the journey in order to gain an education. Although he was a Turkish Muslim, he was of an age not to be the object of romantic or sexual attraction for her.

Uncannily, the two sisters had a similar encounter with another Turkish boy during a charitable function organized by Ottoman women in Istanbul, as described by Nazli Begum on 8 September 1908. True to form, and in a scene that contrasts with the Paris opera encounter in significant ways, Nazli Begum noticed an aristocratic lady with her son and daughter seated near her:

> After the play started the little Mubarak Beg said something to his mother [Farid Pasha's wife][32] and aunt, the meaning of which was that he had seen us in Paris. Then he came and began to talk to us. I have not seen such intelligence and sharpness in any child in my life. God give him a long life. He will become a famous man one day. Now he is twelve or thirteen years old. He understood everything that was said and asked questions, and was conversant with contemporary politics. The love for his country and fellow countrymen was astonishing. I was captivated by his lovely and serious conversation. He is an amazingly charming child and so well educated. Truly he is the best example of the education of upper-class Turks. Such a small creature so easily introduced all us ladies to each other. He is an expert in introductions. His manner is completely experienced but a childish quality was also visible. He asked for my card to find out my name and then ceremoniously gave me his card ... The introductions were made! He asked such questions about India that we looked at him in astonishment. He said that he only lived in Paris for his education; afterwards he would never live there. Eastern manners and western delicacy have combined to make this child very pleasing. He kept asking us whether he could do something for us, whether he could call a servant or carriage. He was ready to help us in every way. He spoke perfect French with the correct pronunciation. These people live in Nishantash. I have called him over to our place.[33]

Like Atiya, Nazli Begum was enchanted by this intelligent and polite boy

31. Fyzee 2010a, 120.
32. This Ottoman gentleman can tentatively be identified as Damad Ferid Pasha (1853–1923), who was the grand vizier under Mehmet VI (r. 1918–22).
33. Nazli Begum 1909, 269–70.

who would one day become a promising and capable citizen of the Muslim world and the Ottoman Empire.

A few days later, on 11 September, Nazli Begum writes, "[W]e had called Mubarak Farid Beg and he came exactly on time. The child talked about all sorts of things. He is a mine of information. He answered our questions with such intelligence and swiftness that I was stunned. He is a darling child. He invited His Highness [the Nawab] and us all on behalf of his parents, brother and sister."[34] The next day, at a party at Farid Pasha's mansion in Nishantash, she writes, "Little Mubarak Beg came with energy and said, 'Come, sahib, come' and took us along. He is of an age that he can go into both the *haramlik* [women's quarters] and *salāmlik* [men's quarters]. He took His Highness to the side of the *salāmlik* area and led us to the door of the *haramlik* where his mother and sister were waiting to welcome us."[35] The young ephebe helped the sisters negotiate their movement between the gendered spaces in a cultural setting that was familiar yet foreign. He also seemed to have brought out the maternal instinct in the sisters who were both to remain childless throughout their lives.

As mentioned above, the figure of the adolescent boy calls to mind an emblematic poetic figure from Persianate literature. The fair-skinned Turk was the cupbearer and quintessential beloved of Muslim males and is frequently encountered in Persian, Ottoman, and Urdu poetic texts.[36] Although he is sometimes the object of desire by men in poems and real life, for the Fyzee sisters he poses no sexual threat, rather by speaking to them directly and intelligently he empowers them as "masculine" women. In fact, Atiya was conscious of and admired masculine women, describing them in her diary, as well as discussing the topic in some detail with the scholar Maulana Shibli Numani in various letters.[37] In a replay of the age-old poetic relationships the Fyzee sisters appropriated a masculine role and redefined it on their own terms. By this time in history, the dalliance with beardless boys had been abandoned by Indian, as well all Persianate, men under the influence of European modern ideas that considered such a relationship to be deviant. In Nazli Begum's case, her appropriation of the responsibility of composing the "official" travelogue, that in other cases a princely ruler may have done himself or have assigned to a secretary, is a strategy to protect

34. Nazli Begum 1909, 274.

35. Nazli Begum 1909, 275.

36. I have in mind here the beardless male beloved in the Persian poetic tradition who is the object of the poet's affection, but who is also in some senses sexless: see de Bruijn 1990. Afsaneh Najmabadi discusses this figure, also known as *amrad,* in the context of historical transformations in early modern Iran in her book (Najmabadi 2005, 15–6).

37. Lambert-Hurley and Sharma 2010, 53.

herself from her passive husband and even to assume symbolic power in the relationship. Outside the native state of Janjira, she was the cosmopolitan, English-speaking guide who was in charge, suggesting on another level that the problem with their relationship was not so much her barrenness but his lack of masculinity.

The travels in Europe and the Ottoman Empire would have long-term consequences for the Fyzee sisters. They returned from their travels with a better understanding of their own desires, and the role of men in their lives and the world at large. Nazli Begum was soon divorced from her husband, with some people ascribing blame to Atiya for interfering in her sister's personal life. Atiya ultimately gave up on Iqbal and in 1912 married an Indian Jewish artist, Samuel Rahamin, who converted to Islam for her. It would seem that their travels allowed the two sisters to come to terms with their frustrated desires and come to a better understanding of their own selves. Besides the immediate effect on their lives, what were the abstract implications of the voyage of the two sisters, for them as well as for the readers of their narratives? As articulated in one study on women's travel writing and gender, "[The] perception of the heroine's identity in terms of the masculine/feminine binary structure appears complementary to the periphery/centre axis and may reveal both national and gender challenges as the sources of self-discovery".[38] The gendered impulses behind the behavior and reactions of the sisters, especially Nazli Begum, were complex and transgressed normative roles, and thus they challenged not only the geographic and social sphere around them, but also the emotional roles assigned to women of their time. According to Indrani Sen, "[T]he image of the Indian woman was constantly being re-constituted and ... while at one level she was *proscribed* for her sensuousness and other alleged 'moral' failings, she was at another level also held up as a *prescriptive* model of feminine behavior."[39] Women were expected to save men from becoming dissipated and in this way they were good subjects of the British Empire, which functioned as a training ground for men, while continental Europe, a foreign space for many Indians of the time, was a dangerous place that could corrupt men and feminize them.

The revulsion caused by the sight of the American dandy in decadent Paris represents the opposite end of the emotional spectrum to the usual expression of wonder and delight that new experiences and people traditionally elicited in travelers. If the West was precariously balanced between the capable and the morally decadent male, Istanbul represented the seat of

38. Eugenia Gavriliu 2001, 83.
39. Sen 2002, 62.

the caliphate and the repository of everything that was fine in Islamic and Persianate culture, in which Muslim women like themselves could re-enact traditional masculine roles. For the most part, the Fyzee sisters viewed Muslim men in Turkey and Egypt, like their British counterparts, as capable, well-mannered and good people. In the Muslim utopia that they saw in the Ottoman Empire, the beardless males and eunuchs who also transgressed gender lines in terms of movement between social spaces were non-threatening and positive, thus empowering the women's sense of their own identity. The young Muslim boys whom Atiya and Nazli encountered during their travels were symbolic figures who facilitated the enactment of the sisters' role as Muslim travelers in a world where previously only men had the privilege of encountering newness or to engage in relationships with beardless youths. Interacting with the young boys in a joyful setting and writing in detail about these encounters was another way of subtly challenging the established social order. In the end, it would seem that the literary trope of delight in early twentieth-century travelogues of Indian Muslim women survived as a feature of older texts to be deployed in a new setting, while the disgust regarding the crisis of masculine values and gender identities was a new element that is the reaction to the changing world around them.

Appendix

Travel narratives by South Asian women:[40]

1870. Nawab Sikandar Begum of Bhopal, *A Pilgrimage to Mecca* (Urdu; only the English translation survives)

1883. Pandita Ramabai, *Inglandcā Pravāsa* (Marathi)

1885. Krishnabhabini Das, *Inglande Bāngamahilā* (Bengali)

1889. Pandita Ramabai, *Yunāited States chī Lokasthiti āni Pravāsvrutta* (Marathi)

1901. Nandkunvarba, Rani of Gondal, *Gomandal parikramā* (Gujarati)

1906–07. Atiya Fyzee, *Zamāna-yi tahsīl* (Urdu)

1909. Begum Nazli Rafiya of Janjira, *Sair-yi Yūrop* (Urdu)

1909. Sultan Jahan Begum of Bhopal, *The Story of a Pilgrimage to Hijaz* (Urdu)

1909. Ummat al-Ghani Nur al-Nisa, *Safarnāma-yi Hijāz, Shām o Misr* (Urdu)

40. Dates refer to the year of publication, not the actual year of travel.

1911. Maimoona Sultan, *Siyāsat-i Sultānī* (Urdu); 1913. *A Trip to Europe* (English)

1915. Hariprabha Takeda, *Bāngamahilar Jāpānjātrā* (Bengali)

1915. Sarala Devi Chaudhurani, *Burmājātrā* (Bengali)

1916. Sharatrenu Devi, *Parashye Bāngaramanī* (Bengali)

1921. Sunity Devee, *The Autobiography of a Princess* (English)

1926. Sughra Humayun Mirza, *Safarnāma-yi Yūrop* (Urdu)

1932. Durgabati Ghose, *Paschimjātrikī* (Bengali)[41]

Works Cited

Blanton, Casey (2002), *Travel Writing: The Self and the World,* New York: Routledge.

de Bruijn, J.T.P. (1990), "Beloved," *EIr* IV: 128–9.

Dutt, Romesh Chunder (1896), *Three Years in Europe, 1868 to 1871, with an account of subsequent visits to Europe in 1886 and 1893,* Calcutta: S.K. Lahiri.

Feldman, Jessica R. (1993), *Gender on the Divide: The Dandy in Modernist Literature,* Ithaca: Cornell University Press.

Fyzee, Atiya (2010a), "Zamana-i-tahsil: a translation," in: *Atiya's Journeys: A Muslim Woman from Colonial Bombay to Edwardian Britain,* New Delhi: Oxford University Press, 109–236.

—— (2010b), *Zamāna-yi tahsīl: 'Atīya Faizī kī nādir o nāyāb khudnavisht,* ed. Muhammad Yamin Usman, Karachi : Idāra-yi Yādgār-i Ghālib.

Gavriliu, Eugenia. (2001), "Gender Influences on the Construction of Otherness in Olivia Manning's *The Balkan Trilogy,*" in: Vita Fortunati, Rita Monticelli, Maurizio Ascari (ed.), *Travel Writing and the Female Imaginary*, Bologna: Pàtron Editore.

Lambert-Hurley, Siobhan and Sunil Sharma (2010), *Atiya's Journeys: A Muslim Woman from Colonial Bombay to Edwardian Britain,* New Delhi: Oxford University Press.

Majeed, Javed (2007), *Autobiography, Travel and Postnational Identity: Gandhi, Nehru and Iqbal,* New York: Palgrave.

Mandal, Somdatta (2010), "Introduction," in: *The Westward Traveller*, Durgabati Ghose, Hyderabad: Orient BlackSwan.

Moore-Gilbert, Bart (1996), *Writing India, 1757–1990: The Literature of British India,* Manchester: Manchester University Press.

41. See Mandal 2010 for a survey of Bengali women's travelogues.

Mottahedeh, Roy (1997), "'Ajā'ib in *The Thousand and One Nights*," in: Richard C. Hovannisian and Georges Sabagh (ed.), *The Thousand and One Nights in Arabic Literature and Society*, Cambridge: University of Cambridge, 29–39.

Najmabadi, Afsaneh (2005), *Women with Mustaches and Men without Beards: Gender and Sexual Anxieties of Iranian Modernity*, Berkeley: University of California Press.

Nandy, Ashis (1983), *The Intimate Enemy: Loss and Recovery of Self under Colonialism*, New Delhi: Oxford University Press.

Nazli Begum (1909?), *Sayr-i Yurop*, Lahore: Union Steam Press.

Sen, Indrani (2002), *Women and Empire: Representations in the Writings of British India, 1858–1900*, Hyderabad: Orient Longman.

Sharma, Sunil (2004), "The City of Beauties in the Indo-Persian Poetic Landscape," *Comparative Studies of South Asia, Africa and the Middle East*. 24/2: 73–81.

—— (2006), "Atiya Begum and the Mystery of the Beloved's Identity in Shibli Nomani's Persian Ghazals," in: *Poetry's Voice, Society's Norms: Forms of Interaction between Middle Eastern Writers and Their Societies*, ed. Andreas Pflitsch and Barbara Winckler, Wiesbaden: Reichert, 105–19.

Tavakoli-Targhi, Mohamad (2001), *Refashioning Iran: Orientalism, Occidentalism and Historiography*, New York: Palgrave.

—— (2002), "Eroticizing Europe," in: Elton L. Daniel (ed.), *Society and Culture in Qajar Iran: Studies in Honor of Hafez Farmayan*, Costa Mesa: Mazda, 311–46.

Ideological Voyages

Nationalism, Colonialism and Identity in the Works of Qāẓ̤ī ʿAbdul Ġaffār

Daniel Majchrowicz

REPLETE WITH LIVELY DESCRIPTIONS of suggestively-clad British women and voracious Italians with noodles dangling from their mouths "like cows eating grass," Qāẓ̤ī ʿAbdul Ġaffār's 1924 travelogue of a journey to Western Europe, *Naqsh-i firang*, significantly complicates the trope of the "lustful savage." In a creative reversal of Orientalist discourse, ʿAbdul Ġaffār questions the idea that the so-called "passionate Turk" was defeated by his own licentiousness, for if this were possible, he asks, wouldn't Europe have fallen long ago? He ventures still further, interrogating, and ultimately rejecting, many received notions of Western superiority inherent in colonial propaganda.

A prominent figure in Urdu literature in the early and mid-twentieth century, ʿAbdul Ġaffār (1888-1955) was also a journalist, political activist and intellectual. His accomplishments include the publication of several newspapers and popular novels, short stories, a report on Operation Polo, and the translation of the Indian constitution into Urdu. In this essay, I will explore how he combines his literary and political interests using two related genres — the travelogue and the autobiography — to negate colonial propaganda and formulate a nationalist self-identity. The essay is divided into two sections. The first traces ʿAbdul Ġaffār's earliest elaboration of an anti-colonial discourse within *Naqsh-i firang*. This critique is innovative, couched in a temporal narrative faithful to the generic expectations of the modern Urdu travelogue. The second observes the maturation of this discourse and its manifestation in ʿAbdul Ġaffār's unfinished autobiography. From these two sections emerges the image of a talented author and anti-colonial theorist who deftly employed first-person narrative accounts to fashion trenchant attacks on colonial institutions.

Nationalism and anti-colonial thought in *Naqsh-i firang*

The Urdu travelogue emerged in the early to mid-nineteenth century, but

Qazi Abdul Ghaffar and family. (Courtesy Omar Khalidi.)

reached the age of its maturity in the last decade of that century.[1] By the early 1900s, countless travelogues were being produced in Urdu by writers famous and unknown. At this time, it was one of the most popular genres in Urdu and provided readers with accounts of contemporary conditions of countries across the world, but especially in the Middle East and Europe. 'Abdul Ġaffār is thus not unique in choosing to record the details of his journey in the chronological style popular at the time. Of course, many before 'Abdul Ġaffār had used the *safarnāma* to proto-nationalistic ends, but few can compare with the intensity and complexity of his critique of colonialism, put forth during a period of surging nationalist sentiment in India. The publication of *Naqsh-i firang* in 1924 postdates the fracturing of a delicate moment of cooperation and unity between various Indian independence movements. The work describes his travels to London, France, Switzerland and Italy over a two month period in the spring of 1921 as a member of the Khilafat Committee's delegation to the prime minister of Great Britain, Lloyd George, who was involved in negotiating the dissolution of the caliphate in Istanbul. The Khilafat Movement in South Asia had emerged to protect this sacred institution. Over time, it developed into one of the earliest concert-

1. Metcalf 1990, 87.

ed nationwide movements for independence in India. Public subscriptions were collected to aid the effort, and wealthy sponsors promoted the goals of the movement.[2] 'Abdul Ġaffār, along with the Agha Khan and several other delegates, was sent to London to dissuade the Prime Minister from taking action against the Caliphate. They failed.

Naqsh-i firang was written after 'Abdul Ġaffār had returned to India, a fact that accounts for the palpable bitterness that pervades his prose. Bitter, but purposeful, *Naqsh-i firang* is the masterpiece of a conscientious artist preparing an eminent literary yet ultimately political work. One of the finest littérateurs of Urdu in the twentieth century 'Abdul Ġaffār was also a journalist and public figure. *Naqsh-i firang* is at every moment carefully weighted and precisely written to account for the delegation's failure. But beyond this immediate goal, 'Abdul Ġaffār hoped to share with his readers what he had learned about the realities of colonialism and the West while abroad. *Naqsh-i firang* (literally the map, mark, impression, or sign of Europe) is designed to call into question a great many myths about the nature of East and West, to use 'Abdul Ġaffār's own taxonomy. This is his primary goal. Although this type of dichotomous discourse is by no means unique to *Naqsh-i firang*, its ferocity and explicitness here make it an exemplary candidate through which to explore how the *safarnāma* became a powerful anti-colonial weapon in the hands of adroit nationalist authors. This section will explore how 'Abdul Ġaffār used the inherent ambiguity of the Urdu travelogue to this end. It will then present several facets of his anti-colonial thought as they are presented in *Naqsh-i firang*.

From at least the early nineteenth century, Indian travel writers often desired to wrest the power to represent India from the British who claimed to monopolize it, as Kumkum Chatterjee's analysis of the emergence of the Bengali travelogue demonstrates. The authors in Chatterjee's sample do this passively by asserting their own images of India and conducting ethnographic surveys.[3] They are often apologetic, writing with the European reader in mind, if only sub-consciously so. As the genre emerged in Urdu, authors such as Shibli Numani spoke more forcefully. Shibli himself claimed to have written his *safarnāma-yi Qunstantaniya o Miṣr o Shām* to educate India's isolated Muslims on the conditions of their brothers in the Middle East. He explicitly notes that colonial restrictions and economic depravity denied Indian Muslims the opportunity to experience these regions firsthand. Worse still, a robust Orientalist literature on Islam had cultivated in India a very particular, and not so appealing, image of Arabs.[4] Shibli's account was

2. See Minault 1982.
3. Chatterjee 2002, 192.
4. Numani 1999, 7.

intended to provide a response to this discourse and present his readers with an accurate picture of conditions of Muslims in the Middle East.

Thirty years after Shibli visited Istanbul, ʻAbdul Ġaffār penned his own trenchant critique of Orientalist "learning." Anticipating a trend that would take several more decades to catch on elsewhere, in *Naqsh-i firang,* the term *mustashriq* (orientalist) is used derisively. Orientalist "scholarship" is ridiculed ad nauseum. As ʻAbdul Ġaffār deconstructs the myth of Orientalist objectivity, he also builds a national identity firmly rooted in a discourse predicated on the irreconcilable difference between East and West. Turning the tables on the wretched *mustashriqīn*, ʻAbdul Ġaffār fashions his own ideology from the very academic fields used to establish Western superiority, such as history, sociology, and psychology. And yet, these intellectual weapons of the West are combined with an awareness of Islamic history and social justice — not to mention the first-person observations of Europe provided by the author — to lead the reader to the ineluctable conclusion that these reified entities, East and West, are hopelessly at odds with one another.

Mirroring at times the passion of Franz Fanon, what this ideology lacks in analytics is made up for with ʻAbdul Ġaffār's literary prowess. His abilities and ideas find a suitable medium in the travelogue, and the result is a compelling polemic against "the West" as a benevolent intellectual power. But beyond that, it was also the *form* of the *safarnāma* that was a crucial element in making ʻAbdul Ġaffār's argument credible to his Indian readership. The Urdu *safarnāma* is a genre of diverse parentage. The confluence of genres and characteristics that inform its modern incarnation irrigated a fecund terrain in which nationalists might sow the seeds of their discourses.

Most travelogues in Urdu during the colonial period were first published not as books, but were serialized in newspapers. Though they may now be thought of as leather-bound instances of literature, their original publication suggests a somewhat more diverse generic provenance that lies somewhere between the literary and the journalistic. Metcalf, for instance, points out that Mumtāz Muftī calls his own travelogue "reportage,"[5] and indeed, even *Naqsh-i firang* is occasionally referred to as such.[6] Moreover, the modern travelogue has been to a great extent influenced by the autobiography, resulting in an emotional travel account based on personal experience.[7] This was only rarely the case in classical Islamicate travel literature.

By locating the autobiographical travelogue in a medium used primarily to inform the community (and indeed, to create the community, in the Andersonian sense) and not simply in a stand-alone volume reminiscent of

5. Metcalf 1993, 150.
6. Suroor 1964, n.p.
7. Metcalf 1993, 149.

other works of literature, a new style of narrative is born. The result can best be described as semi-fictionalized autobiographical reportage. In this form the modern Urdu *safarnāma* becomes an opportune vessel for the dissemination of nationalist ideology, as well as for mediating or debating nationalist principles precisely because it unites the qualities of the autobiography, the traditional *riḥla*, modern journalism, political op-eds, and an informal anthropological gaze. It derives its persuasive power from the fact that it can draw liberally from all of these sources without being particularly beholden to any of them. But above all, it is the slippage between a personalizing, emotional approach that draws on the narrative techniques used in fiction and a generalizing and distancing journalistic prose that purports to inform and feigns neutrality that makes it such a useful weapon for the nationalist writer. In Urdu, it is almost a *sine qua non* to begin an account with the assertion that "this is not a true travelogue." I read this uncertainty as a product of the travelogue's diverse parentage. The generically ambiguous *safarnāma* thrives in the interstices between other genres even as it takes on generic conventions in its own right.

How then does 'Abdul Ġaffār use this generic vagueness to cut the colonial enterprise down to size in the heyday of the Khilafat movement? 'Abdul Ġaffār's approach is to reverse the accusations leveled at India by Orientalists, using the chronological flow of his narrative to pepper the text with instances and experiences that underscore his main thesis, namely, that the East and West are incompatible. Every line of *Naqsh-i firang* seems to revolve around what 'Abdul Ġaffār refers to as the *tafāvut-i rāh*, which we may translate loosely as the "disparity of the paths." Platts' dictionary defines *tafāvut* as "being far apart ... dissimilarity, discordance, disparity."[8] The two paths he refers to are the essentialized categories of *maġrib* (West) and *mashriq* (East). In *Naqsh-i firang*, the *tafāvut-i rāh* is beyond question and all-encompassing.

But it is also tempting to read *tafāvut* as a transitive verb, as in the derivative verb, *tafāvut bolnā*, "to make incongruous or discordant, separate." To my ear, then, the phrase *tafāvut-i rāh* also seems to evoke the idea of intellectually bifurcating two paths. A few decades before, figures like Sir Sayyid Ahmad Khan attempted to reconcile the two through an amalgamation of political passivity, "Eastern culture," and Western learning; but, says 'Abdul Ġaffār, that attempt was a failure. For him, the ineluctable conclusion of these experiments with Western education and "culture" was ample proof of the incompatibility (*tafāvut honā*) of the two traditions, and of the necessity to separate them (*tafāvut bolnā/karnā*). This conclusively is reinforced by 'Abdul Ġaffār's assertion that "at every step [in London] I felt my own infe-

8. Platts 2000, 328.

riority as a black man."[9] The ramifications of this resolution are explicated through the rest of *Naqsh-i firang*. Its rhetoric exhorts the reader to become aware of this *tafāvut*. The British and Indians are so irreconcilably different that the former can never hope to rule the latter with legitimate representation. The reader is encouraged to realize the damage that the imposition of a foreign and malignant ideology causes and to neutralize the negative impact of these cultural apparatuses by distancing herself from the colonizer in whatever way possible. In his autobiography, 'Abdul Ġaffār demonstrates how his failure to do so scarred him, literally and figuratively. Thus, his *safarnāma* and his autobiography are closely connected. The former is the locus of realization, where the violence of colonialism is discovered. In the latter 'Abdul Ġaffār tells his own life-history in light of the revelations he first enumerates in *Naqsh-i firang*.

Much of his campaign to prevent future generations from coming under this hypnotic "Western knife"[10] involved a comprehensive deconstruction of the Orientalist scholarship that rendered the Oriental a subject of scientific enquiry. If this so-called science could be disproven, there would no longer be any ideological justification for British rule, and its exploitative nature would be confirmed once and for all. For 'Abdul Ġaffār, to directly attack this institution was tantamount to questioning the colonialist's ability to either understand or benefit his Eastern subject — to strip the West of Joseph Conrad's "idea at the back of it."[11] If the Orientalist could not know his subject, then the political structure he served could not be representative or legitimate. Nor could it hope to improve the condition of the subject population. The civilizing myth would be debunked. And as Ashis Nandy writes, "colonialism minus a civilizational mission is no colonialism at all."[12]

'Abdul Ġaffār's critique of the Orientalist endeavor begins in the museums and libraries of Europe. Unlike earlier Indian travelers writing in English, he feels a heavy heart and a sense of brooding in these institutions.[13] His visits to prominent museums only reinforce his conviction that the West, despite all of its proclamations to the contrary, simply does not understand the East. He writes, "An Oriental wing was recently opened [in the Louvre]. There are present in it many examples of crafts from the Eastern countries. But at every step one feels that the West cannot understand the East, does

9. 'Abdul Ġaffār often refers to himself as a "black man" in the text, reappropriating the term and asserting his own self-worth through its use.

10. 'Abdul Ġaffār, in Anjum 1996, 28.

11. Said 1979, 32.

12. Nandy 1983, 11.

13. Codell 2007, 176.

not know it, cannot understand it, cannot know it."[14] Despite a wealth of material unrivaled in even the Islamic world, the so-called Orientalist is not able to understand even the most basic principles of Islam or of the Eastern lifestyle. He goes on to say:

> People ask me to what extent I have found the West to be acquainted with the East. Acquaintance?! During the Middle Ages of Europe, eastern peoples were enslaved and brought to Europe. The level of awareness that the European masters of those slaves had of the East then is the same as the level that Europeans possess now. They certainly know that these black human beings live in countries where their commerce and governance are extremely lucrative. But what is this? These people are human. They also have hearts and minds. They are also inheritors of some culture and civilization or other. Their homes must have once been filled with light. They also knew how to rule the world. The capitalists of Europe know nothing of these matters![15]

The idea of a benevolent colonial power on a sacred mission to better the wretched of the earth was accepted not only by many Europeans but by many Indians as well, and 'Abdul Ġaffār goes to great lengths to convince his fellow countrymen of its fallacy. It was also believed that Oriental scholarship was integral to this effort. "I had heard that in Europe the high arts and crafts of Asia were greatly valued, and that the greatest and most intellectual of Orientalists spend their lives researching our conditions." As this myth was popular even amongst many Indians, Qāẓī 'Abdul Ġaffār give various examples from his travels to debunk it. I quote three here.

> Parisians are considered to be very interested in issues related to Islam. I would often meet with a particular aged gentleman who is both extremely wealthy and influential in the government. On day he said to me, 'I am surprised that you people accept foreign rule when that nation's influence is restricted to the coasts of Hindustan. After all, the rest of the nation is free. What does that population do'! Now you tell me. This man is considered to be extremely knowledgeable in the Asian and Islamic fields! I met a young aristocrat who also did journalism from time to time. One day he pronounced that 'India is such a big island! It must be huge!'[16]

It would seem that 'Abdul Ġaffār is only too willing to allow for convenient slippages between the common European and the specialist *mustashriq*. But more disconcerting to him than these individual instances of ignorance are

14. 'Abdul Ġaffār 1924, 105.
15. 'Abdul Ġaffār 1924, 141.
16. 'Abdul Ġaffār 1924, 142.

the essentializing, and essentially incorrect, representations of the East being broadcast across France and beyond. 'Abdul Ġaffār had a keen eye for entertainment, and often went to plays, shows and films. In Europe, though, he was often displeased with what he saw.

> It was one of my habits that whenever a movie or theater show was advertised as having an "Asian story" then I would always go to watch it. It is no exaggeration [to say that] lakhs of rupees are spent in preparation for each and every show in Europe, and it is only made ready after years of research and investigation. They read books and study history. They look at buildings. They learn about the traditions and customs of people. Only after all this is the drama brought on to the stage. But as far as Asia is concerned, what is the result? One day I heard that there was to be a movie played in the cinema about Solomon and the Queen of Sheba. According to my custom, I went to watch it. And what do I see, but a large gathering in the magnificent durbar of Hazrat Sulaiman[17] in which the attendants are wearing strange sparkly, sequined outfits. There are Iranian rugs spread about. French glass-work has been set in place, like the *darbar* of some Mughal king. Bilqīs[18] enters, and it seems as though her ensemble had just been ordered moments before from some fancy store in Paris. She is wearing high-heeled shoes. Her head is uncovered. And in the European fashion, her chest is half-exposed. And this is supposed to be Bilqis! (*Aur yeh Bilqīs hu'ī!*). I sat there cursing all those sculptors of the East, those wretches (*kambakht*) who spend entire lifetimes understanding our ways and then put high-heels on Bilqīs' feet.[19]

Regarding its representation of modern Islamic Asia (or Africa), the total exoticization of Islamic practices in French cinema is undeniable. 'Abdul Ġaffār writes:

> I chanced to see another movie which included a scene as a gift to the viewers — a vignette of the traditions and customs of some Islamic country. Muslims praying were depicted throughout the movie. What I should say is that they were standing up straight with their hands pointing directly at the sky (this meant they were doing *niyyat-bāndhī*). Immediately after, they dropped on to the ground (*paṭ leṭ gaye*) (this motion included both *rukū'* and *sujūd*) and then got up, dusting off the hems of their garments. This is what they called prayer (*namāz*). God [alone] could understand these pretenders who make such grand claims to intimate knowledge of the East. The reality is that they don't even know

17. The biblical king Solomon.
18. The Queen of Sheba.
19. 'Abdul Ġaffār 1924, 143.

> the ABCs (*abjad*) of our lives. There are many Muslim subjects under the French government in whose cities French rulers and traders spend their entire lives. Thousands of Arabs are employed by the French army. Even then, no French Orientalist has ever been able to learn the proper way of praying.[20]

This extended tirade against the *mustashriqīn* is concluded with an exhortation to action and a warning for the future should India fail to act soon:

> It is my belief that the European nations do not possess the ability to understand foreign nations (*aqvām*). They are unable to make themselves aware of any aspect of our lives, although their technological and commercial advancement has made them the masters of our fates. And they believe that it is the natural right of the white nations (*aqvām*) to rule over the black peoples. The worldwide movement of the new age is the result of, and answer to, that belief. And this is the one answer that can be given to those narcissists. And which should be given.[21]

This is the closing paragraph of *Naqsh-i firang*. It unquestionably exhorts the reader to take action and give a final rejoinder to the overbearing European races that have imposed their wills and traditions upon the East. These parting salvos are exceptionally explicit about the task that lies before the nascent nation, but the tenor of the entire narrative is no less emotive. The reverse of Said's assertion then also rings true in *Naqsh-i firang* that "every statement made by Orientalists or white men conveyed a sense of the irreducible distance separating white from colored, or Occidental from Oriental."[22] Victim though he was, 'Abdul Ġaffār had learned his trade from the best.

This is the damning discourse that 'Abdul Ġaffār deftly embeds into the narrative structure of his travelogue. Yet he does not drop the thread of the *tafāvut-i rāh,* even when describing the quotidian aspects of life in Europe. His first-person descriptions of meals, meetings and meanderings all circle back to the undeniable chasm between colonial subject and the metropole. In *Naqsh-i firang*, 'Abdul Ġaffār reveals that the hypocrisies of the West permeate to its very roots (which, he notes elsewhere and with derision, begins with the wolves Romulus and Remus). By foregrounding his personal experiences as an eye-witness to the West within the travelogue, 'Abdul Ġaffār claims to be a particularly qualified observer. Few of his readers would have visited Europe, and even of those who had, few would have met the Prime Minister. His presence in London lends his agenda an individual touch that

20. 'Abdul Ġaffār 1924, 144.
21. 'Abdul Ġaffār 1924, 144.
22. Said 1979, 228.

augments its efficacy and impact on the reader and serves as a buttress for his anti-colonial rhetoric. Consider the following passages intended to give the reader an impression of what it feels like to visit London, something almost none of his readers would ever experience.

> The only impact that my first sight of the capital of Great Britain was able to make on me was that, as a black man, even in the land of freedom and liberty I had the status of a slave. In the land of the nation which claims to have erased the name and mark of slavery from the face of the earth in the nineteenth century, every inch of soil bears the worst signs of economic, social, civil, and political slavery which are instructive (*'ibratnāk*) to those insightful enough to see them. The revolting god of slavery is still firmly in place in the temples of power and materialism, the only difference being that now it has been made more presentable and been bestowed with deceitful clothing. In this land of the free I saw signs my own enslavement at every step. And in the corridors of the government of the Prime Minister, degradation and shame chase after every subjugated nation. I was never interested in London. *Al-ḥamdu lillāh!* For as long as I stayed in London, my disassociation with the city only grew.[23]

While in an earlier era, Sir Sayyid clearly manipulated the realities of his trip to make a European voyage sound more appealing to the ambitious Muslim hoping to benefit from the West's advanced technological capacity, in the 1920s 'Abdul Ġaffār would tear down any delusions that the reader may have of the glories of living or traveling in Europe.

> Several times the thought crossed my mind that I should go and see a meeting of Parliament one day, where the decisions governing the fate of India are made. And it wasn't any difficult task. But then I thought about what I would witness and hear if I went there. I'd see two or three hundred civilian and military rulers of India who only utter "aye" or "nay" when the time comes for making decisions regarding issues related to India. They know nothing more than this: that they and a few thousand of their friends are shepherds of 32 crore human beings.[24]

There is nothing to recommend the reader and upwardly-mobile Indian who wishes to visit London. Like its denizens, London is a city of *makr* and *fareb* (shrewdness and deception). It is bereft of any redeeming virtue: "It has only statesmanship and politics, worldwide conquest and administration, [things] which an unbiased human nature would call by another name."[25]

This extreme distaste for English custom and society is tremendously

23. 'Abdul Ġaffār 1924, 42.
24. 'Abdul Ġaffār 1924, 38.
25. 'Abdul Ġaffār 1924, 38.

useful in ascertaining just what beliefs lay behind the generalizing ideology of the *tafāvut-i rāh*. Given the profuse use of the terms "East" and "West," one might be inclined to conclude that this disgust would manifest itself evenly throughout 'Abdul Ġaffār's tours across Europe. In reality, 'Abdul Ġaffār was quite comfortable on the Continent. He adored Paris and worked there for a number of years. This is not to say that all of his moral edicts were thrown overboard while crossing the channel, for many of his observations in France comprise a significant segment of his critique of Western society. But in that country he did not see himself as a subject, undoubtedly because of the heavy burden he believed he carried on his back as a victim of British imperialism. It was England, not France, that had lynched his grandfather in 1857. The West may have some positive characteristics and ideas, but nothing positive could be ascribed to England proper. Unlike Sir Sayyid Ahmad Khan, 'Abdul Ġaffār uses *his* travelogue to convince his readers *not* to visit England. He concludes:

> It is useless to write about what London is like. If any Indian brother should desire to see Europe and his pockets are filled with excessive amounts of money, and he has plenty of free time from the tumult of daily life, then he should certainly go. But he should remember that British life is a mirror in which the color black appears to look even blacker![26]

Should the inquisitive and adventurous Indian chose to make the journey, though, he would be sure to discover England's depravity as every turn. 'Abdul Ġaffār, using an evocative literary palate drawn from Urdu poetry, creates this impression by narrating a caricature of England's (self-described) virtues. If, for instance, the colonial apparatus engineered the perception that while the Indian aged, the Company servant was forever young, then Qaẕī 'Abdul Ġaffār attempted to overturn this perception in the eyes of his readers. In his description of England there is an almost obsessive tendency to draw the reader's attention to the old, decrepit and handicapped of society. He writes of Brighton:

> There are two types of people that can be seen here next to the waves and the ocean. They are either extremely old men and tremendously decayed women who are trying to elongate the weak and decomposing fibers of their lives in the salubrious ocean climate, or otherwise young men and women drunk in the intoxication of young age, who hear in the waves of the ocean the melody of youth, and who are completely unaware of the dangers of approaching senility. In old age the desire to remain alive

26. 'Abdul Ġaffār 1924, 40.

> becomes very powerful. I saw thousands of handicapped and disabled persons who sat by the ocean from dawn till dusk making public their desire. The young boys and girls would look at them and laugh, unaware that one day that day would come for them as well.[27]

He elaborates, enumerating bandaged men cavorting about in wheeled chairs. Others have arms in casts or are missing eyes and limbs. These were, of course, the victims of the recently ended World War I. The entire scene is characterized by a sort of humorous morbidity: the elderly futilely attempt to elongate the remaining sinews of their lives while the impotent veterans of yet another pointless European feud gaze longingly at the transient bazaar of coquetry and youthful beauty that surrounds them. What better allegory to debunk the myth of a powerful and fecund English masculinity?

The few examples I have presented here represent only a fraction of a more comprehensive, nationalistic attack on colonial rule. It is sufficient to say that at nearly every moment of *Naqsh-i firang,* "those with the eye to see" could discover the *tafāvut* between East and West, as ʻAbdul Ġaffār had. The discovery of this *tafāvut* germinated a deep consternation at the prevalence of colonial influence on Indian life, and ʻAbdul Ġaffār, in the years after his journey, would eventually find its mark even in his childhood. That is, the experiences that ʻAbdul Ġaffār narrated in his travelogue enabled him to discover the hidden hand of colonialism at work throughout his life. In following the development of this belief as it spread to his own sense of personal identity, I now turn to the culmination of the discourse begun in *Nasqh-i Firang* and explore its manifestation in that sister-genre of the travelogue, the autobiography.

Self, Identity and the West in *Bar mā chunān guzasht*

ʻAbdul Ġaffār began his autobiography *Bar mā chunān guzasht* (It Happened to Me Thus) late in his life but unfortunately never completed it; it was only published in excerpts years after his death. Despite its brevity, one immediately finds connections to the discourses begun in his earlier travelogue. Here he traced the influence of colonialism on the formation of his character and the trajectory of his life. ʻAbdul Ġaffār understood himself to have been violated and victimized by the West. But he also simultaneously recognized that the violence wrought on him was due in good part to his own inability to resist its allure. This is the allure of which he had attempted to disabuse his readership years earlier in the pages of *Naqsh-i firang*. In this piece he is

27. ʻAbdul Ġaffār 1924, 91.

singularly concerned with the deleterious effects of colonial rule on a personal level. In one of his first paragraphs, ʻAbdul Ġaffār recounts the earliest memories of his childhood and interprets them as auguries of a contentious, suspended existence between two worlds (*na ghar kā na ghāṭ kā*). His words are worth quoting here in full.

> The first thing that I remember [from my childhood] is the corner of our house where my father's pencil-sharpener was kept. I tried to sharpen one of his pencils and ended up giving my index finger (*kalma kī unglī*) such a severe surgical incision that the mark is still visible now, fifty years later. In the blink of an eye, the sharp blade removed a chunk of my finger, such that even the bone came apart and the flesh was left hanging off. In those days, the "*Rājas* knife" was famous. This was the first Western knife whose blade I tested on my finger. At that time I wasn't a poet, and hadn't heard this *miṣra'*
>
> انگلیاں فگار اپنی خامہ خوں چکاں اپنا
>
> ungliyā<u>n</u> fi<u>g</u>ār apnī, <u>kh</u>āma <u>kh</u>ū<u>n</u>-chakā<u>n</u> apnā
>
> My fingers are wounded, the pen is dripping my own blood.
>
> Perhaps it was a game of the Invisible [*ġaib*] that the story of my life would begin from the tip of a wounded finger![28]

Here, as elsewhere in his autobiography, ʻAbdul Ġaffār clearly privileges the role of the West, which is to him synonymous in the Indian context with colonialism. For him, it is no coincidence that his wound was inflicted by a product of the West, of colonialism. The phrase "this was the first Western knife" goes beyond mere suggestion to assert that he was often scarred by the "blade" of the West and its agent in India, colonialism. It is tempting to read into this allegory a certain Freudian element pointing towards colonial discourse and Orientalist scholarship, a return to the question of virility addressed earlier in this paper. Here, the colonial knife performs an allegorical castration of the *kalma kī unglī* (index finger) which is, significantly, the very finger used to attest to one's belief in *tauhīd* or the unity of God, but also in writing, giving witness, *shahādat*. At an age when circumcision is traditionally performed on Muslim boys, ʻAbdul Ġaffār instead becomes the victim of a West that seeks to emasculate and enslave him. This metaphoric circumcision marks the beginning of an internalized struggle between two imagined antipodes that would last a lifetime. Ironically though, it is this allegorical castration that would empower him to speak out, to reproduce.

28. Anjum 1996, 28.

The profundity of 'Abdul Ġaffār's argument here is multiplied by the line of poetry he cites. Most Urdu readers would immediately realize the significance of this *miṣra'* by recalling the hemistitch that precedes it. The full couplet by the poet Ġalib (1797–1869) reads thus:

درد دل لکھوں کب تک جائوں ان کو دکھلا دوں
انگلیاں فگار اپنی خامہ خوں چکاں اپنا

dard-i dil likhūn̲ kab tak, jā'ūn̲ un ko dikhlā dūn̲
ungliyān̲ figār apnī, k̲h̲āma k̲h̲ūn̲-chikān̲ apnā

For how long can I write of the pain of my heart? I should go and show him.
My fingers are wounded, the pen is dripping my own blood.

In one reading of this couplet, the pen is dipped in the lover's own blood, his fingers wounded and bloody from ceaseless writing. Or perhaps, as in 'Abdul Ġaffār's childhood, the lover has severed his own finger while sharpening the reed. In her explication of this couplet, Frances Pritchett suggests the lover may have sharpened his own finger instead of his *qalam* and used it to write his tale in his own blood.[29] In any case, the couplet is a captivating indictment of the limitations of writing. Paper, ink, not even blood are sufficient to represent the struggle and plight of the lover. The pain of his heart can never be captured in either prose or poetry. It can only be directly experienced, just as 'Abdul Ġaffār's own insights came from experiencing the duplicity of England first-hand. Moreover, the lover is not even moved to compassion by the sight of missals composed in human blood. Like the cruel lover of the classical *ġazal*, rebuffing yet ever demanding Ġālib's eternal sacrifices, colonialism makes great demands of 'Abdul Ġaffār yet never allows him full access or parity. And unlike the classical lover, 'Abdul Ġaffār has given up his quest for the unattainable. He is allowed a glimpse of the beloved, the magical allure of the unknown is shattered, and the hope for union, *viṣāl*, deflated.

But his internal suffering was not without fruit. In this passage, 'Abdul Ġaffār learns to address his victimhood through the empowering act of self-expression, while simultaneously acknowledging the inherent limitations involved in that act. Despite these, and even as he gives voice to his own victimization, he acknowledges that his power as an individual to fight for political and social change is enabled by the very blood which finds its way into the tip of his pen. His blood is dulled and dried upon the paper, but the passion which accompanied its inscription is unmistakable even today in

29. Pritchett 2008.

Naqsh-i firang and his other works, such as the famous *Lailā ke khuṭūṭ* (*Laila's Letters*, 1932). His livid prose exudes the ferocity and energy of the moment of the empowering dis-finger-ment.

At another, perhaps more profound, level, we can read into this passage a mythification of the self from the Hindu tradition that mirrors 'Abdul Ġaffār's contested relationship with colonialism. Here, the mythical epic sacrifice of the colonial subject is emphasized. In the Sanskrit epic *Mahābhārata*, Eklavya, a low-caste prince, masters the skill of archery from a clay image of Dronāchārya. Just as he begins to rival Arjuna, the *kshātriya* disciple of Dronāchārya, he is required to offer his right thumb as *dakshina* for his discipleship, rendering his skill useless. 'Abdul Ġaffār mythifies his own sacrifice in a similar way. His finger is excised by the West in exchange for certain abilities that were taught to him and which enabled him to notch arrows into the bow of his prose and journalism. In viewing his own sacrifice as a heroic one, he is able to recover his own dignity in the writing of his autobiography. In a sense, his existence and understanding of self is being reasserted as he interprets his own past in terms of this enormous sacrifice. He is then able, through his writing, to restore to himself the dignity that he possessed at birth. But the path to this re-appropriation of self is a harrowing one, a point emphasized by 'Abdul Ġaffār as he brings his account to a close. He writes:

> This game has many other aspects, too. For example, my attempt to hide that finger in the hem of my *kurtā*, my *kurtā* turning a deep purple color, and its revealing the secret of this first wound. And then the realization brought about by my father's agitation that the incident was serious and my life in danger! While making my way through the journey that is life I have often contemplated this first experience with a sharp blade![30]

Here again, we find a reference to the "blade" of the West. As is seen in *Naqsh-i firang*, the representative of the West in India, colonialism, has had a deleterious effect on its subjects by imposing an unjust rule upon them. This rule was justified by the project of the *mustashriqīn.* In *Bar mā chunān guzasht*, 'Abdul Ġaffār foregrounds this event to highlight the recurrence of colonial violence on its Indian subjects.

Another event from his childhood provides further evidence of the dangers of ignoring the doctrine of the *tafāvut-i rāh*, which connects European culture and learning generally with the colonial project in India. Like the incident with the knife, his run-in with trousers would provide a foretaste of the traumatic years to come. Even more than in the previous passage, here

30. Anjum 1996, 28.

'Abdul Ġaffār speaks with a candidness and element of self-mockery that acknowledges his own fascination with the West.

> A second event that occurred during that same period now seems extremely full of meaning. Perhaps you might, in your opinion, call it a *fāl-i bad* (a bad omen). The first time I ever wore Western clothes, I was struck by a severe blow. What happened was that my father was a servant for the state of Bhopal and he was returning after spending some time away. I went to the railway station to welcome him back with my cousin. In the run from the door of the carriage to the platform I took a sharp fall. The mark of that incident remained on both of my knees for quite a long time. Often, when I would go strutting about in clothes stitched in Bond Street through the bazars of London and the grand boulevards of Paris I would recall that first experience wearing Western clothing. That day my knees were broken, and today my eyes have been burned out by constant confrontations with the flame of Western culture.[31]

Again we encounter 'Abdul Ġaffār rereading his childhood as premonitory, viewing this incident in allegorical terms that require little elucidation. The issue of clothing, like so many other external representations of culture, comes to hold a primary significance for 'Abdul Ġaffār. It is significant that after his return from London he decided to abandon Western attire entirely. By the time he wrote his autobiography, this childhood accident had come to represent decades of cultural contention and conflict and his slavish hypnotism to the allure of the "flame of Western culture."

Like many other writers of his period, 'Abdul Ġaffār felt that the Indian male educated in both the Western and traditional systems was unable to attain mental maturity. Like the by-product of a failed composite education system, 'Abdul Ġaffār, with the body and rhythm of an Indian but inappropriately attired as an Englishman, is unable to run. The unfamiliar garb constricted his movements and tripped him, arresting his forward momentum. His fall while running towards the train is then to be read as an allegory for a foolish desire to emulate the ways of the West. Not only did he fail to catch that train (and thus parity with the idolized modern West which would never accept fully accept him), he also was forced to bear the scar of Western violence on his body as a physical attestation of his victimhood for nearly fifty years. He also argues that although he eventually learned how to move about in this restricting costume and to dance to a Western tune, he was just as impeded by it as an adult as he was as a child. Initially, only his knees suffered, but this *fāl-i bad* is read as the event which inaugurated a

31. Anjum 1996, 27–8.

long series of events that would burn his eyes out from constant confrontations with "the flame of Western culture."

Yet, the same experiences that would submit Qaẕī ʻAbdul Ġaffār to a lifetime of struggle and confusion would also provide him the means to narrate and resolve that contentious existence through the act of writing. The same blood which would leave a deep-purple stain on the hem of his *kurtā* enabled him to speak out against colonialism, imperial domination, and gender inequality in a unique and forceful manner. As ʻAbdul Ġaffār was fond of quoting:

ہر چند ہو مشاہدہ حق کی گفتگو
بنتی نہیں ہے ساغر و مینا کہے بغیر

har cand ho mushāhida-yi ḥaq kī guftugū
bantī nahīn̲ hai sāġar o mīnā kahe baġair

No dialogue of the witnessing of Truth can exist
without recourse to wine and the goblet.

Earlier, we encountered another couplet by Ġālib which lamented the limitation inherent in using the act of writing to describe the reality of one's own emotions or state. Here, we find that that reality can only be expressed, however approximately, with recourse to analogy and allegory. ʻAbdul Ġaffār's invocation of these two couplets by Ġālib is indicative of his own relationship with the act of writing. He recognizes its inability to render an accurate account of the subject, but affirms that an approximate vocalization of reality, or the Truth, can be rendered through the medium of allegory and other literary devices. In *Naqsh-i firang*, ʻAbdul Ġaffār uses his own literary abilities and the framework provided by the *safarnāma* to approximate the reality of British imperialism, Orientalism and the entire colonial project.

Edward Said wrote that "if you feel you have been denied the chance to speak your piece, you will try extremely hard to get that chance."[32] In *Naqsh-i firang*, ʻAbdul Ġaffār creates his own space for speaking back to colonialism. Ranajit Guha has argued that "when a victim, however timid, comes to regard herself as an object of injustice, she already steps into the role of a critic of the system that victimizes her. And any action that follows from that critique contains the elements of a practice of resistance."[33] Although ʻAbdul Ġaffār is in no way timid, he has recognized his own victimization and is all too willing to step into the role of the critic. He does so in all of his writings, but this is most palpable in this first-person works. In *Naqsh-i*

32. Said 1979, 335.
33. Guha 1997, 59.

firang, he capitalizes on the form of the travelogue to make his critique while also disabusing his readers of their misconceptions of the West. In his autobiography, *Bar mā chunān guzasht*, this discourse is further developed and cast into allegorical terms to capture, in more encompassing and evocative terms, the critique he originally presented in his travelogue.

Works Cited

Anderson, Benedict (2006), *Imagined Communities*, London: Verso.

Anjum, Khāliq (1996), *Qāẓī 'Abdul Ġaffār, ek mumtāz nasrnigār*, New Delhi: Anjuman-i Taraqqī-yi Urdū (Hind).

Chatterjee, Kumkum (2002), "Discovering India: Travel, History and Identity in Late Nineteenth- and Early Twentieth- Century India," in: *Invoking the Past: The Uses of History in South Asia*, Delhi: Oxford University Press, 192–230.

Codell, Julie F. (2007), "Reversing the Grand Tour: Guest Discourse in Indian Travel Narratives," *Huntington Library Quarterly* 70/1 (2007): 173–89.

Ghaffār, Qāzī 'Abdul (1989), *Laila ke khutūt aur Majnūn kī dā'irī*, Karachi: al-Musallam Publishers.

—— (1924), *Naqsh-i firang: ya'nī, aqsā-yi maghrib kī sair ke dilāviz tā'ssurāt*, Lahore: Darulisha'at-i Panjāb, 23 Apr. 2008 <http://bibpurl.oclc.org.ezproxy.lib.utexas.edu/web/18741>.

Guha, Ranajit (1997), "Chandra's Death," in: Ranajit Guha (ed.), *Subaltern Studies Reader*, Minneapolis: University of Minnesota Press, 34–62.

Metcalf, Barbara D. (1990), "The Pilgrimage Remembered: South Asian Accounts of the hajj," in: Dale F. Eickelman and James Piscatori (ed.), *Muslim Travellers: Pilgrimage, Migration, and the Religious Imagination*, Berkeley: University of California Press, 85–110.

——(1993), "What Happened in Mecca: Mumtaz Mufti's Labbaik," in: *The Culture of Autobiography*, Stanford: Stanford University Press, 149–67.

Minault, Gail (1982), *The Khilafat Movement*, New York: Columbia University Press.

Nandy, Ashis (1983), *The Intimate Enemy: Loss and Recovery of Self under Colonialism*, Delhi: Oxford.

Nu'mānī, Shiblī (1999), *Safarnāma-yi Rūm o Misr o Shām*, A'zamgarh: Ma'rūf Press, Shiblī Akademī.

Platts, John T. (2000), *A Dictionary of Urdū, Classical Hindī, and English*, New Delhi: Munshiram Manoharlal Publishers.

Pritchett, Frances (2008), *Desertful of Roses*, 19 Apr. 2008 <http://www.columbia.edu/itc/mealac/pritchett/00ghalib/043/43_05.html?>.

Said, Edward, (1979), *Orientalism*, New York: Vintage Books.
Suroor, A. A. (1964), "Humour: Modern Urdu," *Indian Writers in Conference*, (ed.) Nissim Ezekiel, Bombay: P. E. N. All-India Center, 209–15.

From the *House with Wisteria* to *Inside India*

Halide Edib's Journey to the Symbolic

Roberta Micallef

ON JANUARY 9, 1935, INDIAN MUSLIM INTELLECTUALS invited the Turkish intellectual Halide Edib Adıvar to Delhi to give a series of lectures. Her friend and host Dr. Ansari asked her to share her observations about India with the world. In 1937 with the publication of *Inside India*, Halide Edib reluctantly added travel writing to her impressive body of works that include literature, history and philosophy, political essays, and social criticism.

Halide Edib Adıvar begins *Inside India* by explaining that this work is an exception to her rule "not to write anything about a country not her own beyond personal impressions, and that very rarely." She explains that she broke this rule by writing *Inside India* because:

> I felt India to be nearer to my Soul-Climate than any other country not my own. It was not merely because I am a Muslem and there are Muslems in India. Even among Hindu friends who have kindly opened their homes to me, a people whose social structure is so different from my own, I felt entirely at home. And it is this sense of belonging in a spiritual sense which has made me take the liberty of writing about Indians so freely.[1]

Inside India is a remarkably rich text. The first Indian travel narrative by a Turkish woman has been described as "the most eloquent statement on Indian society and politics in the 1930s."[2] A British critic, H. Grey, wrote in 1937:

> It is illuminating for British readers to look at modern India through Madame Edib's unprejudiced eyes.... Madame Edib lived in close intimacy with both Hindus and Muslims, and shows insight into the problems and personalities of both camps. In town and village this trained observer picks out the significant feature, and records it in terse phrases...[3]

1. Adıvar 2002, 3.
2. Hasan 2002, x–xii.
3. Gray, H. 1938, 566–7.

A portrait of Halide Edib. (Public domain image available on Wikimedia Commons at: http://commons.wikimedia.org/wiki/File:Halide-edip-adivar-b3.jpg)

Inside India is an equally valuable resource in what it reveals about this obscure period of Halide Edib's life. I read *Inside India* as the third segment of Halide Edib's life story. In this text, Halide Edib returns to the maternal space of her early memoirs and ascribes meaning to the empty mother-daughter relationship that marks that segment of her memoirs. In India her unwavering challenges to patriarchal authority represented by the British Empire and its representatives, as well as to extremists of various Indian camps continue. I am aware of the criticism garnered by Julia Kristeva because of her book *About Chinese Women*.[4] Nevertheless, Kristeva's views on women and the semiotic and symbolic as articulated in this work and Halide Edib's story complement one another in part and challenge and complicate each other in other parts. Therefore I find discussing these texts in relation to one another valuable.

Although I am concerned primarily with *Inside India*, I will also discuss two other texts: *House with Wisteria: The Memoirs of Halide Edib* (1926), and *The Turkish Ordeal* (1928). These two texts illustrate Edib's progression from the semiotic to the symbolic and provide information that is crucial for my argument. All three volumes were published while Edib and her husband were in self-imposed exile (1925–39).[5] Halide Edib writes in *The Turkish Ordeal* that after a tense scene with Mustafa Kemal she decided to write her memoirs "in English simply and honestly." We must ask ourselves whether Edib felt that she could not be honest in Turkish. Furthermore she writes that she completed the first volume, *The Memoirs of Halide Edib*, while she was still in Ankara.[6] Edib wrote all three texts that I refer to as segments of her life story in English first. They are all first-hand accounts where the genre absolves her from having to be objective. While autobiographies and travel narratives are expected to be truthful, they are also understood to be subjective. Halide Edib published *The Memoirs of Halide Edib* and *The Turkish Ordeal* while she was in familiar England.[7] She published *Inside India* (1937) in France where she was doubly alienated.[8] The translation of *The Memoirs of Halide Edib* was serialized in 1955 but it was not published in its entirety in Turkey until 1963. *The Turkish Ordeal* appeared in book form in 1962 after having been serialized from 1959–60 in Turkey.[9] Both texts were

4. Kristeva 1977.

5. The Adıvars went into voluntary exile in 1925 when all opposition to the Republican People's Party was suppressed. In 1926 Dr. Adıvar was found to be involved in the "Izmir attempt" and sentenced to death in absentia.

6. Adıvar 1928, 190–1.

7. Erol 2003, x–xii.

8. Adıvar 2002, 4.

9. Erol 2003, xiii.

translated by the author herself and differed from their English counterparts. *Inside India* has never been published in its entirety in Turkish. Only parts of the Turkish version *Hindistan'a Dair* was serialized in *Yeni Sabah* in 1940–1.[10]

Over the course of the years between *The Memoirs of Halide Edib* and *Inside India*, Halide Edib's speech transforms from intense echolalia to the articulate, sophisticated if anachronistic speech of a well-educated, cosmopolitan intellectual. In Kristevan terms, Edib's speech travels from pre-Oedipal speech to that of an accomplished participant in the symbolic. Kristeva argues that men and women have a different relationship to language and hence the mother. The semiotic is the real and significant pre-oedipal period during which the child does not distinguish herself from the mother. The symbolic introduces difference, and thus the possibility of subjecthood, but through alienation and subjection to paternal law.[11] In terms of the development of speech, the pre-Oedipal phase corresponds to an intense echolalia, first in rhythm and then in intonation, before the phonologico-syntactic structure is imposed on the sentence.[12]

Pre-Oedipal Speech

Throughout the first chapter of her memoirs Halide Edib refers to herself as "she" and narrates what "she" remembers.[13] In this chapter, she is a young child and she often has physical reactions to stimuli; she is rendered speechless or, when she is moved to extreme passion or anger, she is reduced to howling like a dog. The color yellow induces stomachaches. The cruel maid tortures her and "she" remembers the "helpless terror, the speechless agony of fear."[14] Her memories of her mother are those of a woman who is trying to socialize her daughter and to civilize her. Even when she is hurt, her mother's "caressing" represses her howl.[15] In one such memory, her mother is cutting her fingernails. She is cutting them too short and it is painful but Halide, who feels like howling, does not do so because of her mother's gentle voice. Halide loses her mother to consumption as a young child. Her mother is no longer there to repress her howl. The moment that Halide Edib herself

10. Adak 2005, vi.
11. Kristeva 1977, 57.
12. Kristeva 1977, 29.
13.. Sibel Erol presents an extensive reading of Halide Edib's usage of "she" and "I" in the *Memoirs* and the *Turkish Ordeal* in her introduction to the *Memoirs*.
14. Adıvar 2005, 8.
15. Adıvar 2005, 4.

sees as a defining moment, "a symbol of her life-long temperament,"[16] occurs because she misses her recently departed mother so dreadfully much. "She" has no one to cuddle with at night and "she" feels alone. Her father is at the palace attending to his duties. After having been silent for a long time, she utters a statement: "I want my father!" She describes her voice rising in "piercing howls of pain." She continues howling and sobbing "louder and louder, wilder and wilder," until she is taken to the palace in the middle of the night. In a town under strict curfew this little girl gets through sentries, guards, gates and reaches her father who is spending the night at the royal residence.

According to Kristeva, women either over-identify with the mother and live silently incarnate existences or have over-identified with the father and become militants of the structuring systems of society. The oedipal phase brings language, the symbolic instance, the ban on auto-eroticism, and the recognition of the function of the father.[17] The girl can either identify with her mother or raise herself to the symbolic stature of her father. The symbolic order, the order of verbal communication, is a temporal order. Women cannot gain access to the temporal scene, that is, to political affairs, except by identifying with the values considered to be masculine dominance and such. Those more bound to their mothers, more tuned in as well to their unconscious impulses, refuse this role and hold themselves back, sullen, neither speaking nor writing, in a permanent state of expectation punctuated now and then by some kind of outburst; a cry, a refusal, an "hysterical symptom". They remain in an eternal sulk before history, politics, society: the symptoms of their failure, but symptoms married to a new marginality or to a new mysticism.[18] The speech of women who have not given up the maternal can make itself heard only through bodily manifestations, gestures, cries, hysterical symptoms.[19]

Oedipal Speech

Halide Edib was raised primarily by her father. Her father tried out his Anglophile ideas about childrearing on her. She remembers envying the other children's Turkish attire and food. She had to eat and dress according to British fashion. However, she did grow up in the women's quarters of a Turkish Muslim household and her maternal grandmother continued to be an

16. Adıvar 2005, 9.
17. Kristeva 1977, 28.
18. Kristeva 1977, 37–8.
19. Kristeva 1977, 57.

important element in her life even after her mother's death. Her memoirs abound in descriptions of the women that she spent time with and the gardens and kitchens of the various households that she frequented. In 1901, upon graduating from the American Girls' College, she married Salih Zeki, her much older math and physics tutor. She describes him as a brilliant man who made many contributions to the intellectual debates of his time as well as to the field of mathematics. Rather than claiming the symbolic stature of the father, at seventeen she chose to identify with the maternal or rather the idea of the maternal. She married a much older, well-educated, "modern" man like her father.

Edib describes her early marriage as traditional and herself as an obedient young bride: "no Circassian slave...could have entered upon our common life in such an obedient spirit as I did."[20] It is clear from her text that she was very much in love with her husband and that she wanted this marriage to work.

> My life was confined within the walls of my apartment. I led the life of the old-fashioned Turkish woman. For the first few years I even ceased to see father's old friends whom I had known as a child. I belonged to the new house and its master, and gave the best I had, to create a happy home and to help him in his great work.[21]

In 1902 she had her first nervous breakdown: "I believed I was quietly fading away, and I waited for the end."[22] She had a second case of "mental disorder" in the fall of 1906. Part of her cure was a move to Antigone (Burgaz in contemporary Turkish) where she and her husband found a house that was identical to her grandmother's house. She writes that she went there as an invalid and recovered both in body and mind. She describes her recovering from her mental disorder as the conquest of her "mature self over the foolish whims and the precocious mind of a rather ridiculous young girl."[23] The 1908 Constitutional Revolution brought many changes, including new opportunities for women. Halide Edib sees this as another important moment in her life: "In the general enthusiasm and rebirth I became a writer."[24] Her contemporary Yakub Kadri Karaosmanoğlu, an author, intellectual, and diplomat, remembers noticing her first not because of what she had written but because she dared to publish with a man's name attached to hers. In his memoirs of his youth and literature, Yakub Kadri writes that he was

20. Adıvar 2005, 166.
21. Adıvar 2005, 167.
22. Adıvar 2005, 170–1.
23. Adıvar 2005, 186.
24. Adıvar 2005, 214.

intrigued by this woman who for the first time ever broke the taboo of attaching a man's name to hers and published as Halide Salih.[25] She was not writing as the daughter of a man or as a "lady" Halide hanim. She was simply writing as a woman with a first and last name. She was claiming her right to a public space as a woman in her own right. Here she begins her transition to the symbolic. In 1910 her husband's taking a second wife led to her asking for a divorce. Her love for and concern about the well-being of her two sons is an undercurrent that runs through the first two volumes. The sons are not major characters in any of the three volumes discussed in this paper but their presence is felt in the first two volumes: "I was determined to live, and not leave them to the sort of life which children have when their mother is dead or crushed in spirit."[26] Halide Edib then sent her sons to the United States with some help from American friends to get a good education and to be safe during the tumultuous period that would follow.

The Transition to the Symbolic

Chronologically *The Turkish Ordeal* covers four of the pivotal years in Turkish history 1918–22. *The Turkish Ordeal* is the tale of the Turkish war of independence or what Hülya Adak[27] characterizes as a defense of Halide Edib, whose reputation was tarnished in *Nutuk*, Mustafa Kemal Atatürk's narration of the war of independence. Ayşe Durakbaşa sees it as an alternative history written from a female perspective.[28] During these four years of active participation in the national struggle Halide Edib's unified adult public-speaking voice emerges. In 1918 she returns to Istanbul from Syria where she has been setting up schools and orphanages. She teaches Western literature at Istanbul University. She joins a secret society, *Karakol*, which smuggles weapons to Anatolia.[29] When Istanbul is occupied in 1920, she and her second husband, Adnan Adıvar, escape to Anatolia. After the Treaty of Sèvres at the conclusion of World War I, the Ottoman Empire was divided among the Allies. On August 5, 1921, Mustafa Kemal is chosen to lead the army that would bring independence to Turkey. Halide Edib sends Mustafa Kemal a telegraph on August 16, 1921, asking for a position at the front and she is immediately sent to the Western front. During the national war of independence, Edib works as a public speaker, journalist, translator, writer, editor, nurse, and soldier. As compensation for her services, she is promoted

25. Karaosmanoğlu 1990, 239.
26. Adıvar 2005, 255.
27. Adak 2003, 511.
28. Durakbaşa 200, 144.
29. Uyguner 1968, 5.

to sergeant major in the Nationalist Army.[30] After the victory of August 30, 1922, she marches into Izmir with the victorious Turkish army.

The Turkish Ordeal is the text that introduces us to a more mature, self-confident Halide Edib who is in the process of making the transition from the semiotic to the symbolic. This is a transition period because she still refers to herself in the third person when she is describing public speeches she gives in service to the Turkish national cause. Her "I" is still not a unified "I."

Halide Edib sees herself as the personification of Turkey when she climbs the steps of the platform in Fatih, where she is to give her first public speech: "All eyes were concentrated on the little shabby figure which moved slowly up the five steps of the platform...Here she was, Turkey in black, her cheeks pale, her eyes sorrowful, her shoulders bent. Yet she was stronger than the victors and her and their force and joy."[31] As simply Halide Edib she is still not comfortable claiming the right to speak in public. As a Muslim Turkish woman she is about to break many taboos by uncovering her face and speaking in public in front of an audience of men and women. She has not yet elevated herself to the status of the father. She removes herself from herself in order to perform her duty: "I hardly thought it was my voice speaking. I listened to what it said as a creature aloof, believing in and comforted by its message as much as any one of the crowd below."[32] She describes herself as being someone other, someone extraordinary on these occasions.

About a speech at Sultan Ahmed on June 6, 1919, she writes, "I believe that the Halide of Sultan Ahmed is not the ordinary everyday Halide...That particular Halide was very much alive, palpitating with the message of Turkish hearts, a message which prophesied the great tragedy of the coming years."[33] She is not yet comfortable in claiming an equal space or voice in the company of men. Upon being asked to participate in a meeting by the National Block, she describes the men in these terms: "All seemed above six feet, all were finely dressed, and all had some past pages of Turkish history attached to their records in some way or another."[34] In contrast she describes herself as the "pygmy, in a black charshaf, earnestly [I] tried to find a corner where I would not be seen."[35]

It is the departure from Istanbul as well as the extraordinary condition of the national struggle that allow her to begin her transition to the symbol-

30. Adak 2003, 511.
31. Adıvar 1928, 24.
32. Adıvar 1928, 28.
33. Adıvar 1928, 31.
34. Adıvar 1928, 37.
35. Adıvar 1928, 37.

ic. What facilitates this transition may be the number of surrogate mothers that she finds in Anatolia. Perhaps what Sibel Erol identified as the search for the absent mother[36] in the *Memoirs of Halide Edib* is fulfilled in Anatolia. Although mothers and their role as peacemakers are recurring motifs throughout this book, in Anatolia Edib finds mothers who take care of her. In the early chapters of the book, which take place in Istanbul, mothers are the civilizing elements and peace-makers. In one of many such examples, "two packs of children, Turks and Christians, stood facing each other, and among them stood four women, two of them Turkish and two Christian, all poorly dressed, all fraternizing, all begging their group and the other to stop fighting."[37] Edib's interpretation of this scene is: "Was it an allegory of a world which was to supersede our own, where all the women of all nations would stand before their boy packs and stop fights?"[38] She herself helps a Greek boy get out of a Turkish street without being beaten.

As she is breaking from the semiotic, making the transition to the symbolic, she rediscovers the mothers of Anatolia who become her surrogate mothers. She is travelling under harsh conditions that are challenging both physically and mentally. Anatolia has been battered and burnt and showing its scars. The nationalists are facing opposition on many fronts. Although she never complains, she finds herself exhausted. On many occasions she is welcomed and nursed back to health by older women. In Samandra they are welcomed by a peasant woman who says: "welcome my daughter."[39] Halide's interpretation is that "it was the mother in her that was trying to warm the miserable little refugee woman."[40] In the village of Kutchuk Kaymaz, she falls to the ground as she enters the home of a peasant woman who catches her and lays her down on pillows and feeds her soup with a spoon "like a baby."[41] The war of independence has allowed her to recreate herself in the most extraordinary way. The shabby pygmy of the earlier chapters is brave and tough and stands up even to Mustafa Kemal and what she calls "his despotic tendencies." Halide Edib derives much of her strength from the support and tacit approval that she receives from the older women in Anatolia.

Toward the end of the text Halide Edib gives a speech which she recollects in the first person. This is, by her own admission, the speech that she most enjoyed giving. This speech saved "a slut" from being lynched by an angry mob. By her own admission this was a "wild" speech and one where

36. Erol 2003, xxi.
37. Adıvar 1928, 55.
38. Adıvar 1928, 55.
39. Adıvar 1928, 93.
40. Adıvar 1928, 93.
41. Adıvar 1928, 115.

she was not a split "I": "So I went ahead and harangued and enjoyed myself immensely. I have never enjoyed a public speech as much as I did that wild one I made on the veranda. It is the only public speech where I gesticulated, fell into demagogics, dramatized and scolded and scorned and appealed."[42] Edib's description sounds very similar to Kristeva's description of the woman who makes it to the symbolic realm. According to Kristeva such a woman becomes the most ardent bureaucrat or most extreme revolutionary. Here Edib took on the role of an extremist. Although Edib is not narrating this in the third person, one gets the impression that she is role playing. She knows what to do to save this woman and she does it.

And yet the transition is still incomplete. When she returns to Istanbul she again reverts to referring to herself in the third person when she is participating in anything extraordinary for the sake of her nation.[43]

Inside India: In the Symbolic

Inside India was published in 1937 after Edib had spent twelve years in exile and seven years after she had published *The Turkish Ordeal*. The Halide Edib who travels to India is a mature woman over the age of fifty. Her voice is confident and scholarly. In her memoirs we have a steady progression from the domestic to the public, from the maternal to the paternal, from over-identifying with the maternal to over-identifying with the paternal. The Halide Edib who wrote *Inside India*, at least as she represents herself, is a woman who was able to synthesize the semiotic and symbolic without becoming an extremist. She has made peace with her mother and she has risen to the stature of the father in the symbolic not by rejecting her mother but rather by making peace with her. If she found surrogate mothers in Anatolia, in India she finds surrogate daughters.

Halide Edib's *Memoirs* and *The Turkish Ordeal* simply begin on page one. Neither book has a preface or an introduction. The reader has to get through several layers before reaching the narrative *Inside India*. Halide Edib frames *Inside India* with a preface and an introduction. The author is concerned about the reader's interpretation of information she provides. In the preface, Edib frames for us her gaze of whose limitations she is well aware: "The conclusions I have reached may not be right. What I say about India need not be the truth as the Indians themselves see it, but it is the truth as I see and believe."[44] Mary Louise Pratt argues convincingly in *Im-*

42. Adıvar 1928, 259.
43. Erol 2003, xxxiv.
44. Adıvar 2002, 18.

perial Eyes: Travel Writing and Transculturation that travel books written by Europeans about non-Europeans created the "imperial" order at home.[45] Pratt's work explores the contribution of travel books, even seemingly innocent ones such as the intersection of Linneaus' travel writing and plant classification system and formations of subjectivities, in light of imperial projects.[46] *Inside India* allows us to examine how a non-European traveler negotiates travel and the formation of subjectivity in the absence of an imperial project. Halide Edib is not part of a foreign imperial conquering race that has come to experience an exotic land and she is not a male. She is forthright about what she knows about India and how it might impact her gaze. Halide Edib as an older Muslim woman has access to women in purdah and she often stays in the women's section of households that continue to practice purdah, but she does not exoticize purdah or dwell on it. The occult only merits a passing sentence. She is invited to participate in an event involving the occult and she declines to do so.

In the introduction Halide Edib tells us about all her encounters with India and Indians preceding her arrival in India. She has met India in the fantastic tales of her childhood and the stories of her English governess. She has met Indians who came to help the Ottoman armies returning from devastating wars. She has met Indian soldiers who came to the Ottoman Empire as part of the British armies. She has encountered many contrasting Indias and Indians. They do not form a coherent image. *Inside India* is divided into three parts: India Seen through Salam House, India Seen on Highways and Byways, and India in the Melting Pot, which is not part of the travel narrative but rather an objective account of her encounter with Gandhi and his place in the Indian political landscape.

The title of the book itself, *Inside India,* suggests many different possibilities. Prospective readers may expect to be shown an India to which only an expert has access or they may expect this narrative not to be a superficial description of India but rather a more complicated, nuanced account from inside, perhaps from the ultimate interior, the home. Indeed the first section of the book is titled "India through Dr. Ansari's house." However, Dr. Ansari's home is not simply a domestic space. His home functions as a bridge between the inside and outside and between people of different political persuasions, races, genders, and nationalities. Gandhi and Lord Irwin have had meetings in this home. The shadow cabinet has met here. East and West have met in the drawing room of this house. Edib meets well-known women and politically active women from East and West here. But even this

45. Pratt 1992, 3.
46. Pratt 1992, 25–7.

house has its secluded areas and as an older Muslim woman Halide Edib belongs to a small minority that has access to the apartments of Begam Ansari who chooses to maintain purdah. The only man Begam Ansari sees other than her relatives is Gandhi. Halide Edib identifies with Begam Ansari and her adopted daughter Zohra. The author respects Begam Ansari's choice to remain in purdah and not to stand in the way of Zohra's emancipation. Halide Edib envies Zohra and Begam Ansari's relationship. The author finds that Zohra with one foot in the past and the other in the future is facing the same difficulties that she faced as a young woman but that, unlike herself, Zohra has a mother to guide her through this difficult stage.[47] Edib's admiration for what she perceives as the flexibility of Indian Muslims with regard to women's position is evident throughout the book. She appreciates the fact that women are allowed to decide for themselves whether they should remain in purdah or not. Halide Edib comments on the top-down modernization effort in the Republic of Turkey, which included clothing reform by banning veiling and scarves in Turkey. It is in Chapter Three that she makes her thoughts on women in India clear and, in an interesting way, she also comments on women that Kristeva might have classified as having overly identified with the paternal.

The chapter titled "Sorojini Naidu and Other Indian Women" captures her thoughts on women's emancipation and the condition of women in India, which are reemphasized throughout the book with her comments about encounters with women and women's clubs. In Salam House there are two other women guests; one of them is Sarojini Naidu, "the foremost Indian woman of the present day, the best known Eastern woman in politics."[48] In many ways, based on the description of Naidu provided by men, Naidu is the Kristevan revolutionary woman who is more fanatic than any man, the woman who has over-identified with the paternal. The male head of the Chicago Forum says to Edib: "I always believed India to have a meek and submissive spirit, but Mrs. Naidu upset my notion."[49] Edib takes the time to point out that this woman has many dimensions and moods. The Mrs. Naidu Edib describes is a well-rounded person and what he has seen is only one dimension. To Halide Edib she is a woman of many moods, sometimes cruel, sometimes tender; aggressive in pursuit of nationalism and in expressing it and yet capable of a universality of spirit, a comprehension of humanity. Indian men call her Akka, older sister. Perhaps the question should be whether the flaw is in the way she is being perceived by the head of the Chicago

47. Adıvar 2002, 18–9.
48. Adıvar 2002, 25.
49. Adıvar 2002, 26.

Forum. Is Mrs. Naidu perceived as being overly strident because she does not adhere to his stereotypes about India and Indian women? Through Mrs. Naidu, Halide Edib meets many other women of all castes, religions, and ethnicities in the Ansari drawing room. She meets nationalists, reformers, teachers, and students. She is delighted that women of different backgrounds can come together. She is impressed with Begam Mohammad Ali, who "will not be hustled. She wants change, but in her own good time."[50] Halide Edib also met with the Purdah Club. She is brutal with them, not about Purdah but about being good citizens and doing good for their community: "What do you mean I thought by dressing so beautifully and sitting idle instead of helping, working, teaching. ... And all this costly food. ... Why, they could calculate the weekly cost, and spend it on providing meals for the poorer students of Jamia."[51]

Although Halide Edib may have placed herself firmly in the symbolic in this book, she also valorizes female space in it. That Halide Edib has made peace with the maternal and female space is evident on many levels in Chapter One and emphasized throughout the rest of the book. In the first section of *Inside India*, Halide Edib delights in describing the gardens, the animals, and the people she encounters but she is very brusque when it comes to monuments, especially those marking empires. Monuments that pay homage to conquering, great men and their armies are often dismissed abruptly. Zohra accompanies her on her touristic trips in Delhi: "She both humanized and dramatized for me the great monumental edifices which would otherwise have been only heaps of stones more or less artistically arranged."[52] Indeed in the next chapter, which is devoted in its entirety to monuments, the reader becomes well-acquainted with her disdain for "heaps of stone." She finds palaces oppressive "with or without royalty in them." It is again the gardens, the symbol of female space and fertility, that catch her eye. When visiting an old fort, she is enthralled when they suddenly find themselves "in the lovely gardens."[53] She is not even particularly impressed by the Taj Mahal. Her comment is, "The supreme irony for the Westerner is that it was a Muslem who erected this eternal monument to woman!"[54] Regarding British architecture her comment is that no one will ever come to India to see the architectural remains of British rule. Their contribution would be found elsewhere.[55]

50. Adıvar 2002, 29.
51. Adıvar 2002, 32.
52. Adıvar 2002, 19.
53. Adıvar 2002, 20–1.
54. Adıvar 2002, 23.
55. Adıvar 2002, 24.

Gandhi and the two women who are closest to him introduce her to new masculinities and femininities. In the next three chapters, which are devoted to her meeting with Gandhi, the trio around him and his activities, she expresses her admiration for a different type of leadership and masculinity. Mahatma Gandhi offers a "third way," one that is perhaps neither maternal nor paternal. This is a man whom women in purdah meet and allow into their apartments. His is a movement that is not centered on leaving behind monuments but on improving the circumstances of the poor. Halide Edib describes the reverence and the love for Gandhi. Her portrayal of Gandhi provides quite a contrast to the portrait of Atatürk drawn in *The Turkish Ordeal*: 'Now now now ...' was saying Mahatma Gandhi to the women, 'you don't mean that...,' trying all the time to prevent those who embraced his feet from kissing his knees. At least so it seemed to me from where I was."[56]

Gandhi and the women around him have given up worldly pleasures. This is an asexual masculinity but still there is a gender delineation. Quite simply he has a name whereas the two women are "sister," and they serve his needs. We come across the Kristevan archetypes in Halide Edib's descriptions of Gandhi's wife, Sister Kasturba, who is no longer his wife, and his adopted daughter, Sister Miraben. They are both titled "sister," which changes their relationship to one another as well as to Gandhi. While the author describes them in and of themselves and in relation to Gandhi, she does not comment on the relationship between Sister Kasturba and Sister Miraben. In Sister Kasturba's description we find "the revolutionary woman." She is described as more "Gandhi than Gandhi himself." Halide Edib does not chide her for this; in fact, she contextualizes Sister Kasturba by describing her life and what Gandhi's politics has meant for her as a wife and a woman. Sister Miraben, on the other hand, is another "daughter," she has not risen to Gandhi's position but, according to Halide Edib, she is a "great woman," who has given up herself for a different cause and taken on a new identity. And yet there are questions about whether this upper-class British woman has really been accepted or not. Sister Miraben complicates the Kristevan scheme because she has not chosen to stay in her own frame. She has aligned herself with another "father." She cannot be accused of being a strident revolutionary at home because she has left home. Symbolically, Sister Miraben has rejected her own maternal and paternal path. She has created her own route. By assuming the right as an individual to determine her own fate she has chosen to enter the symbolic but she has not become a "revolutionary woman," as postulated by Kristeva's theory.

Halide Edib introduces us to different types of men and intellectuals in

56. Adıvar 2002, 58.

the following two chapters, which describe the university (Jamia Millia Islamia) or the Jamia men and their ideas. She is well received even if at times challenged and questioned by her audience. That she is firmly in the symbolic and that she has assumed the same rights as the father are obvious. Her lectures are attended by significant intellectuals and political figures. She is not treated as an honorary male but simply as an important intellectual. She reflects on the political and social landscape in India and she is deeply concerned about the potential religious conflicts. She wants to see an India that is united and not torn apart by religious conflict.

Halide Edib's comments on India are reflective of her sentiments on what has been taking place in Turkey since independence. Religion was strictly controlled by the state after the Republic was established. Religious institutions were stripped of their financial resources and power base. Halide Edib argues for balance in society and the necessity for religion and science to coexist. She also argues that women should not be rushed into change or forced into it. She argues that education is important and should be emphasized for men and women.[57] Halide Edib illustrates her point regarding the importance of women and education by describing a scene in which the laying of the foundation stone of the new Jamia building is taking place. Halide Edib is observing the masses, which include school children. The youngest child is to lay the foundation stone. School children are watching. First they are well behaved but then they start getting fidgety. The teachers who sit among them don't do anything: "A little girl of seven restored order. She was a puny creature with sharp black eyes. Her eyes glared, and certain ribs felt her sharp elbows stuck into them. There was no more fidgeting. She seemed to me a symbol of the modern Indian woman, asserting her rights by proving her ability to make her men behave."[58] The little girl acts, whereas the adults are given to apathy. At the same time this little girl, who is more concerned with imposing order than the adults, is perhaps a good example of the female who over-identifies with the paternal.

The second section of the book is titled "India Seen on Highways and Byways." In this section, Halide Edib is travelling in the parts of India that have a significant Muslim population. This is a travel narrative within a travel narrative. Each chapter is named after the city she is visiting. Again it is not the great historically important places that catch her attention, but rather the gardens and the people and their ideas that are of significance for her.

In this section she is not based in a single home and when visiting homes she often finds herself eating with the men. In Aligarh she comments that

57. Adıvar 2002, 63.
58. Adıvar 2002, 72.

the Muslim University has produced men who look modern on the surface but are mostly fanatical and stagnant in mind.[59] Again she could well be describing her fears for her home country where modernization from above may be producing citizens and leaders who look modern but who have not internalized democratic values. She warns that both Hindu and Muslim should consider religion seriously. She is concerned about the two communities' ability to coexist once the unifying enemy, the colonizer, has left.

Halide Edib's descriptions of her encounters with women in Lahore remind the reader of her sentiments on women as peacemakers in her earlier works. Here again the reader senses her appreciation of the Indian approach to women's emancipation. In Lahore, where she is welcomed by thousands, she is the guest of a rich landowner in whose house strict purdah is practiced. She eats only one meal with the women in strict purdah but she makes much time for them. Begam Shah Nawaz is her hostess and takes her to visit a college for young women in purdah. At a party by a women's club or clubs she writes, "once more I thought how much better women all over the world understood each other than men."[60]About the harems in the purdah homes she writes:

> One saw three definite generations with three definite thoughts and ways of life. Grandmothers, entirely old-fashioned; mothers, though still absorbed in their homes, yet interested in women's education and proud of their English-speaking daughters who were out of Purdah; such daughters who were entirely emancipated.[61]

Fiction written by Halide Edib often includes characters who are hypocrites or charlatans who fool innocent people by claiming religious authority. In Lahore she is shocked and horrified when she discovers that Muslim women are denied the right to inherit by their own community, which has adopted Hindu inheritance laws. In her speech here she harangues her listeners and deals with the hecklers. In Lahore she finds a surrogate daughter when she dines in the house of a doctor, a member of the Association which invited her to Lahore. After dinner he brings her a "precious bundle" and asks her to name his seven-day-old daughter Halide: "That miniature creature in green silk has moved me almost to tears, and in a strange way tied me to Lahore. For whatever happens in that city the destiny of a human being called Halide will be affected by it."[62]

Again her disdain for armies and war shines through when she is taken

59. Adıvar 2002, 81.
60. Adıvar 2002, 85.
61. Adıvar 2002, 86.
62. Adıvar 2002, 89.

to the Khyber Pass. She has no interest in such places but more of an interest in people and the impact of various armies and civilizations on people. What she chooses to highlight about her visit to the Khyber Pass is the flitting image of a little Afridi girl, a dirty and poor beggar who is incredibly pretty even though she is covered in grime and with other children who are not particularly attractive: 'What is the explanation of the child's extraordinary beauty?' I asked. 'A handsome ancestor in the army of Alexander the Great,' was the answer."[63]

It is also in this chapter that she makes a reference that suggests that she went through the Kristevan revolutionary woman phase. She tells us in commenting on an ascetic that:

> I want to digress and confess to an incurable weakness for extreme puritanism, even for asceticism. Yet I know that they often lead to hypocrisy and intolerance in the first instance; and to self-righteousness, or withdrawal of the best moral element from human intercourse in the second.[64]

Her fiction works are peppered with such characters both male and female. For example, Rabia's mother and grandfather in *The Clown and His Daughter* are both deeply religious and terribly intolerant, self-righteous, and unpleasant.

In Lucknow she finds much to admire and much to despair about. Once again in this city, which is admired for its beautiful women, she finds lovely gardens and orchards. She admires Begam Wasim's housekeeping and is in awe of the camaraderie and respect among mother and children in this house. But it is the trip outside of Lucknow that brings despair and trepidation for the future of India. Here she witnesses extreme poverty. Here she sees what Gandhi is fighting against. She realizes that "95 per cent of India is semi-starving in order to keep the 5 per cent middle-class, rulers, or whatever else they may be."[65]

Her stay in a Hindu home in Benares is equally felicitous and again takes her to a garden that brings her back to her childhood with her grandmother: "The moment I crossed the gate I was in the garden of my childhood. Whether it was a trick of memory or a reality, the trees were all acacias, the trellises were wisteria, the flowers the same as my grandmother grew in her garden at Beshiktash."[66] She encounters Hindu, Muslim, and the remnants of Buddhist Benares. She is again wondering how it is that Hinduism drove out

63. Adıvar 2002, 96.
64. Adıvar 2002, 98.
65. Adıvar 2002, 113.
66. Adıvar 2002, 114.

Buddhism and assimilated everything but Islam.[67] This for her is a topic that India must deal with in order to have a promising future.

The temple of Kali, which she visits while staying in Calcutta, is the one monument she comments on extensively. Significantly, Kali is a female deity. She is the goddess of destruction and death. As Halide Edib describes her, however, she is the Kristevan revolutionary woman who is dominated by the brain without the heart and who follows orders heartlessly or science without religion or ethics. She is the paternal taken to the extreme:

> For the adherents of every religion, alas, have an unnamed Kali in their hearts. Destruction is as much an instinct as love in the human heart. The question is whether the divine commandment of every religion which says 'Thou shalt not kill...' or the man-interpreted precept which says, 'Thou shalt kill...' is going to prevail in the end.[68] Kali is the domination of the brain without the heart.

Hyderabad demonstrates for her clearly the difficulties India will face in nation building. She visits an orphanage where the children cannot eat together. Out of respect for the Hindus the majority Muslim population in Hyderabad is intent on showing that the Hindu children's dietary laws are being followed. Halide Edib warns that this situation may create complications for the future. Another incident that takes place in Hyderabad demonstrates that Halide Edib has moved out of the extremist position regarding the Ottoman dynasty. Her hostess Lady Amina's dear friend turns out to be the Ottoman princess whose family Halide Edib helped oust from Turkey.[69] She likes the princess and admires her but feels the need to justify her feelings by comparing the princess to Mehmet the Conqueror: "Strange that of all the members of that somewhat degenerate family she has inherited from the strongest and ablest of the dynasty."[70] The princess is a much loved reformer who has never lived in purdah. She exemplifies everything that the republican government declared it wanted the modern Turkish woman to be, namely, educated, intelligent, chaste, and devoted to service.

The trip is complete with the return to Bombay and a description of a woman singer whose song about the motherland reduces Halide to tears. The sight and thought of women of all backgrounds fighting for the independence of India reminds her of the Turkish struggle for independence.[71]

67. Adıvar 2002, 125.
68. Adıvar 2002, 139.
69. Princess Hatice Hayriye Ayşe Dürrüşehvar (1914–2006) was the daughter of Sultan Abdūlmecid II, who was exiled to Paris by the new rulers of Turkey in 1924.
70. Adıvar 2002, 146–7.
71. Adıvar 2002, 155.

Is it the thought that she does not have a homeland to which to return after the struggle and suffering that saddens her?

Halide Edib's remarkable and informative travel narrative which clearly demonstrates that she has claimed her place in the symbolic ends rather abruptly. Perhaps because she is not returning home there is no return voyage, simply a statement about the end of a visit:

> Thus ended my visit to India ... When I have digested it all, I must give my report as an objective eye witness of India in the year of grace 1935, I said to myself.[72]

Indeed her next monumental trip would be her return to Istanbul on March 6, 1939.[73]

Works Cited

Adak, Hülya (2003), "National Myths and Self-Na(rra)tions: Mustafa Kemal's *Nutuk* and Halide Edib's *Memoirs and The Turkish Ordeal*," *The South Atlantic Quarterly*, 102/2–3: 509–27.

—— (2005), "Introduction: An Epic for Peace," in: *The Memoirs of Halide Edib*, Piscataway, NJ: Gorgias Press, v–xxvii.

Adıvar, Halide Edib (2002), *Inside India*, New Delhi: Oxford University Press.

—— (2003), *House with Wisteria: Memoirs of Turkey Old and New*, Charlottesville, VA: Leopolis Press.

—— (2005), *The Memoirs of Halide Edib*, Piscataway, NJ, Gorgias Press.

—— (1928), *The Turkish Ordeal*, New York: The Century.

Çalışlar, Ipek (2010), *Halide Edib Biyografisine Sığmayan Kadın*, Istanbul: Everest yayınları.

Durakbaşa, Ayşe (2000), *Halide Edib: Türk Modernleşmesi ve Feminizm*, Istanbul: İletişim yayınları.

Erol, Sibel (2003), "Introduction," *House with Wisteria: Memoirs of Turkey Old and New* vii–xxxvi.

Gray, H. (1938), "*Inside India* by Halide Edib," *International Affairs (Royal Institute of International Affairs 1931–1939)*, 17: 566–7.

Hasan, Mushirul (2002), "Introduction," in: *Inside India*. New Delhi: Oxford University Press, ix–lx.

Karaosmanoğlu, Yakup Kadri (1990), *Gençlik ve Edebiyat Anıları*, İstanbul: İletişim Yayınları.

Kristeva, Julia (1977), *About Chinese Women*, tr. Anita Barrows, New York: Urizen Books.

72. Adıvar 2002, 160.
73. Çalışlar 2010, 400.

Pratt, Mary Louise (1992), *Travel Writing and Transculturation*, N ew York: Routledge.

Uyguner, Muzaffer (1968), *Halide Edib Adıvar: Hayatı Sanatı Yapıtları*, İstanbul: Varlık yayınevi.

Contributors

Omar Khalidi was a staff member of the Agha Khan Program for Islamic Architecture, MIT's Department of Architecture. He was born and raised in Hyderabad, India, and educated at Wichita State University (B.A. 1980). He lived in Riyadh, Saudi Arabia, and worked at King Saud University in the 1980s, and then moved back to the United States to obtain an M.A. at Harvard University, 1991, after which he earned a Ph.D. at University of Wales at Lampeter, Wales, UK, in 1994. He authored several books and articles on Islam in America, mosque architecture, and the culture and history of Hyderabad. Dr. Khalidi frequently lectured on a variety of subjects at various forums in the United States, Europe, the Gulf States, Malaysia, India and Pakistan.

Mana Kia is currently a Postdoctoral Fellow at the Center for the History of Emotions at the Max Planck Institute for Human Development in Berlin. She received her Ph.D. from Harvard University in History and Middle Eastern Studies (2011), where she wrote a dissertation called "Contours of Persianate Community, 1722–1835." She has published articles on eighteenth-century Persianate cultural history, modern Iranian history, and gender and sexuality in Iranian historiography. She is generally interested in comparative and connective social and cultural histories of West, Central and South Asia (eighteenth-twentieth centuries).

Daniel Majchrowicz is a Ph.D. candidate in the Study of Indo-Muslim Societies in South Asia in the Department of Near Eastern Languages and Civilizations at Harvard University. He completed his B.A. in Spanish literature and political science, as well as his M.A. in Asian Studies, at the University of Texas at Austin. His current research focuses on Urdu travel literature and language politics in South Asia. When not reading the travelogues of others, he is a traveler himself, and is currently collecting material to begin writing his own *safarnāma*.

Roberta Micallef received her Ph.D. in Comparative Literature from the University of Texas at Austin in 1997. Micallef is currently a Master Lecturer at Boston University, where she teaches Turkish language and literature courses as well as courses in Women's, Gender, and Sexuality Studies. Micallef has contributed chapters to a number of books on Turkish and Turkic culture and literature in addition to publishing articles in the *Journal of Mus-*

lim Minority Affairs, the *American Associaton of Teachers of Turkic Languages* and *Orientaliska Studier*. She has also contributed to *Oxford Islamic Studies Online* and *Worldmark World Religions*. Her current research involves nineteenth and twentieth-century Turkish travel narratives and Turkish women's life-writings. She is also engaged in translating Turkish literature into English. An active member of the Turkish language teaching community, Micallef has received a STARTALK award to train teachers of Turkish and awards to produce teaching materials.

Sunil Sharma is Associate Professor of Persianate and Comparative Literature at Boston University. He received his Ph.D. from the University of Chicago. He was the Bibliographer for Persian at Harvard University's Widener Library and has held fellowships at the Wissenschaftskolleg zu Berlin, Aga Khan Program in Islamic Architecture at Harvard, and the Jawaharlal Nehru Institute of Advanced Study (New Delhi). He is the author of two monographs: *Persian Poetry at the Indian Frontier: Mas'ūd Sa'd Salmān of Lahore* (2000), and *Amir Khusraw: The Poet of Sultans and Sufis* (2005); two collaborative works: *Atiya's Journeys: A Muslim Woman from Colonial Bombay to Edwardian Britain* (2010; with Siobhan Lambert-Hurley), and *In the Bazaar of Love: The Selected Poetry of Amir Khusrau* (2011; with Paul Losensky); and co-editor of a volume of essays, *Necklace of the Pleiades: Studies in Persian Literature Presented to Heshmat Moayyad on his 80th Birthday* (2007; with Franklin Lewis). He has co-curated several exhibitions at Harvard University. His research interests are in the areas of Persianate literary and visual cultures and travel writing.

Daniel Sheffield received his Ph.D. in Iranian and Persian Studies from Harvard University in May 2012. He specializes in medieval and early modern Zoroastrian religious history in Iran and India. His dissertation, entitled *In the Path of the Prophet: Medieval and Early Modern Narratives of the Life of Zarathustra in Islamic Iran and Western India*, is a historical study of the discursive practices by which Zoroastrians in Iran and India struggled to define their communal identity through constructions of the life of Zarathustra, the central figure of their religion. During 2008–09 he held a US Department of Education Fulbright-Hays Doctoral Dissertation Research Award to investigate Pahlavi, Persian, and Gujarati manuscripts at the First Dastoor Meherjirana Library, Navsari and the K. R. Cama Oriental Institute, Mumbai. His publications have appeared in *Bulletin of the Asia Institute* 19 (2009); *Journal of the K. R. Cama Oriental Institute* (2012); and *The Blackwell Companion to the Study of Zoroastrianism*, ed. Michael Stausberg and Yuhan Vevaina (forthcoming). In 2012, he joined the Princeton University Society of Fellows as a Link-Cotsen Postdoctoral Fellow and lecturer in Near Eastern Studies.

Thomas Wide is a D.Phil. candidate in Oriental Studies at Balliol College, Oxford University. He holds a B.A. in Classics and Oriental Studies from Oxford, and an M.A. in Middle Eastern Studies from Harvard University, where he was also a Kennedy Scholar. He is currently writing a dissertation on transnationalism in early twentieth-century Afghanistan, using travelogues in a variety of languages. He also makes history and current affairs documentaries for the BBC.

General Bibliography

Translations

Abu Taleb, Mirza (2005), *Westward Bound: Travels of Mirza Abu Taleb*, tr. Charles Stewart, ed. Mushirul Hasan, New Delhi: Oxford University Press.

—— (2009), *Travels of Mirza Abu Taleb Khan in Asia, Africa, and Europe, during the years 1799, 1800, 1801, 1802, and 1803*, tr. Charles Stewart, ed. Daniel O'Quinn, Peterborough, Ont.: Broadview Press.

—— (1984), *Safarnāma, Masīr-i Tālibī fī Bilād-i Afranjī*, Urdu tr. Sarwat Ali, New Delhi: Qaumi Council bara-yi Urdu Zaban.

Alawi, Amir Ahmad (2009), *Journey to the Holy Land: A Pilgrim's Diary*, tr. Mushirul Hasan and Rakhshanda Jalil, New Delhi: Oxford University Press.

Farahani, Mirza Mohammad Hosayn (1990), *A Shi'ite Pilgrimage to Mecca: The Safarnameh of Mirza Mohammad Hosayn Farahani* [1885–6], ed., tr. and annotated by Hafez Farmayan and Elton L. Daniel, Austin: University of Texas Press.

Fyzee, Atiya (2010), *Atiya's Journeys: A Muslim Woman from Colonial Bombay to Edwardian Britain*, New Delhi: Oxford University Press.

Ganeshi Lal (1976), *Siyahat-i-Kashmir, Kashmir nama, or Tarikh-i-Kashmir* [1846], *stage-wise account of journey from Ludhiana to Srinagar and return to Simla via Mandi, contemporary and eye-witness record of the historical importance of the places visited in general and social, political, and economic conditions of the Valley in particular*, tr. and ed. Vidya Sagar Suri, Chandigarh : Punjab Itihas Prakashan.

I'tisāmuddīn, Mīrzā (1827), *Shigurf namah i Velaët, or, Excellent intelligence concerning Europe: Being the Travels of Mirza Itesa Modeen in Great Britain and France*, translated from the original Persian manuscript into Hindoostanee, with an English version and notes by James Edward Alexander, London: Printed for Parbury, Allen.

—— (1995), *Shigarfnāma-yi vilāyat*, Urdu tr. Amir Hasan Nurani, Patna: Khuda Bakhsh Oriental Public Library.

—— (2002), *The Wonders of Vilayet*, tr. Kaiser Haq, Leeds: Peepal Tree.

Khair, Tabish, Martin Leer, Justin D. Edwards and Hanna Ziadeh (ed.) (2006), *Other Routes: 1500 Years of African and Asian Travel Writing*, Bloomington: Indiana University Press.

Khan, Muhammad Fazil (1993), *The Uzbek Emirates of Bukhara & Khulum in the Early 19th Century as Described in an Indian Travelogue, Tarikh-i-Bukhara (1812 A.D.)*, tr. and ed. Iqtidar Husain Siddiqui, Patna: Khuda Bakhsh Oriental Public Library.

Najaf Kuli Mirza (1839?), *Journal of a Residence in England : and of a Journey from and to Syria, of Their Royal Highnesses Reeza Koolee Meerza, Najaf Koolee Meerza, and Taymoor Meerza, of Persia*, tr. with explanatory notes by Assaad Y. Kayat, London : W. Tyler.

Nasir al-Din Shah (1874; reprint 1995), *The Diary of H. M. the Shah of Persia during His Tour through Europe in A. D. 1873*, tr. J. W. Redhouse, Costa Mesa, CA: Mazda.

Sayyāh Muhammad ʻAlī (1998), *An Iranian in Nineteenth Century Europe: the Travel Diaries of Haj Sayyah, 1859-1877*, tr. Mehrbanoo Nasser Deyhim, Bethesda, Md.: Ibex.

Sikandar Begum, Nawab of Bhopal (2008), *A Princess's Pilgrimage: Nawab Sikandar Begum's A Pilgrimage to Mecca*, (ed.) Siobhan Lambert-Hurley, Bloomington: Indiana University Press, 2008.

Sultan Jahan Begum (1909), *The Story of a Pilgrimage to Hijaz*, Calcutta: Thacker, Spink.

Wolfe, Michael (ed.) (1997), *One Thousand Roads to Mecca: Ten Centuries of Travelers Writing about the Muslim Pilgrimage*, New York: Grove Press.

Studies

Afshar, Iraj (2002), "Persian Travelogues: A Description and Bibliography," in: Elton L. Daniel (ed.), *Society and Culture in Qajar Iran: Studies in Honor of Hafez Farmayan*, Costa Mesa, Cal.: Mazda, 145–62.

Alam, Muzaffar and Sanjay Subrahmanyam (2007), *Indo-Persian Travel in the Age of Discoveries, 1400–1800*, Cambridge: Cambridge University Press.

Anderson, Jaynie (ed.) (2009), *Crossing Cultures: Conflict, Migration and Convergence*, Melbourne: Miegunyah Press.

Anvar, Sadīd (1987), *Urdū adab meñ safarnāma*, Lahore: Maghribi Pakistan Urdu Academy.

Asiltürk, Baki (2009), "Edebiyatın Kaynağı Olarak Seyahatnameler," *Turkish Studies* International Periodical for the Languages, Literature and History of *Turkish or Turkic* 4/1–I: 911–95.

—— (2000), *Osmanlı Seyyahlarının Gözüyle Avrupa*, İstanbul: Kaknūs Yayınları, Istanbul.

Bentley, Jerry H., Renate Bridenthal, and Káearen Wigen (ed.) (2007), *Seascapes: Maritime Histories, Littoral Cultures, and Transoceanic Exchanges*, Honolulu: University of Hawaii Press.

Bhattacharji, Shobhana (2008), *Travel Writing in India*, New Delhi: Sahitya Akademi.

Bose, Sugata (2006), *A Hundred Horizons: The Indian Ocean in the Age of Global Empire*, Cambridge: Harvard University Press.

Burton, Antoinette (1998), *At the Heart of the Empire: Indians and the Colonial Encounter in Late-Victorian Britain*, Berkeley: University of California Press.

Chandra, Nandini (2007), "The Pedagogic Imperative of Travel Writing in the Hindi World: Children's Periodicals (1920–1950)," *South Asia: Journal of South Asian Studies* 30.2 (Aug.): 293–325.

Chatterjee, Kumkum (1999), "Discovering India: Travel, History and Identity in Late 19th and early 20th Century Colonial India," in: Daud Ali (ed.), *Invoking the Past: The Uses of History in South Asia*, Delhi, Oxford University Press, 192–230.

Clark, James (2002), "ʿAbd-Allāh Mostawfī in Russia, 1904–1909," in: Elton L. Daniel (ed.), *Society and Culture in Qajar Iran: Studies in Honor of Hafez Farmayan*, Costa Mesa: Mazda, 189–214.

Codell, Julie F. (2007), "Reversing the Grand Tour: Guest Discourse in Indian Travel Narratives," *Huntington Library Quarterly* 70: 173–89.

Daniel, Elton L. (2002), "The Hajj and Qajar Travel Literature," in: Elton L. Daniel (ed.), *Society and Culture in Qajar Iran: Studies in Honor of Hafez Farmayan*, Costa Mesa: Mazda, 215–38.

Digby, Simon (1999), "Beyond the Ocean: Perceptions of Overseas in Indo-Persian Sources of the Mughal Period," *Studies in History* 15: 247–59.

Dumont, Peter (2010), "Western Exoticism in the Accounts of Ottoman Travellers in Europe," in: Rahilya Geybullayeva and Peter Orte (eds.), *Stereotypes in Literatures and Cultures: International Reception Studies*, Frankfurt am Main: Peter Lang.

Eickelman, Dale F. and James Piscatori (1990), *Muslim Travellers: Pilgrimage, Migration, and the Religious Imagination*, London: Routledge.

Ekhtiar, Maryam (1996), "An Encounter with the Russian Czar: The Image of Peter the Great in Early Qajar Historical Writings," *Iranian Studies* 29/1–2: 57–70.

Euben, Roxanne L. (2006), *Journeys to the Other Shore: Muslim and Western Travelers in Search of Knowledge*, Princeton: Princeton University Press.

Findley, Carter V. (1998), "An Ottoman Occidentalist in Europe: Ahmed Midhat Meets Madame Gülnar, 1889," *American Historical Review* 103/1: 15–49.

Fisher, Michael H. (2004), *Counterflows to Colonialism: Indian Travellers and Settlers in Britain 1600–1857*, Delhi: Permanent Black.

—— (2007), "From India to England and Back: Early Indian Travel Narratives for Indian Readers," *Huntington Library* 70/1: 153–72.

Ghanoonparvar, M.R. (1993), *In a Persian Mirror: Images of the West and Westerners in Iranian Fiction,* Austin: University of Texas Press.

—— (2002), "Nineteenth-Century Iranians in America," in: Elton L. Daniel (ed.), *Society and Culture in Qajar Iran: Studies in Honor of Hafez Farmayan,* Costa Mesa: Mazda, 239–48.

Göçek Fatma Müge (1987), *East Encounters West: France and the Ottoman Empire in the Eighteenth Century*, New York: Oxford University Press.

Green, Nile (2004), "A Persian Sufi in British India: The Travels of Mirza Hasan Safi 'Ali Shah (1835–1899)," *Iran: Journal of Persian Studies* 42: 201–8.

—— (2009), "Journeymen, Middlemen: Travel, Trans-Culture and Technology in the Origins of Muslim Printing," *International Journal of Middle East Studies* 41: 203–24.

—— (2011a), *Bombay Islam: The Religious Economy of the West Indian Ocean, 1840–1915,* New York: Cambridge University Press.

—— (2011b), "The Madrasas of Oxford: Iranian Interactions with the English Universities in the Early Nineteenth Century," *Iranian Studies* 44: 807–29.

Grewal, Inderpal (1996), *Home and Harem: Nation, Gender, Empire, and the Cultures of Travel,* London: Leicester University Press.

Haag-Higuchi, Roxane (2001), "Touring the World, Classifying the World: The Iranian Ḥājj Sayyāḥ and his Travel-Writing, in: *Erzählter Raum in Literaturen der islamischen Welt. Narrated Space in the Literature of the Islamic World,* (ed.), Roxane Haag-Higuchi and Christian Szyska, Wiesbaden: Harrassowitz, 149–60.

Hanaway, William L. (2002), "Persian Travel Narratives: Notes towards the Definition of a Nineteenth-Century Genre," in: Elton L. Daniel (ed.), *Society and Culture in Qajar Iran: Studies in Honor of Hafez Farmayan,* Costa Mesa: Mazda, 249–68.

Hece: Aylık Edebiyat Dergisi (2011), "Gezi Özel Sayısı" [Travel Special Issue], 15 (174–6): 6–519.

Herzog, Christoph and Raoul Motika (2000), "Orientalism "*alla turca*": Late 19th /Early 20th Century Ottoman Voyages into the Muslim Outback," *Die Welt des Islams* 40/2 (July): 139–95.

Hooper, Glenn and Tim Youngs (ed.) (2004), *Perspectives on Travel Writing,* Aldershot: Ashgate.

Khan, Gulfishan (1998), *Indian Muslim Perceptions of the West during the Eighteenth Century*, Karachi: Oxford University Press.

Khazeni, Arash (2010), "Across the Black Sands and the Red: Travel Writing, Nature, and the Reclamation of the Eurasian Steppe, circa 1850," *International Journal of Middle East Studies* 42: 591–614.
—— (2007), "On the Eastern Borderlands of Iran: The Baluch in Nineteenth-Century Persian Travel Books," *History Compass* 5/4: 1399-1411.
Kılınç, Berna (2003), "Yirmisekiz Mehmed Çelebi's Travelogue and the Wonders that Make a Scientific Centre," in: Ana Simões, Ana Carneiro, and Maria Paula Diogo (ed.), *Travels of Learning: A Geography of Science in Europe*, Dordrecht: Kluwer, 77–100.
Kosambi, Meera (2003), "Introduction, Returning the American Gaze: Situating Pandita Ramabai's American Encounter," in: *Pandita Ramabai's American Encounter: The People of the United States (1889)*, Bloomington: Indiana University Press, 3–46.
Lambert-Hurley, Siobhan (2005), "Out of India: The Journeys of the Begum of Bhopal, 1901–1930," in: *Bodies in Contact: Rethinking Colonial Encounters in World History,* (ed.), Tony Ballantyne and Antoinette Burton, Chapel Hill: Duke University Press, 293–309.
—— (2006), "A Princess's Pilgrimage: Nawab Sikandar Begum's Account of Hajj," in: Tim Youngs (ed.), *Travel Writing in the Nineteenth Century: Filling in the Blank Spaces*, London: Anthem, 107–37.
—— (2008), "Afterword: Muslim Women Write Their Journeys Abroad," in: *A Princess's Pilgrimage: Nawab Sikandar Begum's A Pilgrimage to Mecca*, Bloomington: Indiana University Press, 155–71.
Lambert-Hurley, Siobhan and Sunil Sharma (2010), *Atiya's Journeys: A Muslim Woman from Colonial Bombay to Edwardian Britain*, New Delhi: Oxford University Press.
Leask, Nigel (2002), *Curiosity and the Aesthetics of Travel Writing, 1770–1840: 'From an Antique Land'*, Oxford: Oxford University Press.
Mahallati, Amineh (2011), "Women as Pilgrims: Memoirs of Iranian Women Travelers in Mecca," *Iranian Studies* 44: 831–49.
Mahdavi, Shireen (2002), "Hājj Mohammad-Hasan Amīn-al-Zarb: Visionary, Entrepreneur, and Traveler," in: Elton L. Daniel (ed.), *Society and Culture in Qajar Iran: Studies in Honor of Hafez Farmayan,* Costa Mesa: Mazda, 269–84.
Mahmūd, Khālid (1995), *Urdū safarnāmoñ kā tanqīdī mutāla'a*, New Delhi: Maktaba-yi Jāmi'a.
Majeed, Javed (2007), *Autobiography, Travel and Postnational Identity: Gandhi, Nehru and Iqbal*, Hampshire: Palgrave Macmillan.
Mandal, Somdatta (ed.) (2010), *Indian Travel Narratives,* Jaipur: Rawat.
Metcalf, Barbara D. (1990), "The Pilgrimage remembered: South Asian

accounts of the hajj," in: Dale F. Eickelman and James Piscatori (ed.), *Muslim Travellers*, Berkeley: University of California Press, 85–110.
—— (1993), "What Happened in Mecca: Mumtaz Mufti's Labbaik," in: Robert Folkenflik (ed.), *The Culture of Autobiography: Constructions of Self-Representation*, Stanford: Stanford University Press, 149–67.
Mohanty, Sachidananda (ed.) (2003), *Travel Writing and the Empire*, New Delhi: Katha.
Motadel, David (2011a), "The German Other: Nasir al-Din Shah's Perceptions of Difference and Gender during His Visits to Germany, 1873–89," *Iranian Studies* 44: 563–79.
—— (2011b), "Qajar Shahs in Imperial Germany," *Past and Present* 213: 191-235.
Nadvī, Mas 'ūd 'Alī (1960), *Hindūstān 'Araboñ kī nazar meñ*, A'zamgarh: Dār al-Musannifīn.
Mukhopadhyay, Bhaskar (2002), "Writing Home, Writing Travel: The Poetics and Politics of Dwelling in Bengali Modernity," *Comparative Study of Society and History* 44: 293–318.
Nag, Anindita (2003), *Leaving "Home": Gender, Nation and Empire in the Travels of Krishnabhabini Das, Toru Dutt and Pandita Ramabai*, Thesis (M.A.), University of Memphis.
Ortaylı, Ilber (1992), *19. Asırdan Zamanımıza Hindistan Üzerine Türk Seyahatnameleri*, Ankara Üniversitesi Siyasal Bilgiler Fakültesi Dergisi 47: 271–7.
Papas, Alexandre, Thomas Welsford, Thierry Zarcone (ed.) (2012), *Central Asian Pilgrims: Hajj Routes and Pious Visits between Central Asia and the Hijaz*, Berlin: Klaus Schwarz.
Pearson, Michael N. (1996), *Pilgrimage to Mecca: The Indian Experience, 1500–1800*, Princeton: Markus Wiener.
Pratt, Mary Louise (1992), *Imperial Eyes: Travel Writing and Transculturation*, London: Routledge.
Quraishī, Qudsīa (1987), *Urdū safarnāme, unnīsvīñ sadī meñ*. Delhi: Maktaba-yi Jāmi'a.
Rahimieh, Nasrin (2001), *Missing Persians: Discovering Iranian Cultural History*, Syracuse: Syracuse University Press.
Rahmān, Bushrā (1999), *Urdū ke ghair mazhabī safarnāme*, Gorakhpur: Siddiqurrahman.
Rajabzadeh, Hashem (2002), "Japan as Seen by Qajar Travelers," in: Elton L. Daniel (ed.), *Society and Culture in Qajar Iran: Studies in Honor of Hafez Farmayan*, Costa Mesa: Mazda, 285–309.
Rao, Velchura Narayana, and Sanjay Subrahmanyam (2003), "Circulation, Piety, and Innovation: Recounting Travels in Early Nineteenth-Century

South India," in: ed. Claude Markovits, Jacques Pouchepadass and Sanjay Subrahmanyam (ed.), *Society and Circulation*, Delhi: Permanent Black, 307–56.

Rastegar, Kamran (2007), *Literary Modernity between the Middle East and Europe: Textual Transactions in Nineteenth Century Arabic, English, and Persian Literatures*, London: Routledge.

Ringer, Monica M. (2002), "The Quest for the Secret of Strength in Iranian Nineteenth-Century Travel Literature: Rethinking Tradition in the *Safarnameh*," in: Nikki Keddie and Rudi Matthee, (ed.), *Iran and the Surrounding World, 1501-2001: Interactions in Culture and Cultural Politics*, Seattle: University of Washington Press, 146–61.

Sājid, Kamāl (1995), *Urdū safarnāma, tahqīqī va tanqīdī ja'iza*, Muzaffarpur: Kitabistan.

Sen, Amrit (2008), "The Persian Prince in London: Autoethnography and Positionality in *Travels of Mirza Abu Taleb Khan*," *Asiatic* 2/1: 58–68.

Sen, Simonti (2005), *Travels to Europe: Self and Other in Bengali Travel Narratives, 1870–1910*, New Delhi: Orient Longman.

Sohrabi, Naghmeh (2011), "Looking behind Hajji Baba of Ispahan: The Case of Mirza Abul Hasan Khan Ilchi Shirazi," in: *Untold Histories of the Middle East: Recovering Voices from the 19th and 20th Centuries*, (ed.), Amy Singer, Christoph Neumann and Selçuk Akşin Somel, London: Routledge, 159–75.

—— (2012), *Signs Taken for Wonder: Nineteenth Century Travel Accounts from Iran to Europe*, Oxford: Oxford University Press.

Stöcker-Parnian, Barbara (2010), "An Unusually Long Way to the Kaaba: Reflexions in the Safarnāma-ye Makka of Mehdīqolī Hedāyat," in: *Many Ways of Speaking about the Self. Middle Eastern Ego-Documents in Arabic, Persian, and Turkish (14th–20th century)*, (ed.), Ralf Elger and Yavuz Köse, Wiesbaden: Harrassowitz, 103-14.

Tavakoli-Targhi, Mohamad (2001), *Refashioning Iran: Orientalism, Occidentalism, and Historiography*, New York: Palgrave.

—— (2002), "Eroticizing Europe," in: Elton L. Daniel (ed.), *Society and Culture in Qajar Iran: Studies in Honor of Hafez Farmayan*, Costa Mesa: Mazda, 311–46.

Ursinus, Michael (ed.) (2000), "Ottoman Travels and Travel Accounts from an Earlier Age of Globalization," *Die Welt des Islams* July 40: 133–334.

Vanzan, Anna (2002), "Mīrzā Abu'l Hasan Khan Sirāzī Ilcī's *Safar-nāma ba Rūsīya:* The Persians amongst the Russians," in: Elton L. Daniel (ed.), *Society and Culture in Qajar Iran: Studies in Honor of Hafez Farmayan*, Costa Mesa: Mazda, 347–57.

Wasti, Syed Tanvir (1991), "Two Muslim Travelogues: To and from Istanbul," *Middle Eastern Studies* 27/3: 457–76.

Wright, Denis (1985), *The Persians amongst the English: Episodes in Anglo-Persian History*, London: I. B.Tauris.

Yapp, M. E. (1992), "Europe in the Turkish Mirror," *Past & Present* (Nov.) 137: 134–55.

Youngs, Tim (ed.) (2006), *Travel Writing in the Nineteenth Century: Filling the Blank Spaces*, London: Anthem.

Index